DANCING WITH GOD

DANCING WITH GOD

AMERICANS WHO HAVE BEEN TOUCHED
BY THE DIVINE

STEVE WALL

ST. MARTIN'S PRESS ❧ NEW YORK

To My Grandmother

VANGIE HOPPES GRAYSON

I Love You

Book design by Gretchen Achilles

All interior photos by Steve Wall, except those on pages 1–17, which are © 1998 by
Ken Touchton and are used by permission.

Library of Congress Cataloging-in-Publication Data
Wall, Steve.
    Dancing with God : Americans who have been touched by the Divine /
Steve Wall. — 1st ed.
      p. cm.
    ISBN 0-312-18562-6
    1. Spiritual biography — United States. 2. Wall, Steve. 3. United
States — Religion — 1960– I. Title.
BL72.W35   1998
200'.92'273 — dc21   98-2881
           CIP

First Edition: July 1998

10 9 8 7 6 5 4 3 2 1

CONTENTS

Acknowledgments
ix

Foreword
xi

1. GEORGE AND LITTLE WILLIS
ATLANTA, GEORGIA
1

2. SARAH PHILLIPS
HAMPTON, VIRGINIA
29

3. PARKER TATE
SHELBY, NORTH CAROLINA
43

4. FLOYD JUSTICE
TOCCOA, GEORGIA
75

5. GERMAINE CURLEY
PICAYUNE, MISSISSIPPI
97

6. WILLIAM J. McFARLANE
OUTSKIRTS OF SAN ANTONIO, TEXAS
119

7. GWEN SCOTT
ALBUQUERQUE, NEW MEXICO
143

8. *FERNANDO MERCADO*

SAN ACACIA, NEW MEXICO

177

9. *BOB SHERRILL*

CHATTANOOGA, TENNESSEE

189

10. *PETER FREED*

CHATTANOOGA, TENNESSEE

205

ACKNOWLEDGMENTS

There are those to whom I cannot say "Thank you" enough. If I could actually shout on paper I would freely do so. It is my hope that writing my thanksgiving here will make it just a bit louder.

B.J., I love you with all my heart and soul. And there's more. Without you this book would not exist. You listened lovingly and intently, without losing your patience, when I needed a sympathetic ear. You read the early drafts until you almost dropped from exhaustion, even after ten to twelve hours at your own job and after an hour's drive home on top of that. You cautiously advised me on each chapter as it was completed and you painstakingly did the preliminary editing when you had many other things demanding your attention. And I know you did all of this out of love and a sincere belief in the value of the material. So I say thank you from the bottom of my heart.

To Robert Weil, the editor of this book, I bow in appreciation for your love of books and your commitment to the authors with whom you work. Your caring shows. Along with that you can know that I, for one, believe you to be one of the most important editors of our day. So saying thank you, alone, would come across as sounding so thin and flat. Therefore, I am compelled to add, Bob, you have inspired me to do more than I'm capable.

A special thank you goes, also, to others at St. Martin's Press. It is a pleasure, indeed a great honor, to have worked with Andrew Miller in matters relating to the editorial and production processes of this book, and Gretchen Achilles in designing the book and showing tremendous artistry in doing so.

Ray Stott of Richmond has contributed to this book as well, but his work will not be immediately obvious. Yet he has helped to make it better by doing what he does with great talent. Ray printed all of my photographs. To him, I say thank you for being the artist you are. And I cherish your friendship.

Finally, my gratitude goes to all those whose stories are included in this book. All I can say is thank you for sharing your dance with me. And now the world can take part in that dance with you.

FOREWORD

Late one night, just after my grandmother had gone to bed but not to sleep, she heard steps. Two people were coming up the stairs. Immediately she sat straight up in bed. No one, she reasoned, should have been in her house. So she imagined it to be robbers or, worse still, murderers. Then, the unexpected. She couldn't believe it. The sounds seemed strangely familiar. Each time a foot touched the creaking boards, she grew more and more aware that something was not right. One of the two had to be her father. She just knew it. There was no question in her mind. Her father had a way of walking, a pattern she had grown to recognize over the course of the fifty years she had lived. So she became terribly alarmed. She told herself it couldn't be. Her father was dead. He had been buried earlier in the week. Now she was shaking scared.

Even her scream of "Who is it?" didn't stop them. They came on. Up the staircase. And opened the door to her room. In panic she closed her eyes for fear of what she might see. Yet still they came. Right up to the side of where she lay. Then one of the two spoke.

"Vangie. Vangie. Vangie," the one whispered, calling her name three times.

She refused to answer. If she could have moved, she wouldn't have dared in hopes that they would just leave. But that didn't make the apparition go away. Nor did it keep the one man from speaking. He went on.

"We're not here to hurt you or scare you. We would never do that. But your father asked me to come with him. He has to talk with you. It's important. He pleads that you will let him tell you this one last thing. But you have to give him permission." Then he added, "Will you let him speak?"

My grandmother was mortified. So she refused to acknowledge either of them. And until she died some sixteen years later, she regretted it. As long as she lived, she wondered what it was her father had wanted to say to her. But two things she never questioned: that it was her father who came into her room that night, and that the man who spoke had been an angel sent by God as a messenger.

Once she told me her story, she pleaded with me to be always aware of God. That He was real. And she impressed on me to be open-minded to the possibility of angels. Since she was never one to exaggerate or tell me anything other than the truth as she saw it, I believed, without question, she had been visited by an angel that night. And do I believe it to this day? I do. Beyond any doubt.

Since then I have often wondered if there were others who have seen God, been touched by celestial beings, felt angels' breath, talked with the saints. If my grandmother did, I reasoned, there must be. To them, I determined, I would go.

Mine is a life of journey. Of wandering. The passion to go has always been there. But it has been more than just to see what was over the next hill. It was to get to the horizon. To the edge.

In all my years, I found that mysterious precipice always eluding my grasp. Tricking me. Teasing. Moving beyond my reach. Nonetheless I still harbored a secret hope that I'd find the meaning of it all. God. So I was forever enticed to take yet one more step. Then another. And another. As a journalist I traveled on assignments to Europe, the Middle East, India, Vietnam, Japan, and Australia. Time and again I went to Central and South America. Although I told myself that I was covering war, famine, poverty, natural disasters, and indigenous cultures to show others what was happening around them and at the far reaches of the globe, there was another reason. I was looking for something or, I should say, someone. In reality I was looking for at least one manifestation of the divine and that *someone* would be my guide to understanding the sign.

The point of giving up finally came. But something drew me on, almost against my will. So, after waging a fierce battle with myself, I yielded. One thing I promised myself, however, was there would be no more expeditions to the end of the world. But I would commit to another journey. One that would take me to the brink. I would go to those who believed they had been visited by the divine.

From a child I had heard stories. Some raised the hair on my arms. Gave me the shivers. Caused my heart to race. Prompted dreams in the middle of the night. This thanks to my grandmother. She had been the first to take me into her confidence. And in so doing, she turned my thoughts forever toward God. It was a story I would never forget.

This book, then, is a record of that journey. It is a trip I will never forget. And by reading it you will discover what I found. As to where I went and how I got there, only intuition was my guide. Sometimes it came as a thought, such as heading for Louisiana and the Mississippi Delta in search of a religious commune I knew about. On getting there, I learned the leader had died and the group had disbanded. Yet that expedition led me to someone else. Now, because of that adventure, Germaine Curley's story is a part of this book.

Then there was the impulse to pick up the hitchhiker in Texas. I thought when I slammed on the brakes I had lost my mind. Who in his right mind stops for anyone by the side of the road? Never me. But I did. And I must say that my life was enriched because I did.

I learned to be very careful of making vows. Promises are easily made. Breaking them means facing the consequences. I've kept some and I've reneged on a few. One that I broke is a subject within the chapter on Peter Freed. You may be absolutely amazed at what you discover when you read the moving conclusion to his and my chance meeting. Did I say "chance"? It could be that there was more at work than anyone would suspect.

One after another I found individuals who had remarkable stories to tell. Sometimes someone would suggest a person to go see because of a rumor, or it was a personal acquaintance who had been touched by God. At times I would turn down a road for no justifiable reason at all. And because of that, I would encounter someone who would open up and share his or her secret revelation.

Broaching the subject of God was never easy. There is no right way to do it. The question "Have you seen God lately?" opened me up to ridicule. On one occasion I was shouted at in condemnation for my blasphemy. I was told, "Worship God! You'd better just worship God. There's only one true God and He's going to punish you for even asking that question."

Others inched away from me, apparently in fear for their lives. They must have thought I was going to be struck by lightning, and they didn't want to be too close to the fireworks. Or they may be found guilty by association when God pronounced his judgment on the wayward sinner I surely must be.

Yet there were many who were drawn into the conversation because of the subject being God. The vast majority of people were excited about exploring the meaning of life and entertaining the possibility of divine visitations. I never met one, however, who doubted the existence of God. These more than compensated for whatever conflict the others sought to stir up.

Along the way something happened in my thinking. After you finish your reading, you may come to the same conclusion. My religion taught me that all the holy texts had already been written. When they were finished, that was it. Signed and sealed. Etched in stone. History. And at the close of that age, divine inspiration became a thing of the past. I didn't believe it then, and I surely don't believe such things now. Not after completing this journey. Not after coming face to face with those who saw and heard and felt what they did. And they were willing to talk about it even if it meant sacrificing careers, losing social standing in their communities, being confronted with ridicule. So I know, and you may entertain the idea, too, that the divine narrative is ongoing.

Don't get me wrong. I'm not trying to say, or even imply, that this book is a holy text. It's not. But what happened to those whose stories are recorded here is part of an endless saga. That is the way it was meant to be. Yet you will have to decide for yourself. In the least, you will be moved by those whom you encounter here. At times you will want to laugh, and may. Occasionally you may feel someone's pain, another person's joy. More than likely you will sense the unraveling of what we all consider to be the mysterious, as I did many times. And at the end of your reading journey, you could even conclude that there is divine intervention in all our lives.

DANCING WITH GOD

1. GEORGE AND LITTLE WILLIS

ATLANTA, GEORGIA

All of their backs were up against the wall. Shoulder to shoulder they stood—Atlanta's homeless—as if lined up for an interrogation. Every so often a police cruiser crept by, the officer eyeing the ragtag group of men. Occasionally the patrol car stopped, the officer rolling down his window to shout out, "Get back against the building. How many times do we have to tell you? Don't block the sidewalk! If we have to tell you again, any one of you, we'll run you all in. Then you'll for sure get nothing to eat tonight."

Murmuring, a few cursing under their breath, everyone obediently pressed his body harder against the rough-sided bricks of the old church. Apparently pleased with himself, seeing in amusement that his command had been followed, the officer inched his car forward. With a quick look back, double-checking for any rebels in the small crowd, he sped forward with a twisted grin, satisfied that he had been taken seriously.

The old man beside me, his amiable expression turning to a scowl, said, "The cop'll be back. Every ten or fifteen minutes. Like clockwork, I tell you. Watch out for 'im. Got 'is orders."

"What?" I retorted in disbelief.

"Hate," the homeless old man barked as he leaned over to look me dead in the eye. "The city hates us. Every cop around's got orders. We're scabs. Sores of the city."

Quickly I darted my eyes away from his penetrating gaze. A fear suddenly rose within me. A nervous twitch seized my left shoulder. The old man's gaze rolled from off my face and over to the twitch. He was momentarily captivated, not wanting to look but unable not to. Struggling to take a deep breath, I tried to calm down. If I didn't, I knew the old man would sense that something was amiss.

"Say," he said, trying hard not to laugh but laughing anyway, "you get that much?" He jerked his shoulder furiously, mimicking my twitch.

Returning the laugh in real relief, I stammered, "Only when I can't help it."

Suddenly we were both laughing so hard the other men nearby gathered around, wanting in on the joke. As my alarm of being discovered dissipated, I prayed hard that they would assume I was one of them.

For a long time the old man seemed to ignore me, and I stood alone in the crowd. Doubts again began to arise. I was at war within, first telling myself that I had been accepted by this army of the homeless, then arguing that everyone, including the friendly old man, would soon turn on me for pretending to be one of them. Weeks earlier I had become obsessed with an idea—to witness, firsthand, God at work. Where better to do that, I thought, than among those who say they have been "called" by God? I would hit the street as a homeless person. My initial immersion into the world of the "God-called" and that of the "down-and-outs" would be a visit to the gospel rescue mission as one in need. In that way I would see both sides and be able to draw my own conclusions from my experiences.

Acceptance, if no more than tolerance, would be a big issue. I had to be in everyone's mind, including my own, what I appeared to be. For clothes I dug through my own old discards and pulled from the bottom of boxes at the back of my closet a yellowing white shirt, more polyester than wool creaseless pants with a permanent wallet mark on the backside, a big imitation leather belt, and a pair of scuffed shoes. Then, by chance, I happened upon a forgotten stained, nearly threadbare, knee-length army raincoat my uncle had given me from his military days years earlier. After I had donned the attire, slicked down my unruly hair, and rubbed newsprint over my face for a "many miles on the road" look, the transformation was complete and I believed myself ready for my wanderings into the world of the homeless. Only the gnawing feeling in the pit of my stomach caused me to hesitate as I took one last look in the mirror. When I did, I was shocked. I was hardly recognizable, even to myself. My family gasped in disbelief as I emerged from the bathroom. I passed the first, and most important test: My own family hardly knew me. I knew that had they encountered me on the street, they probably would have looked away. As a result of my new attire, I actually felt my self-esteem begin to falter. The slide was real; there would be no pretense about it.

Feeling a bit unsteady, I asked my close friend from college days and fellow magazine photographer, Ken Touchton, to accompany me on my trips. To disguise my own very real fears that I might, for some reason, run into trouble, I suggested, as an excuse, he document the experience. He agreed, much to my relief, and I rested comfortably in the knowledge that I would have a way out should I need one. We both acknowledged

that we should not arrive at the same time, so as not to arouse suspicion. He would drop me off a few blocks from the mission and I would walk in alone. At no time would we be seen together around or in the mission. He would photograph, as a special project with the management's permission, the operation of the rescue mission. I would be just another face in the crowd. When the evening was over, he would leave after I did, retrieve his car, and pick me up where he had left me off earlier. But for most of the evening he would be there, and that would be my great consolation.

Now standing against the building on the chilly windblown street in Atlanta, my mental mind game continued without any concern as to what was going on around me. A hand tapping my side drew me back to reality. Looking down and only half alert, I discovered the old man had poked me awake. A touch of fear—fear of my having been discovered—caused me to look at him from the corner of my eye. He stared straight ahead, not looking at me, so for a moment I could study him.

Wrinkles covered his entire face. A whisp of snow-white hair was all that remained on his otherwise balding head. His eyes spoke without the necessity of words a deep sadness. Years of hard times seemed to have settled permanently in the dark bags sagging down over his protruding cheekbones. His thin, pale lips quivered uncontrollably in the chill. Over and over he shifted from foot to foot to stir the circulation, a vain attempt to keep warm.

Then, when I failed to respond to his first tap, he poked me once again. This time his jab was harder. Immediately I glanced down at the chapped hand. When I did, he opened his bony fingers. In his withered palm were a few coins. I blurted out, "What's that for?"

"Take it," he demanded, his words coming from deep in his throat. His abrupt change in tone was his feeble attempt at trying not to arouse attention to what he was doing. "Take it, boy," he growled, his breath nearing a pant.

"What for?" I asked, truly puzzled at the generosity of his surprising offer.

Like a swift kick he poked me again. "Take it. You look like you're hungry. Just look at yourself."

And he went on. "The food in there'll kill you. Down there at the joint on the corner you can get a cheap hamburger. Can always get some water to wash it down if you buy something first. Better than dying on the food inside here. Besides, you'll starve on the rations here. Now take it and get going. If you're still hungry, come on back and try to live on this stuff."

"I can't take all your money," I whispered.

"You think I'm crazy just 'cause I'm old? Well, I might be old, and that's the truth, but I ain't crazy. Not stupid, either. I'll share, but I ain't going to give you all I got."

Without flinching this time, and certainly without the twitch, I bravely looked him in the eye. Dead center. Then, with courage, and I meant it, I said, "Thank you, but I'm not taking your money. I'll wait and eat with you. If you can do it, so can I. How's that?"

Balling up his fist and shoving it in his ragged pants, he thrust his right hand at me for a shake. "Name's George." A second later, almost as an afterthought, he added, "You're okay for a stranger."

"And mine's Steve. Glad to know you." He placed his aging hand in mine, and we shook for the longest while. Self-consciously we broke off at the same time and stood silent even longer, lost in thought, our backs hard against the wall.

"George," I said abruptly.

"Huh?" he coughed.

"I'm going in now. It's getting cold and I've got to take a leak."

His robust laughter caught me off guard. He started coughing and couldn't quiet down. A wiry guy next to him pushed him forward, causing him to stagger in a free fall toward the curb. As I grabbed him, the man slapped him hard right between the shoulder blades. Stunned, George coughed once more, wheezed, and bent down to grab his knees for balance. Once he finally caught his breath, he bellowed in laughter again. He turned his now blue-red face to look at me, his bloodshot eyes ablaze. Past the rheuminess I saw a mischievous streak in his gaze. In a flash I could see a liveliness that must have been there in his youth. Some things just cannot be hidden. Hard living—the drinking, the disappointments of life, and the passage of years—had overtaken him, and yet his sense of humor had never died.

"Son," he said, "you're the funniest I've ever known. We're going to get you a stage and charge admission. Every one of us'll have a clean room tonight. Hell, we'll keep it a week and we'll have dough left over." Pulling a stained handkerchief from his back pocket, he blew his nose and with the same rag wiped the rolling tears from his eyes.

"What's so funny?"

"You're joking?"

"No," I said. "No, I'm not. All I said was that I'm cold and got to take a leak and I'm going in now."

"Please." He held up his hand as a command for me to stop, as if he couldn't take any more. Fighting for a breath, his body quaking, he choked back a laugh and said, "You for real? You don't know nothing, do you? Just don't know nothing! Well, go ahead. Give it a try. I'll wait for you here, if you don't mind." Then, jabbing the fellow beside him who had chopped him in the back, he nodded for him to watch.

Shaking my head, bewildered at George's behavior, I sauntered past three or four men, who turned toward me to glare. Self-consciously, I bolted for the building's main entrance. Looking over my shoulder before grasping the doorknob, I saw that George had moved from his place to the bottom of the steps to watch. He blinked hard and smiled what seemed like a terribly wicked grin. I grabbed the knob and instinctively started to enter. But the door wouldn't budge. Locked tighter than a safe. Frustrated, I shook it hard. Nothing but glass rattled. Determined, I clamped down and twisted and pulled and pounded with a fierceness that surprised me. Nothing. The door was locked solid. There was no way I could force it. Nevertheless I was not going to give up. I was cold and I seriously had to get to a rest room.

Letting go of the doorknob, I stood motionless and contemplated what to do next. Maybe, I thought, if I knock loud enough, someone'll come to the door and my problems will be over. Placing my hands over the sides of my face and pressing against the glass, I could faintly see into the old structure. After holding the pose for what seemed an eternity, I finally got a glimpse of a man walking down the darkened hallway. This is my chance, I told myself, and I let go with a barrage of pounding. The figure stopped and turned around. I pounded again and motioned for him to come, thinking he could surely see me if I, however faintly, could see him. With militarylike steps, he marched up to the door, turned the deadbolt, and flung open the door. With a scowl burrowing deep across his forehead, he demanded, "What do you want?"

"Sir," I timidly responded, "it's cold out and I've really got to use the rest room. Could I come in for a little while?"

"*Read the sign!* You blind or something?" He began closing the door. Just before it went shut, I stuck my foot between it and the frame. The next thing I knew pain was shooting up from my foot as he pressed harder to close the door.

"I don't know about a sign," I protested. "All I know is I've got to go."

The door swung open and I was standing face to face with a very belligerent man. In an undignified manner, he jerked his arm up and poked my chest with a long, spearlike finger and slowly angled it over to a nondescript sign. The faded letters stated, DOORS OPEN AT 5 P.M. Under that proclamation there was a further warning: NO ONE PERMITTED TO ENTER BEFORE DOORS UNLOCKED.

"Can I use the rest room? I'll leave—"

"Read the sign! No exceptions. None!" With a drop-dead look, the man in the spotless, wrinkle-free suit with coordinated tie added with pinched sarcasm, "Please remove your foot."

"Can I ask one more question?"

"I told you the rules. Now what is it?" he said, very impatiently.

"You got the time?"

"You got another hour. That what you wanted to know?"

Dejected, feeling a lot less human, I turned toward the street once more. George was waiting, his expression of deepest heartfelt sympathy. He slammed his hand down on my shoulder as I approached. "Let me show you something," he said. "I thought you knew. Sorry. Come on, I know you got to take a leak. I'll show you to the only place you can go around here, and it ain't to the hamburger joint. They won't let you in 'less you buy first. Everybody wants money. The world's gone mad, but when Nature calls, she calls."

Walking me past all the other faces, George turned very kindly. "Son, you ain't been out long, have you?"

"Out? Out long?" I repeated, thinking he was asking if I'd just gotten out of prison.

"On the street," he explained as we continued to walk. "Could just tell you're new to the jungle." He grinned and nodded knowingly.

At the uphill end of the church building, George abruptly stopped, his withered, wrinkled hand still on my shoulder. Then he said, "Biggest thing you got to do is find a wall to piss against without getting caught. They'll call it exposing yourself if you do. To me, it's just nature . . . natural." With that his hand slid from off of me and his bony finger became a tool of direction. "There it is. It's all we got, but it's our wall," he intoned. Then he went on, "We take turns. One stands to watch out for cops while the other goes."

Between the two buildings, there was just enough room for a person to walk. A path had been worn weed-bare by a constant stream of thin soles pounding the ground to the far end. "That's our rest room, if you want to call it that. Go on and relieve yourself. If nothing else, you'll feel better. Hit a fly or two. There'll be a swarm of 'em. Nobody'll miss 'em." And he turned his back on me to stand guard.

"Just made it," George announced as I reemerged from the dank passageway a minute later.

"Whew, you're right. What a relief."

"No, no," he protested as we returned to the line of men. "Looky yonder. He's back, or another just like 'im."

Moving around George's huge, although slightly stooped, frame, I glimpsed what he was staring at with amused delight. The cop was back, only this time he didn't yell out, he just glared. The effect was enough. All of us backed up against the wall, and several men raised their hands as if waving in good will. A few faces down from me a skinny fellow grinned and said through yellow-dark teeth, "Yessiree, boss!" complete with a mock salute. I craned my neck to get a better look at who was so bold, then turned away quickly. I couldn't bear the sight. The man was in great need of a dentist, and I was sure he hadn't seen one in years. His mouth was raw, a real mess, and I knew he must have been in constant pain, probably excruciating at times.

So caught up in being on the street, I had temporarily forgotten about Ken, my friend and protector. Suddenly I was seized with alarm. I had not seen him since I jumped out of his car earlier. "He's left me," was my immediate thought, my reasoning having left me. Thinking the worst had always been my first reaction. But then, with second thoughts surfacing, I guessed he had made his entrance while I was taking care of "business" in the alley. It was the plan, after all, that he would deal from the administration's position and I would be on the street. I knew, at least I prayed, that I'd see him inside. And with that I let my concern, for the time being, pass.

"Hey. Hey. Watch out. Watch the cars. Now hurry." The shouting grabbed my attention and I frantically searched out the commotion. George squeezed out of his space and elbowed me hard.

"Looky! Looky there," he sang. "If it ain't Little Willis. Knew he'd be here. Got to meet 'im. Nobody like that little black man."

"How's that?" I asked, carried away in the excitement.

"God's little wonder," he answered with more pride than I'd seen.

In the midst of honking horns and squealing tires, a small, frail creature zigzagged like a maniac across the busy street. George and a few others raised their arms, hands reaching for the sky as if in godly praise. Then, just as quickly, they stretched them out as they would do to receive a blessing from the pope. Excitement spread among most of the men lining the sidewalk.

One by one Little Willis passed the eager men. Fingers touched. Hands shook. Arms grabbed. Then Little Willis got to George and his face lit up. There was a long hug, with Little Willis's head catching somewhere at the older man's rib cage.

"Been lookin' for you, old man, all over the place," Little Willis complained. "Don't never do that to me again. Had me scared out'a my wits."

"Just laying low," George tried to explain. "Not been feeling good lately."

Little Willis grabbed George again and squeezed tight. Backing away a step or two, he looked George over, his hands holding George's arms just above the elbows. "What's this?" Little Willis blasted. "You shaking. You cold. Where's ya coat? You freezing."

"Lost it. Can't find it nowhere. Lived without it before, can do it again. We'll get indoors in a little while, then it'll make no difference."

Little Willis was indignant. "No, no, no, no. Told you never again. You gotta have a coat. You get a chill and die, then what'll Little Willis do? You my friend."

"Ah! Shut up, little man," George whispered in a forced deep, gravely voice.

"I thought giants like you was smart. Know otherwise now, you old man. You ain't so smart after all. Can't fool Little Willis. He knows what he knows. Little Willis gotta take care of ya."

"I told you I'd be all right."

Little Willis would have nothing of it. Shaking his fist at the kindly giant, he roared, "Stay here. Don't go nowhere, man. I'll be back. Ain't goin' far."

Before George could respond, Little Willis was already in the middle of the street. In a run, he yelled, "Goin' ta gets you a coat. Stay here." And he swung around a building like a whirlwind and was gone, just that fast.

"Never saw anybody like Little Willis," I mused. "What's with him?"

"He's crazy. Crazy as a loon," George said, then after a pause added, "Ain't nobody like 'im. Always doing when ain't nobody else ta give a damn. Brought me medicine last winter and kept me from dying. Should've let me go but didn't." Nervously brushing his eyebrows, to keep attention from his watery eyes I figured, he went a little limp, saying, "I ain't got nothing for 'im . . . to pay 'im back, but he's my friend. Probably the only one in the world." George went silent and never mentioned Little Willis again.

Time passed. George continued to say nothing to me or anyone else. The cool air turned toward cold. Little Willis didn't return. Another police cruiser crept by. More and more men stumbled up and the group grew into a sizable, subdued crowd. Then someone shouted that the doors were being unlocked and all of us lined up like schoolchildren.

"Warmth and food," I said out loud, adding, "finally!"

Before I could finish saying my sentence, the guy in front of me whirled around to bump me chest to chest.

"That's what you think, buddy?"

"Ye-e-s," I stammered, not knowing what was coming next.

"Think again," he blared. "Got news for you," he went on, his face nearly touching mine. "It's the hot seat first. We got to hear the sermon on hell before there'll be any eating." Then angling back on the heel of one shoe and leaning forward on the toe of the other, he twirled back around to rejoin the march of the outcasts.

A real character, I thought, continuing to keep in step with the others. Feeling the heat before I ever passed over the mission's threshold, I breathed deeply and let out a sigh of relief—a relief just shy of that I had felt when I let go in the cavernlike alley between the two buildings. But more surprise was still to come.

As I entered along with the others, I caught a whiff of what smelled deliciously like food intertwined with the musty odor of old hymnals, aging wooden pews, disinfectant, perspiration, and bad breath. The combination would have stopped me in my tracks had it not been for the spiffily dressed staffer. As each of us approached him, he, in a very determined authoritarian tone, commanded we go into the sanctuary for "a very short message," as he put it. The guy outside had been right after all. It was sermon time, and everyone dutifully shuffled in. But I rebelled.

With a boldness I was not accustomed to, I requested, "I'd like to go on and eat, if I could."

"Sorry," he responded in surprise. "Eating's later."

"What if I'd like to pass on the message?"

Taken aback, he quickly regained his lines. "You'll have to leave. Rules! The service is first."

"No choice?"

"Absolutely not. That's just the way it is."

Holding up the human traffic line, I began to hear grumbling behind me: "What's the hold-up? Move on. Go on in." So as not to alienate those I had come to consider as my comrades, I relented, went into the jammed sanctuary, found a seat, and waited to face the music along with everyone else. But it wasn't music that we got. It was a full-fledged, earth-shaking, hellfire-and-brimstone sermon delivered with fervent passion by a local preacher invited in just for us.

The preacher droned on and on about sinners and saints, Jesus and the devil, and heaven and hell, but all I could think about was the hand-painted banner on the wall over his head behind him. What did it mean? In Gothic English lettering it read, BUT FOR THE GRACE OF GOD . . . The three little dots after GOD held my undivided attention throughout the "very short message" the staffer had "requested" we attend. Although the last amen had been said in benediction, I sat contemplating the three dots. Four or five men kneed me to get around me between the crammed-together pews. In desperation one shook me by the shoulder to get me going and I did. As I moved along, it suddenly hit me what the dots stood for: "I could be like you."

It was the minister's words that brought it together. He'd said, "Sin! You're where you are because of sin. Sin, I tell you! And you're like you are," he'd continued, "because you've disobeyed God's law. Rejected Jesus' love."

That preacher had told us what that "But for the Grace of God . . ." meant. The phrase was saying, "We good Christians could be like you," meaning like "us" on the street.

"What a thing to do to us, make us feel even more unworthy, less human," I lectured

to everyone. But no one listened. They just went single file on through the old building, not seeming to care. They'd been here before, I reasoned in my own head.

"Drop it," I said out loud and rushed to catch up to the meandering line as it stretched down the hall to a hotel-like front desk. There the men slowed to a snail's pace and eventually to a stall. No one, however, was going into the dining room. That meant that no one was being allowed to eat, not just yet anyway.

Nearing the desk, I could hear the question "You spending the night?," then "That way" or "Transient. Down the steps." Whatever the response the staffer would wave with a flourish and then point one way or the other, and each man would follow according to the command he was to follow. Eventually it was my turn.

"Overnighter?" I was asked, just like everyone else.

"What do you mean?" I asked. "Is this like a hotel?"

"Renting a bed or not?"

"Does it cost?" I asked.

"Renting usually does," the staffer barked.

"I just wanted something to eat," I said, confused.

"Transient! Down the steps."

"Is that where I'm supposed to eat?"

"I don't have time for this," the official said, his voice rising an octave. "Meal's later. Move on."

Out of the corner of my eye, I could see Ken moving through the dining hall with his appointed guide, a young man pointing to this and that, patting him on the back, and introducing him to staff members. Ken didn't see me, but just seeing him was truly a welcomed sight.

"Move on," the desk clerk ordered, interrupting my security.

"Oh," I said. "Can I eat now?"

"No! This is the way it works around here, since this must be your first time. Staff eats first. Next the overnighters. Then the transients. And you're transient." Waving me along, he ended the conversation with, "Down the stairs. Next."

The brightness of the fluorescents faded as I descended the narrow, unlit old stairway. With each step I took, a thick stale dampness rose. A cloud of mildew engulfed me. When I landed on the concrete floor in the basement, I felt as if I had waded into a sea of raw sewage as the disgusting pungent stench of urine permeated my senses. Trying to shake off the shock, I hung on to the railing for balance and to allow my eyes to adjust to the lack of light. Unwittingly, I had entered another world, and it was a dungeon with only a couple of bare bulbs spaced far apart illuminating what I could only call a holding pit for the doomed.

"I can leave any time I want to," I told myself. Then, in a flash and seemingly out of nowhere, the dark side spoke up: "You'll never get out! You no longer exist. You've disappeared."

Then, with short unsteady steps, I made myself move forward. Within a few seconds, my faintness abated and I could see a little more clearly. The scene was surreal. I felt as if I had crossed some invisible line and been turned inside out and was now a part of the shadow side. In the false light, colorless beings with hollow black holes for eyes seemed like demons of the netherworld. Hell is populated, I thought, and it's filled with familiar faces from the street.

"There's coffee back in the corner," someone said, and I thanked him for the good news. Immediately I began pushing my way through the sea of men's protruding legs and jumbled folding chairs, making my way to the far side of the cramped quarters. It was true. There was coffee and I quickly fell into the wait. When it was my turn, the large man behind the cardtable set a cup of greasy brew down in front of me with a splash.

"Quarter," he said, holding out a waiting palm.

I stood speechless and he repeated, fingers rolling a come on, "Quarter! Got people waiting."

Stunned there was a charge at the mission, I backed up and mumbled, "I—I don't have any money." Not only did I not have one single dime, or penny for that matter, I didn't have one iota of identification—nothing to say that I was anyone or that I had ever lived or that I was even alive now.

"Sorry, fellow. Somebody else'll take it," he said sympathetically. "Let's let the others up."

"Oh, well, I'll live," I said with a nervous laugh. Falling out of line, and with the thoughts of coffee on my mind, I searched for a seat. Looking over the confusion, I caught the sight of a sleeveless arm waving high above heads of unwashed hair. I squinted to see better.

"Hey, man! Hey, come on!" came a shout. I thought I recognized the voice. Between the bodies moving about I could see George calling me over. I felt a twinge of excitement. Someone knew me and was actually saving me a seat. A friend among strangers!

"I waited to holler at you till you got your coffee. Been holding you a seat," he said, slapping the chair. "Sit." When I slid in beside him, he looked puzzled. "Where's your coffee? You were in line. Did somebody mess with you and push you out?"

"No," I said, and started to change the subject by saying, "Good to sit."

He was too smart for that. He'd been alive a long time and knew a run-around when he heard one. "Did they run out?" he asked, and went on without allowing me to answer. "Hell, no, they didn't. Those guys got some. What happened?"

Just as I was about to respond, George jumped out of his seat and started walking away. "Wait, George. Where're you going?"

Stopping, he turned around and bent right down into my face. His sagging cheeks quivered. Very sternly he stated, "You didn't have any money. Don't deny it!"

"Well, where're you going? Sit back down."

"Hell, no, I'm going to get a cup of coffee," and he was off. Minutes later he returned, sat back down, and handed me a large cup of coffee. "Don't argue. Take it. I've had some already."

"Okay, if you insist. Thank you," I said, very appreciatively and meaning every word. In spite of the grease, I thought it was rather good and sipped it slowly so as to enjoy every swallow.

"George," I asked dryly, "how were you so lucky to get these seats?"

"Last ones, like I said," he knowingly answered, "but you'll get used to it after a while. Everyone does."

It was not a pretty sight. Our chairs were right in front of the commode. One by one, in a steady procession, men would walk up, wait just beyond our knees for their turn, then step into the cubicle. It was a very public affair because there was only a half wall on one side and no door. The very personal event was open for everyone to see.

"That's awful," I said, taking the shame of the mission on myself.

"Not if you got to go. Better'n outside against the wall."

"What if you got to sit down?"

"Take what you can get," he said in such a way as to indicate he didn't want to talk about it. So I dropped it as a fact of life, but still my stomach churned from the odor, the filthiness, and from the humiliation everyone must have felt trying to use the repulsive facility.

After a moment's silence, George hunkered over, elbows on his knees, and asked, "How'd you end up on the street?"

"Bad times going around . . ." I said, letting my words trail off and not wanting to say more.

"Where you headed?"

"Thinking about Miami," I mused.

No sooner had I let Miami roll off my lips than George was livid. "No. No! Oh, no, don't go to Miami. Not Miami. There's ten thousand on the street in Miami. You'll starve. That's right. You'll starve in Miami. Don't go. Promise me. Go anywhere else, anywhere, but not Miami. You're too young to die and you'll die there, for sure."

George meant every word he was saying. He was absolutely convinced that if I went

to Miami, I'd die from starvation. So I asked his advice, wondering what he would come up with. "What would you do?"

A serious look spread across his wrinkled brow. Lost in thought, I could see his mental wheels turning. I waited silently. He was still pondering what to advise. A light must have gone on somewhere in the back of his mind, because his expression changed, reflecting a hopefulness.

"What do you know how to do?" he asked.

"Not too much," I said.

"What 'ave you done before?"

"I've done some writing. Took a few pictures," I answered.

Almost shouting, he said, "I got it. That's it!"

"What?"

"Look, man, I ain't got nothing, but I get a little pension check from the government every month and I got a lousy room up on the hill. Tell you what I'll do. I'll get you a typewriter and you can bunk at my place and start writing again."

Shocked, I searched for something to say. Anything! I wasn't prepared for his offer, so I stumbled for words, "W—well . . . What'll you get out of that?"

"Don't want anything. You can just write and if you sell any of it, you can give me back a little to pay for the typewriter. Then, if you make a lot, you might want to give me a little extra. That's all. Don't want nothing. Best thing is after a while you can get off the street 'cause sooner or later it'll kill you out here."

I was speechless. While George beamed, I sat dumbfounded, staring off into space far beyond the toilet and the crumbling brick wall behind it. He was a man with an answer, proud of his brilliance, and he was out of his seat and moving around the dungeon shaking hands and talking as if he were a new person.

When the call to eat was announced, George was nowhere to be found in the press to get up the steps and into the dining room. I had lost him completely, so I joined the rush, knowing that he was in the crowd somewhere.

At the top of the stairs I saw my friend Ken with the director. It was a pleasing sight, although by now I had lost my fears and was part of a group, some of whom I had become acquainted with and appreciated. Still, I smiled as I approached him, but he didn't seem to see me. No, he didn't recognize me. Yet he was looking right at me. I wanted to

say, "Hey, it's me," but I didn't just in case it would cause him any problems with the director.

By the time we, the transients, were served, the chicken soup was just soup. There was no chicken left in it. Without complaining we got our generous portion of chicken-less soup, rolls, and coffee. With a tray of food in hand, I scanned the filled room for George but to no avail. He was nowhere to be found, so I scrambled for one of the last remaining seats and took it just ahead of the guy behind me. Politeness vanished with growling stomachs demanding to be filled.

During all the slurping I heard someone far in the back of the room shouting, "George! Old George! Big George, where's you at? It's Little Willis. George!"

The big man stood up and waved. Little Willis nearly jumped a row of eaters to get to him. Over the hum of muffled voices, slurps, and clanking spoons, Little Willis yelled, "I got it! George, I got's your coat. I got's you one."

But Little Willis couldn't get down the aisle where George stood, face aglow. So Little Willis slung the coat to him over all heads in its path. Catching it, George immediately put it on and shouted back, "Thank you, friend."

Little Willis was pleased. It showed on the way he strutted, but he was not finished. Walking around the room, he seemed to be searching for something or someone. Trying to swallow the tasteless soup, I followed his movements. Then, before I knew it, he was at the end of my table, not three bodies away. He had found his man and he rushed him.

"Little Willis is here," he said. "Yes, I be. And I got's it."

The man directly across from me grabbed Little Willis and hugged him. Then Little Willis raised his hand, revealing a brown paper bag. "Here it is."

The bag changed hands and the man sat down as Little Willis, the man with a mission, got in line for his ration.

"Thank you, Jesus," the man in front of me began, and I looked up to see him with his head bowed in prayer. "Thank you for these here chicken necks. And thank you, Jesus, for Little Willis. Thank you, Jesus."

Dumping my trash, I bumped into Little Willis with his bowl of soup and rolls. Just as he was eyeing the seat I had given up, I couldn't resist asking him, "Little Willis . . ."

"That's me, all right." He grinned.

"Tell me. Why do you do that?"

"Do what, man?" he responded, knowing what I was getting at and just a little embarrassed that I would bring it up.

"You know. The coat for George, and the chicken necks."

"I don't do nothing."

I prodded deeper. "Yes you do, and you know it! Why?"

"Little Willis don't do nothing, man. It's the Lord. He gets at me and I just do's what He wants. Besides, if Little Willis don't do it, nobody else goin' ta. I's all they got."

"Now wait, I know there's more to it than that," I injected, knowing he was about to split. He was a man in a hurry and didn't want someone getting too close for his comfort. It was obvious he wasn't one to take any credit or think he was too filled with self. Nevertheless, I pleaded, "What is it that makes you do this?"

"Nobody makes Little Willis do anything, man. I do's it 'cause it's right. 'Cause it comes from the Almighty," he yielded.

Pressing him, I asked, "How long you been helping out people?"

A little irritated at me, he grunted, "All's my life. Never had nothing, but Little Willis got ways ta get 'round that. Don't do no stealing, though," he shot back. "It's the Almighty. The Almighty got his ways."

"Why'd you start helping in the first place?" I questioned on, knowing he could take off on his rounds at any minute.

Little Willis softened, but he was anxious to get out of my investigation. "Man, way back yonder in time, we was below dirt poor. And there was this hard-up family lived next to us. We was all in the same boat. But they never fussed 'bout it. Ever time they got something, they gave us some. They shared. They was just good people. Didn't have nothing to their name, but what they got, they passed some of it around.

"See, man, the old grandmama of that family was reading the Bible all the time. Reading it for herself and to us kids. One thing she read one day was, 'Suffer the little children to come unto me, for such is the kingdom of God.'

"Something stuck to me 'bout that saying. It was like the Almighty shook me and made me pays attention. So I says then and there, whenever I sees suffering wherever I goes, I'm to do something about it if I can, 'cause there's the kingdom of the Almighty." Little Willis stopped. Slowly he looked around the hall. He didn't miss a man in his scan. When his eyes met mine, he raised his right hand and, with his palm out, moved it back and forth. Finally, he added, "These here men is God's children and they's suffering."

Little Willis's eyes filled to shimmer with reflections of all the lights and men moving about. But he didn't let it stop him from adding, "I ain't no man of the cloth, no nothing like that. I be just a plain child of the Almighty. We's all God's children, and I just gotta do what the Almighty expects outta me. Makes no difference what all the reverends say 'bout heaven someday. That's holy talk. Peoples gotta have a little help from time to time in the here and now. The rest the Almighty'll take care of."

Then Little Willis grew edgy and started easing away, but he stopped and leaned toward me. In a near whisper he said, "These here men, they's my family, man." Straightening up, he nearly shouted, "Now I gotta go." And he did, straight to where I had been sitting. After a spoonful of the watery soup, he jumped into a conversation with not one but two or three men around him.

Now ready to go, I looked around for Ken. I had seen and experienced enough. As I started for the door, I saw him with his camera about halfway across the hall. This time he saw me. I nodded and headed for the door.

As I walked by the rows of tables and all the men hunched over their meals, George came to mind and I turned to where he had been sitting. I spoke up above the noise: "George, George! Over here."

The big man looked up and around the room. "George. Here." Assuming his eyesight might be failing, I wondered if he would even recognize who I was.

But I wasn't disappointed. He raised his hand, still clutching his spoon. "Hey, son, come on and sit down."

"Can't," I said. "Got to go."

"Hey, son, I meant every word. You know what we talked about. I meant it and I don't ever forget. You got my word."

"Thanks," I shouted. "Hope to see you around. And I won't forget, either."

Outside the night air was much colder than I remembered. There were no men left on the street. Very few cars were going by, rush hour having passed. By the time I reached the corner, Ken was already in the parking lot and unlocking his car. It would be a few more minutes before he could go around the block, travel a few one-way streets, and come around to pick me up. As I ambled on, I saw a police cruiser slowly making its way down the street. I prayed Ken would reach me before the cops did. I just didn't know if there could be a problem with them or not.

Then I saw Ken make the turn at the traffic light a block away. He was coming, but the cruiser was closer. Just as a searchlight was turned on me, Ken efficiently swung around the officers' car and stopped at the corner. Immediately I picked up my pace toward his car. Grabbing the handle, I jerked open the door and jumped in with a bounce. And slam! "Let's get outta here," I said, feeling like a criminal on the run.

After dropping into first gear, Ken revved the engine and sped away, within allowable limits to be sure. Looking over my shoulder to make sure we were not being followed, I spied the cruiser growing smaller in the distance. The searchlight had gone dark. Safe! I breathed a very welcome sigh of relief and let my head fall back against the seat. Closing my eyes in exhaustion, I desperately sought some much-needed rest. However, none was to come. I was to have no peace.

FLASH! GOD. DOT, DOT, DOT. Flash! Dot, dot, dot. Flash!

It was like an old hotel neon light incessantly blinking on and off. Flash. Dot. Flash. Dot. Flash. Dot. I couldn't shake it. Suddenly, as if in a dream, I was back in the sanctuary at the mission with the banner over the pulpit spread out before me. The three dots at the end of the phrase "But for the Grace of God . . ." held me captive. Trying to shut off the images disturbing my relaxation, I spoke aloud: "It's over!" But Ken didn't hear me. And it really wasn't over.

Flash! The mission. There was the aging George with his sincere offer of a typewriter. And Little Willis. He was holding up George's coat in the dining room and yelling for him over the clatter of seventy-five men chowing down to a long-anticipated

meal. There was the stinking exposed commode and men urinating and defecating in front of a roomful of people, a row of whom were only a foot or two away.

Fighting hard to come to my senses, I struggled to stay put in the present moment. It was no use. So I gave up and was immediately sucked along by the twister. In an instant, I was in the upscale Protestant church I had attended as a homeless man the previous Sunday. I'd picked it because it was one of Atlanta's biggest and fastest growing and was advertised all around the metropolitan area. I could still see the affluent Atlanta neighborhood in which it was located. As for the church, it was one of those traditional brick four-columned houses of worship with a gigantic steeple. Then, in my recollecting, I was inside and in my seat on the back pew.

A firm hand from behind me clamped down on my shoulder. Startled, I turned toward it as an involuntary reflex. When I did, a well-groomed face emitting a strong, overly sweet smell of aftershave met mine. Not only were we face to face, we were nose to nose as he bent down from his standing position. Surprised by my swift reaction, he backed slightly away. Lifting his hand from my old army overcoat, he caught himself and left it to hover just beyond touch. He was prepared to say something, but his words stalled at the tip of his tongue. For both of us, it was an awkward moment, his inability to speak and my wondering what he wanted.

"Sir," he started but stopped when laughing teenagers across the aisle drowned him out. One said too loudly, "And, God, look at his socks, too." The man and I both knew I was the focus of their attention. He sternly waved them quiet and severely lectured through silent moving lips. Patting me with his hovering hand, he lowered his head to my ear and said, "Sir! I'm an usher and I'd like to welcome you to our church. We're so glad you're visiting with us today."

Distracted for a moment by the snickering teenagers, I responded to his kindness. "Thank you. Glad to be here."

Hardly giving me a chance to finish, he took a very deep breath and continued, "I'd kindly like for you to come with me. If you will, that is!"

"Oh, I'm just fine, but thank you very much anyway," I said.

"Oh no, sir," his voice deepened. "I'd like for you to come with me. The service'll be starting soon."

Not sure what he meant by his request, which could have been interpreted as a command, I reiterated, "I'm fine here, but thanks."

His hand came back down on my shoulder. With his chin nearly against my neck, he prodded, "Please come. I'd like to take you to the front, where you can be with others like yourself."

"What do you mean?" I blurted out in surprise.

"There are others"—and he coughed—"other visitors." After a very short pause, he regained his sense of position. "What I mean is you'll be more comfortable at the front. The preacher asked me if I'd escort you down. You're to be his guest . . . to introduce you to the congregation. Please join me and we'll walk together."

"Oh, thanks but no thanks. This is just fine. I like it here. Thanks anyway." I went on and on, it seemed, mostly out of an ever-heightening degree of nervousness.

Realizing I was not going to budge, he left in a huff. The teens giggled but stopped when I turned to them and smiled. Then, disconcerted by what had happened, I looked to the far side of the church where Ken was sitting. He had been watching, and his expression showed his concern. We both shrugged our shoulders at the same time. It was impossible to know what he was thinking, but I was surely wondering what would come next. The wait would not be long.

When the usher had left, he had walked down the aisle closest to the pew I occupied. Before he reached the front, he had been met by another man headed toward the back of the church. Together they huddled for a minute or two. Clearly they were talking about important matters. As one, then the other, would look up, giving me a full view of their faces, there was seriousness written all over them. When they parted, the usher proceeded to exit though a door on the right side of the pulpit. The second man took long extended strides up the red carpet in my direction.

Inconspicuously looking over at Ken, I sighed. He responded by raising his eyebrows as high as he could to make sure I could see over the distance separating us. He had seen the unfolding drama, too. Then, in warning, he motioned toward the approaching man with his head and eyes. Ken sensed he was making straight for me. He was right.

Just as the immaculately dressed man got even with me, without giving any overt indications, he stopped in his steps, turned, and knelt down at my knee. As everyone nearby craned to see what was going on, he reached out to take me by the arm. Ready for the demand that I accompany him to the front, I braced myself. In a very pious voice he said, "I'm a deacon here," and without pausing went on to ask, "Do you know where you'd go if you died tonight?"

Taken aback by his bluntness, I said simply, "I came to see God at work."

He seemed not to have heard me, as he asked again, "Do you know where you'd wake up in the morning if you died tonight?"

"Yes, I believe so."

Then he proclaimed, "God loves you. God really loves you. He loves you so much that He gave His Son to die on the cross for you to save you from your sins!"

"Look—" I said, but he wouldn't let me talk. He jumped right back in.

"You can accept Jesus right here today. He will lift you out of your condition and into the love of His wonderful light. And when you die, you can go to be with Him in everlasting glory."

"Please, these are just hard times. There are a lot of homeless people who would like to have jobs and places to live."

His next words became almost inaudible: "We're praying for you." Going speechless, he bowed his head for a moment. Not saying anything more, he slowly rose from his position, stretched tall, and strolled back down the red carpet, shaking a few eager parishioners' hands as he went.

Jostled by several more deacons and ushers, each identifying themselves as one or the other, I came to understand the meaning of being "on the hot seat." The pitch was always the same, never varying. There was one confrontation after another. Each time I responded kindly with the same answers. In the process I had lost who I was and had become, in my mind, what I represented. Soon the bombardment was over. In the calm I lifted a hymnal from the rack in front of me and thumbed through it aimlessly to collect myself. I had never felt more alone. No one had chosen to sit near me. The rest of my pew remained empty, as did the right half of the one in front of me, although the cavernous hall was packed to capacity. The teenagers across the aisle were the closest worshipers. In my aloneness and vainly attempting to hide, I slid lower and lower in the seat and waited for what would come next.

Fortunately, a few minutes later, the choir began entering the sanctuary from doors on either side of the altar, filling the loft behind it. The congregation immediately stood and altogether started singing, "Praise God, from whom all blessings flow." The service had begun.

For a time I was just another face in the crowd. There were several more songs for the congregation to sing. A prayer. Several arrangements from the choir followed that. Announcements. Introduction of guests with the minister looking my way and holding out, in a period of silent anticipation, for me to stand. I held my seat. Prayer. Collection of the offering. A musical solo special led up to the sermon. But if I thought I was to go unnoticed after that, I was sadly mistaken.

Near the end of the fiery speech, the preacher pounded the podium and shouted at the top of his lungs, "You can get up out of the gutter." Silence. "You can get out of any predicament you're in. You can touch the realm of Glory, live in perfect peace here on this earth, and when you die, you can walk the streets of gold. Wear a crown of jewels. And, in the end, you can sit on the Father's right hand. You can have it all, but don't go to hell. It's hot. A lake of fire. Forever! You can have heaven instead. Think about your soul." Silence.

His eyes closed. Dead quiet in the auditorium. Then, opening his glaring eyes to scan his followers, he stopped with a gaze on me. Stretching out both arms, one squeezing his leatherbound Bible, he raised the Bible high over his head. With the other arm still floating in midair, he pointed his index finger right at me. In a trumpetlike blast, he cried out, "Come down to the altar and accept Jesus right now. It may be your last chance. Take it. Don't go to hell, please. Accept Jesus and rise up from the garbage heap to the mountaintop. I'm waiting to receive you."

Feigning exhaustion, the preacher went limp and clung to the outside edges of the podium. Everyone sat spellbound. No one moved a muscle. All waited in anticipation. Breaking the cloud of silence, the pastor whispered, "Let's pray. Let's pray earnestly, knowing God's Will will be done. He's still on the throne and His Will will be done. There's at least one soul I plead to get saved here today. Everyone stand. Every eye closed, every head bowed. Let's pray."

The minister began his fervent agonizing prayer for the lost to come forward. In concert with him, the organist began the hymn "Softly and tenderly Jesus is calling . . ." And I eased out of my seat and made an exit through the sanctuary's main door.

Once in the fresh air, I breathed so deeply that I felt a little lightheaded. A hint of dizziness soon followed. But I didn't linger, thinking one of the deacons would notice my absence and follow me in order to again attempt my conversion. Half walking, half trotting, I bounded for the street. When I thought myself safe from a possible chase, I stopped in my tracks to get my breath. Bending over, I put my hands on my knees and just slumped there on the sidewalk. Although I knew I was a free man both in and out of the church, I relished my freedom as I had never before. Still, I felt dirty. Not on the outside, but within. I wanted a bath, more to wash away a feeling of being unclean all the way through than to get the soot off my face. I wanted out of the rags I was wearing, as well. I wanted to be "me" again and not the person those people had reacted to just because I didn't look and dress like them.

As I stood alone along the busy street, my thoughts turned from thinking about myself to the members of the church. A great sadness engulfed me. It was such a heavy feeling, I wanted to drop to my knees. But I didn't. Nevertheless, I couldn't get that congregation off my mind. Questions arose as to what would make people act as they did, but I realized I was asking myself things I could not answer. And, as best I could, I started walking toward the meeting place Ken and I had arranged earlier. Soon I was back in the safety of the car with my friend.

After what seemed an eternity we finally started talking. I told him everything about George and Little Willis. Ken said, "You were a brave soul. A brave soul." He paused, as if he wanted to let me know he really meant it.

"I wouldn't know about brave," I countered him. "More like ignorant . . . like fools rush in where angels . . ."

Quickly he added, "It was scary. You totally disappeared into that world. I realized in there it was just one step. I took on a different respect . . ." His words trailed off. Then he said, "It was an awareness that I hadn't had before . . . a few quick moments and you disappeared."

"No kidding. You didn't even know me when I came up from the basement. That scared me. I'd already had my doubts, but right then and there I really thought I might never get out."

"I kept waiting for you," Ken broke in, "and you just walked right by me and I . . . it was like I kept waiting for you to come by, but you never did because you had blended in and I . . . I was . . . I was photographing people and I kept waiting. I knew there was one person I wanted to get in a photograph and that one person never walked by . . . but you did. You virtually didn't exist as the person I knew."

"Oh, God, Ken," I interrupted, "the dungeon!"

"My first thought was, 'Gee, they're going to feed those poor men to the lions later on, and I got to get the hell outta here.' It was frightening. I thought, 'Man, they're down in the pits here.'"

"I nearly panicked when George warned me about the cops. That had me going, you know, when I came out to hook up with you and having the cop car . . .'"

"If you'd gotten picked up by the police," Ken chuckled, "I wouldn't have known you anyway . . . 'I don't know who this guy is. I'm outta here.'"

We laughed, but I looked at him, wondering if that's really what he would have done. No, absolutely not, I decided.

Ken broke my self-indulgent paranoia. "It happens all the time. Had you had an encounter with the cops, you could've disappeared for weeks. You could've literally disappeared for weeks! And when you think about the very act of penetrating the level of society that you did, it was a brave moment in your life."

Ken didn't say anything for the longest while, then he said, "I think you found more of the reality of God with George than you did with the ushers and deacons offering you Christianity or salvation at the church." Then his tone became somber. "George really meant it."

We both paused and I said, "The church! What a revelation."

Rubbing his chin, he said, "It was interesting. The ushers sort of looked at each other and it just struck me funny. The look on their faces was almost, 'Here's an opportunity. We can show God just how good we really are.' I could see it.

"And you were going, 'Wait a minute! Wait a minute!' You were their trophy. I know you were going, 'No! No! I'm like you.'

"For them, you weren't a Christian because God blesses those who follow Jesus. You were poor and dirty. You were homeless. God doesn't let that happen to His people. In their mind God was not listening to you, so you must not have been one of His own. Otherwise, you would have earthly material goods. They didn't want anything to do with you, 'cause they didn't want any of you to rub off on them. I call it 'bump-and-run Christianity.' It was real easy to run up and shove God in your face, try to get you 'saved.' And when you wouldn't, they could clear their conscience with, 'Well, I've done my part.'"

Ken breathed softly. "The reality of that moment—think about it—what if you really were in that position? What if I wasn't sitting in a car two or three blocks down from the church to pick you up? What would've happened to you?"

I knew. Ken didn't at the time, because he was a block away. All he knew was that I was running toward the car with all the effort I could manage. He was shocked when I jerked open the door and yelled for him to drive.

With the way I was dressed, I was in the wrong part of town. The church people had let me know it. Then, when I was making my way to our meeting place, an expensive sports car topped the hill in front of me. As it approached, the driver's and my eyes met. Immediately he floored it. My first reaction was that his accelerator had malfunctioned. That wasn't it. It had to be me, because the young man wasn't watching the floor. His gaze was on me, and his expression was one of outrage.

Only seconds passed, but it had seemed forever. It was as if everything was in slow motion. Sounds intensified. The motor raced louder and louder. I knew the car was speeding faster and faster. Panic seized me, for in that instant I knew he was going to try to run me down. I bolted, but it seemed I was going nowhere. At that point, the car swerved and jumped the gutter, bouncing up onto the sidewalk with a deafening noise.

Now my legs were moving faster than I imagined possible, and I sped into the well-manicured lawn of the huge house to my left. I kept running all the while toward the next corner, just barely missing the car's right front fender. Fortunately, the driver decided not to pursue me into the yard. I would've been a goner.

When the driver saw that he had missed, he wheeled back toward the street and hit the gas again. His tires kicked up dust and tiny pebbles and spewed them as fine grit all over me and into my eyes. Back over the curb he went and on down the broad avenue. Neither he nor I slowed down. All I wanted to do was get to that corner before he could get turned around and head back for another try. And that was just what he had in mind. I could hear him braking at the intersection and spinning a turn. His motor was revving again. That's when I saw Ken's Mustang. My relief almost overtook me before I managed to flip the latch of the door handle.

Ken's face showed his surprise, but before he could question me, I told him in short, fast breaths to "Drive. Drive." And he did. Only after we were out on the main thoroughfare did I feel safe.

After my breathing had become more normal, I said, "God, they'll kill you in this part of town for looking like you don't know God or looking poor or just plain being different."

"Human nature, I guess," Ken had grunted.

Now, a week later, when I reminded Ken of what he had said about human nature, he laughed. Then I said, "After going to that church and now the mission, all I can ask is which nature?"

He knew what I was talking about, but I didn't wait for his answer. I could guess what he would say, so I said it for the both of us. "Think I'll take George's and Little Willis's brand." We both chuckled lightly.

Ken and I had never been closer, yet there was something he couldn't know. Maybe I was trying to hide it from myself in hopes that if I didn't talk about it, it would go away. Yet, deep down inside of me, I knew. I had started something, and these two experiences were only the beginning. And the real journey was ahead of me. I had to find those who had encountered God.

2. SARAH PHILLIPS

HAMPTON, VIRGINIA

Word spread that I was on a mission, although I had told only a few friends that I was searching for people who had seen God. Many dismissed the whole subject altogether, labeled me as strange, and kept their distance. Others drew close in hopes of having a part in the quest. That was the way I found Sarah. It was her sister who suggested I go for a visit. And since she lived in Hampton, Virginia, I wouldn't have to travel far.

I became more interested when I learned that Sarah had died and come back to life. When she was able to talk about it, she told of traveling to another place that was not of this world. Now she was sick again, although she had recovered from open heart surgery and several different cancers in the past.

So, at the urging of her sister, I decided to seek Sarah out. Although I had been told she was a most unusual woman, I was not expecting what I found.

Sarah walked around the house with her bird on her head. As the woman floated from room to room, like a gentle spring breeze, the cockatiel clung to clumps of Sarah's hair to maintain its towering perch on her bobbing head. Jostled about by every step, the bird shifted its weight, first from one leg then to the other, as it struggled to stay balanced.

When Sarah plopped down on the couch, the bird was still there on her head. No matter where she went or what she did, the bird usually rode along. They were so connected that even in conversations with others, whether family, friends, or strangers, Pretty Girl was included, most likely as the center of attention. Sarah made absolutely sure of it. Sometimes right in the middle of a sentence, she would just up and start talking to her bird. She was sensitive that way. She couldn't hurt anyone's feelings, not even those of her feathered companion. And the bird knew things, too. Secrets. Told to her through Sarah's whispers. When it was just the two of them and they were securely alone, Sarah talked right out loud to Pretty Girl. And she believed the bird understood it all. But the bird never told a soul, never gave Sarah away.

Pretty Girl was one of the few things that could bring Sarah a degree of comfort in her otherwise painful life. And as long as Sarah lived and breathed, so she said, she would never allow anything to come between them. The bird meant everything to her. They were forever inseparable.

On the surface Sarah Phillips could be dismissed as an eccentric. There was the duster she wore every day; she never seemed to change out of it. Then there was the bird on her head. Sarah gestured and talked, seemingly to herself, when not another person was around. Only the wise could have known the conversation was between her and her beloved Pretty Girl, who stood gallantly alert just above Sarah's brow. And Sarah just wasn't one to run through the neighborhood correcting misconceptions. Let people think what they would. She knew and that's all that mattered.

When I asked about the bond of love between her and the bird, she jumped to answer. Pretty Girl flew off her head, stayed suspended in the air for a second, and settled peacefully on Sarah's shoulder. "I love everybody and I love everything. My Pretty Girl's just something special. We've been together a long time. See, I raised cockatiels. Sold some, mostly gave 'em away. Had to get rid of all the others lately, 'cause I just couldn't take care of 'em anymore."

Stopping to talk to Pretty Girl, Sarah seemed to forget about my question. So I pressed, "What is it between you?"

For a minute or two she continued talking to the bird as if she hadn't heard me. But she had. I knew it. And she knew I knew it. Nothing further was mentioned for a while, each of us trying to outwait the other. Sarah gave in first, or maybe she had been deciding how she was going to phrase the demand she was to make. She caught me off guard when she spoke up with more of a plea than a condition. "I'll tell you about it, if you'll promise me one thing . . ." and her voice dropped.

We were back to the waiting game. This time, however, I knew I couldn't outwait her. I had to respond. She had thrown me a curve and was going no further until I said yes or no.

"How can I promise you unless I know what I'm promising," I quipped and we both laughed. Then there was a pause. And the waiting.

"If you'll promise me . . ." She stopped again and stared me down, her enormous eyes bulging more than they normally did. Finally she relented in her trademark glare and continued, "Promise me you'll come see me at least once every month for as long as I live."

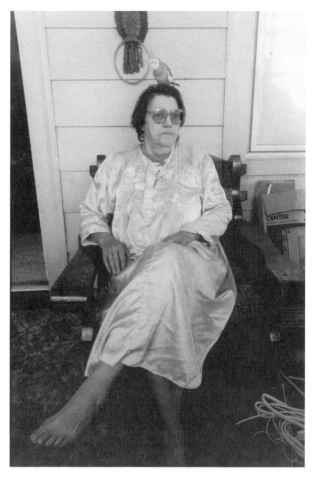

What she wanted was more than a surprise. It was a shock! What's more, she was serious. That, more than anything else, blew me over. Never, but never, had I ever had a request like hers. It left me speechless. She knew it would, and she made it anyway, because she meant it. I knew she meant it. And as I struggled to find a way to handle, really to get out of, her requirement, she watched me as a hawk would. Somewhere inside of me I heard a very vocal voice saying, "You've gotten ahold of a live wire and you're not going to be able to just turn it loose for a long time."

Seeing that my jaw had dropped to my chest, she lurched forward, laughter spilling out like rolling thunder, to take my hand. I couldn't resist her contagious chuckles, so I joined in. Besides, her charm was irresistible.

In the commotion the bird had been momentarily forgotten. Now it flapped and squawked at the top of its lungs. Up and down it flew in desperation, not knowing if or where to land. Startled by the flurry of feathers, Sarah was so overwhelmed in embarrassment, she scrunched her face into a mass of lines and wrinkles to show it. Her hand flew over her mouth like that of a child who had just been caught in some shameful deed.

Guilt covered her entire body. Recovering to rectify her inappropriate actions, she focused all of her attention on Pretty Girl. Immediately, without a second thought, she let go of a nonstop string of baby talk she had no control over. The bird shook in fright. In time, as only she could do, Sarah calmed her faithful cockatiel. Peace returned to the small living room where we sat. The ordeal with the bird was over.

Soon I realized Sarah was reading me as she would a book. She was good at that. She had taught herself to do it through years of lessons learned the hard way. Experiences that hadn't come easy. I felt a little uncomfortable, but I said nothing. Finally, she tried to let me off the hook. "About your promise . . ." she said, creeping back to our stalled conversation.

"A promise is a promise," I interrupted, "and I promise."

Sarah grinned. "Well, when you can't, you'll have to call me. Deal?"

"I promise!"

"I'm a miracle," she started. "Weren't supposed to be here. But I am. And it's a miracle.

"See, I was always just a little bitty, skinny thing. Ninth grade I weighed sixty-five pounds and they wouldn't nobody . . . ah . . . if somebody beat on me, they'd be scared 'cause they thought they'd kill me. Just always so sickly. Couldn't hold anything in my stomach till I was almost grown. I guess I just outgrew it. But I stayed tiny for a long time, never could put on weight, but just look at me now," and she laughed, but did so in such a way as not to ruffle Pretty Girl.

"But you wanted to know about how I love my bird so much, didn't you? I love children and old people and animals. It's just plain wrong to hurt anything, much less the babies and all of them are babies, to me. That's what we're here for is to love 'em all."

With a concerned frown puckering her forehead, she became lost in thought for a moment. "I was always so tenderhearted . . . so little all the time, I thought everybody was mean as they could be. Boy! I had a uncle that was really mean.

"Our big old shepherd dog had a litter of puppies and they were so cute. That mama dog got in a tree stump down in front of the house and had the puppies, and my uncle goes down there. We thought he was going to look at 'em and did you know when we went down there to take 'em food, there wasn't a dog livin'. He killed every one of 'em. I said to myself that I would kill him one day, but I never did. Thank God I didn't. But that did something to me and I never got over it.

"So I watch out for animals, try to protect 'em, take care of 'em. Sometimes they can't get out of the way of people and there's a lot of people who'll hurt 'em. And they're just trying to live like the rest of us. God made 'em just like He made us. So I'm always on the lookout for 'em."

Sarah turned to Pretty Girl and soon was engrossed in cooing to the bird, whispering all manner of gibberish. The bird said nothing but seemed to enjoy the attention. As for me, I allowed my eyes to drift around the room. On every wall hung every conceivable, although not expensive, knickknack, mementos of a life raising and taking care of her children. Pictures graced every wall, table, bookcase, and, of course, the mantel. Trinkets and souvenirs filled vases, ashtrays, and cups. Although the room was cluttered with stuff, nothing seemed out of place. It was arranged just the way Sarah wanted it.

Turning for a minute from the bird, Sarah tapped my leg and went back to playing with Pretty Girl. I understood her actions as a way of saying that she was still there and that I shouldn't get too lost in my own thoughts. Thinking too much could be dangerous. Then, much to my surprise, she let out a laugh and turned to grin at me. Maybe she was reading my mind again.

No one would have ever suspected that trouble was brewing underneath her quick humor and ever-present laughter. I sensed it as soon as I had stepped through the door. Although she had grabbed me with a hug, a kiss, a laugh, that was what she did. She didn't discriminate. It would be the same if it was a grandchild just returning from the store after being gone only a few minutes. Or a long-lost relative, a neighbor, a friend. For that matter, she would do the same for a stranger, like me. She was that way with everyone. It was who she was.

But I knew! There was something going on beneath the exuberant exterior. She wouldn't easily bring it to the surface and expose it. There was just too much there. "Why lay it on others," I could almost hear her say. Even saying it would be too much for her to put on someone else when, as she had put it, "everbody's got their troubles." She just cared too much for others to do that to anyone. That didn't stop me from wondering what was really going on with her, however.

It wasn't that I wanted to pry into her life and pressure her to tell me all of her most intimate secrets, but her sister had suggested that I go see her. "She's lived a hard life," I'd been told, "been through about everything. Had all kinds of physical problems. Operations. But she's never caved in and never given up. Go see her, she'll tell you like she sees it."

Sarah was amazed that I'd wanted to hear about her. "I don't know what in the world I could say," she laughed, "but I'm sure we'll do a lot of talking anyway. We'll drink coffee, smoke, and tell a lotta lies before it's all over." And did she ever laugh at the joke she thought she'd made. I got tickled at her and we both tried drowning the other out with our laughter. That caused us to laugh even harder when, in reality, there was nothing funny at the start. What is reality anyway? It's what you make it, and she was fun.

Sarah's attention was still on the bird, but she knew I was wanting to hear more of her story. "Don't tell me you're just thinking again," she said, startling me. "A penny for your thoughts . . . a penny for your thoughts . . . humm," she sang, "but make it juicy."

Just as I was about to speak up, she strained to push herself up from the soft sofa. Impulsively I reached out to give her a helping hand. "I ain't past getting up by myself," she snapped. "When I am I'll take that hand, 'cause I'll need it then." A strained smile spread across her character-lined face.

She was serious, I reasoned, and joking to hide it. I grinned back at her to cloak my knowing. Before I could make any comment, she murmured, "Been there a couple times. That's why I say I'm a miracle. Ain't supposed to be here, but I am."

"Been where?"

"Dead," she proclaimed, looking down on me from her standing position. "D-E-A-D," she spelled out. "Funeral home was going to be called. They were going to get me a fine coffin. Well, a coffin, anyway," she laughed, "but I fooled 'em, or God did."

Stepping over my feet, she tiptoed past me, breaking the conversation up, and walked to the dining room. "Pretty Girl's got to go in the cage, and I've got to lay down on the couch and give myself a rest," she said as she bent low near the cage. Pretty Girl put up no fuss, knowing the command, and hopped right through the small opening of the roomy cage. There was a rattle of metal as Sarah closed the door and fastened the clasp.

Catching a second wind, Sarah grabbed a rather large plastic bag on her way back into the living room and said, "Don't think I'm on my last leg? Think again. Just look at this."

Sarah held up the bag, and I could see very clearly that she was displaying prescription bottles of every conceivable size and shape.

"Medicine. All medicine," she coughed. "Stuff to put me to sleep, wake me up, keep my heart going, give me energy. That one's a hoot," she barked, and went on. "This one's for circulation and I couldn't live without these here for pains and aches. Got everything

I need in here. May as well just jump in the bag and be done with it. It's what I've come down to."

"You don't look sick to me," I lied.

"Oh, oh, oh, your mother taught you better'n that. I'm going to tell on you." She beamed, pretending she had something on me. Then, stretching out on the couch and throwing an afghan over her swollen legs, she went on. "My troubles now . . . with my body . . . might be coming from me being hungry and sick so much when I was little. I didn't have a good day, I don't think, till I was about eight or nine years old. All I ever remember's going to the doctor and getting shots or the doctor coming out to the house. Everything that came along, I caught it. And that's what I think happened to my body.

"I couldn't eat very much. If it had been good food and we'd got regular meals, it wouldn't have been enough for me, because I couldn't hold enough down till after I was married for the first time. If I ate one bite more than my stomach said to eat, I would just throw up all over everything.

"We'd have to eat cracklin bread with them cracklins that sometimes weren't done. You could crush grease in your mouth. But see, when I had my, what is it . . . pancreas, ah, I was told . . . I wouldn't make it through the operation. I believed in that doctor, but I made it. Not many of those operations have been done. See, I told you, I just get over one operation till I have to get another one. Every time I get in the hospital, my girls think I'm going to die. And I have before, but I came back.

"I had a rough life. I think that's why I'm so sick now. I'll tell you, it's been sixty-seven long years. All us kids, my brothers and sisters, and there were twelve of us, all we ever knew was meanness from my daddy and his brothers and their daddy. My grandpa killed a guy. He was the meanest one man that's ever walked the face of the earth. I couldn't stand him. I think grandpa is the one that caused my grandma's death. He beat her one day when I was up there. Made her wash him a white shirt so he could go out that night. She hadn't washed it, and he said he couldn't wear nothing but white.

"See, he was putting a hood over . . . and that was white. They wore hoods over their heads 'cause he was one of the Klan. Daddy was part of it, too.

"But you know, I didn't know the difference between black kids and white kids and all that. We used to have the cows down in the big pasture and black kids would go with us to round up the cattle and then they'd come and stay with us on our porch all day at a time. They were just like us . . . eat with us and everything else. And I'd run away from home, go to that family that lived over on this side of us. When I grew up, then everybody was racial. But I never was. To me we were all just alike, but not to my daddy. But he beat on everybody, made no difference to him. It was his whole family, they were always look-

ing for excuses . . . just like my mean uncle. He killed his wife and dumped her down a well. That's how mean he was.

"I loved my mother better'n anybody. I couldn't stand for my daddy to beat on her. I didn't ever care much about him after I saw what he did to my mother one time . . . I didn't. I saw him choke her black. I've seen it more than one time, and she still lived with him. He could beat on us kids, but not my mother. When he died, I said, 'Thank God my mother outlived him.' Once I got married and left home, it was years before I went back.

"I was nineteen when I got married. Cecil was just twenty. My children's daddy. He was meaner than hell. He beat me so bad one time I was unconscious. Blood was everywhere. My daughter found me when she got up that morning. She found me lying up on the dresser. He'd thrown me there and left me. I put up with it, 'cause he told me he'd kill me if I told or left him. And, oh, stupid me, I stayed. But not forever. I got a divorce from him. The only reason he left was I just got right beside of him. I had my gun in my hand. I said, 'You go. I'll take you to sign the divorce papers.' I said, 'If you want to live, you go sign the papers.'

"When he went down to the lawyer, the clerk said, 'What made you change your mind to sign the divorce now?'

"He said, 'If you were looking down the barrel of a gun, wouldn't you do something!' See, he didn't want me to say anything until he retired from the army. They could've kicked him out.

"But I'm not going through abuse now, not with my second husband. This one . . . he . . . I could sit down on him and pull his legs out of joint," and Sarah laughed for the first time since she had started her recollections. She probably could have manhandled her husband, but I figured she was only joking to make a point. So I laughed along with her. Then she said, almost as an afterthought, "I'd rather take a beating from anybody as for me to hit somebody else. Now, when it come to my kids, I'd . . ." and she let her sentence die, leaving me to piece it together and decide for myself what she would do. It didn't take much imagination on my part to know the answer. There would be no joking about it, she would take care of her kids whatever the cost might be. With that our conversation dropped off and Sarah dozed. Although I wanted to hear more, I drew back to let her rest.

The next day she and I picked up where we had left off. She was as lively as ever, masking whatever her ailments were in the same manner she had the day before—with barbs, jokes, and a lot of laughter. Not once did she complain. Not once did she appear as a victim.

"So you've seen God," I started.

"Got pretty close," she responded, her big eyes twinkling. "Got close."

"You said you died!"

"More than once," she said, her tone turning very serious. "When I was dead . . . I was dead the last time for seven minutes. I remember it all. When you die, everybody says you go through this tunnel and see a light. I didn't! But I was up in heaven for seven minutes, and it's so quiet and peaceful up there. Man! Everybody just looked at each other and grinned and all . . . just quiet as a mouse.

"I've always been religious." Sarah stopped, catching herself, and started again. "Pretty religious. I used to never miss a Sunday. I believe there's a hell, but I didn't go to it. If I'd have been there, I'd surely have wanted to come back. And at first I didn't want to come back, but I remembered my kids and I knew there were things I wanted to take care of.

"See, the doctors opened me up to work on my heart. They'd done what they were supposed to, but then they couldn't get it going again. I was gone. So everybody had left. They'd already called my house number and was going to tell everybody I was dead. I saw it all. I was in the room. My doctor was still there, though. So he went to the door. Just as he started out, he turned around and said, 'Now Sarah, you listen to me. I'm not going to let you die. James needs you.' James is my husband now.

"I was just busted open. Everything was out like this." She rolled her hands, fingers wide, out from her chest. "Then he just grabbed my heart and did like that." Sarah gestured as if she was kneading dough. Then she continued without even catching her breath. "I just opened one eye and looked up at him. Later he said the side of my jaw moved a little bit and my eye peeped up at him.

"When I came to, I didn't know anybody, though. I couldn't remember nothing. I didn't remember having a heart . . . When I went up to the hospital, I didn't even know it. Then, after the operation, I didn't know anything for another two months. When James took me to the hospital, I didn't even know it. I only remember him saying, 'Go up to the second or third floor and wait for me.'

"When I got off the elevator, well, stumbled off of it, some guy in a white uniform grabbed me. That's the last I remembered until February, 'bout two months later.

"They put the lower section of my heart . . . they took somebody else's. May have been a billy goat for all I know. But when I came to, I asked the doctor what all they did to me. Naturally he couldn't remember day by day. Neither could I. But I got a scar from here up to here. They made all the valves. They just redid everything in there.

"See, why it didn't scare me so bad this time . . . when they first told me I had cancer, it didn't bother me so bad. I've been through everything. I've had cancer twice before. I had it in my elbow and in my womb. All they did was just cut it out. And I got cancer on my leg. That's a skin cancer. It don't grow much.

"Now they say I have lung cancer, but I'm not scared. Next week I got to go in the hospital for them to explore around. But every time I go in the hospital the girls think . . . Well, I've died before. I'm not afraid. There's no need to be, 'cause I've been to where I'd be going. And that's a fine place. But, my kids . . . they're just worried. But I always say, 'Everything's going to be all right.'"

Nodding a yes that everything would be okay, Sarah waved to me mockingly as a child would in teasing a good friend and forced out a false grin. She then waltzed from the room to check on her grandchildren, who were making breakfast in the kitchen. Of course, Pretty Girl was squarely on top of her head, riding high.

After the meal, her sister, who was visiting from North Carolina, began preparing to leave for home. It had been a number of years since the two of them had seen each other and Sarah was pleading with her to stay another day. Soon she realized that it was of no use, and tears welled up in the corners of her eyes. Taking her sister by the hand, she led her into the dining room. All the while she was talking a mile a minute about her bird and the cage and the food. Bending down, she gave Pretty Girl the nod and the bird obliged. Sarah eased the door shut. There were hugs and kisses and Sarah told her sister, "I want you to have Pretty Girl. I know you'll take care of her better'n anybody in the world."

Straight away the sister fussed and fumed. There was no way she was going to take Sarah's most prized possession. Sarah persisted. The sister argued. Sarah demanded. Her sister fought hard against Sarah's appeal. Neither gave an inch. They wrangled on.

"Don't you like birds?" Sarah asked. And the sister nodded. Then Sarah mumbled, "Do this for me. I'm not going to be able to take care of my Pretty Girl. You can do this for me, can't you? I know you'll love her. Please do it for me."

The sister's resistance faded. A deal was made. Sarah promised she would let the bird go for only as long as she was unable to take care of it. They hugged and kissed. Then Sarah helped carry out the bird and cage, giving instructions with every step.

When it was time for me to go, Sarah squeezed me as tightly as she had her sister. Whispering in my ear, she said, "You promised."

Kissing her on her sagging check, I breathed, "Promise."

Then, as quick as lightning, she took off through the house. Rummaging here and there, moving things around on bookcase shelves, peering behind this and that, Sarah became a madwoman. Finally she came back to the door with her hands full, trying not to drop anything. I rushed to her aid to shelter anything that might fall from her thin fingers.

"Now this is for you," she said, and she nimbly handed me a pen and pencil set that she had obviously had for years. "And these are for your family."

There was a tiny vase, a doodad to put on an end table, crocheted doilies, a ceramic frog, and other choice items. Most things had probably been given to her and she was passing them on as gifts, keeping with a grand Southern tradition always to give visitors something to take home with them.

Hugging me again, she beamed. "Tell your family to always remember me when they look at this stuff." She laughed so hard and loud that her straining brought up a round of coughs that cut off her breathing and nearly choked her into a faint right there on the sidewalk.

The following week Sarah checked into the hospital. She had been scheduled for exploratory surgery the same week I had visited with her. I remembered her telling me, "See, I couldn't go to the hospital this week, 'cause you came. Couldn't miss this, now could I?" I smiled at the memory.

Late in the week that she had entered the hospital, I got a call from a member of Sarah's family. During the operation Sarah had lapsed into a coma. The prognosis was not good, but everyone was holding out hope.

Another week passed. She was not responding and the doctors were beginning to hint at the possibility that she would not make it. By the following Monday there were discussions about taking her off life support, but the family held firm. They would wait. And wait they did. But the situation worsened. The doctors said that it was not a good sign. Her eyes had fixed and had to be taped closed. Finally, she was gone.

As I drove to the funeral, I reflected on our talks. One thing about Sarah was that she made a fuss over any and everyone who came through her door. More than anything else,

I remembered what she had said about all those hugs she gave. She said, "I hug all the time. I make people hug me. And when my children leave, even if they come and go three or four times a day, they never leave through that door without me giving 'em a hug and a kiss. And we say we love each other.

"I say, 'One of these days, you're going to walk

out that door and when you walk back in I won't be alive.' And I say, 'I want you to leave knowing I love you.'"

During the simple funeral, attended only by her family, a few friends, and the funeral home staff, a thought came to me. It was the promise I had made to her. Her plea had been, "Promise me you'll come see me at least once every month for as long as I live." Now she was dead. But I was back and it was, without my being aware of it until that moment, exactly within the time frame she had made me promise to keep.

Her words echoed in my mind as I stood by the exposed casket, and I wondered if she had known through premonitions that she would be gone within that period of time. Then, there she was giving Pretty Girl to her sister. She must have known what we didn't. One thing was for sure, she had been a reader. Maybe she could read more than other people.

Some time later I called the sister I had met just to stay in touch. During our conversation I asked about Sarah's pride and joy, Pretty Girl. I envisioned the bird and the sister getting along perfectly. Surely Pretty Girl had adjusted and was enjoying her new home. My tone had been upbeat, but what I heard changed that. Much to my surprise and to the horror of Sarah's sister, the bird was gone. The bird had gotten loose and bolted out of the house through an outside door that had inadvertently been left ajar. Pretty Girl had flown away, never to be seen again.

The sister was heartbroken, and it showed in her voice. I tried to sympathize as best I could, knowing that had she been able to undo the accident she would have. She blamed herself as if it had been her fault.

I knew differently. She would never have let it happen, but nevertheless, she must have felt she had failed in her responsibility to care for the bird, had let her now dead sister down.

Some would dismiss the episode as the bird trying to get back to her home in Virginia. But I saw it differently. Maybe, just maybe, Pretty Girl wanted to be free. To be with Sarah.

3. PARKER TATE

SHELBY, NORTH CAROLINA

Preacher Truelove shouted. He bellowed. And then he ranted and raved. With one breath he belched out fire and brimstone. Warned of eternal damnation. The lake of fire. Proclaimed the coming day of reckoning. In the next, he oozed a fervent sweetness without changing the prophetic tone in his voice. "God is love," he blared. "God is love," he shouted over and over again. He was on a roll and building steam.

In the heat of a blistering August sun, the preacher's suit coat swung open as his arms frantically rose and fell like a bird preparing to take flight. Gesturing with his tattered Bible in one hand and shaking a clenched fist at the end of the other outstretched limb, sweat rolled from his forehead and down his beet-red face. Beads of perspiration dropped from his round nose. His tie-strapped neck was a flood and his worn white shirt collar was soaked through. But neither heat nor age was about to stop him. This was his street corner and he was on a divine mission to save not only the people nearby but the

entire little town. By being at his chosen place on the Court Square every Saturday, he made sure that everyone entering or leaving the county seat heard the message of salvation at least once a week. The way he preached said it all. He was in the middle of Sodom and Gomorrah.

The aging preacher man had a ready-made, although resistant, audience. The town of Shelby was bustling with people. Saturday was the day to go to town. Uptown. And from all over the county, and two or three surrounding ones, they came. Streets were full. Stores were packed. But no one ever seemed to be listening to the preacher. If anyone was, no one dared show it. All made every effort to steer clear of him. Even to shun him. Unofficially the man was an embarrassment. Had he been a member of one of the half a dozen powerful prominent families running the town, it might have been different. He could have been passed off as just being a little eccentric. But because he stood outside the circle of the local high society, he was barely tolerated.

But he was there on the corner and in broad daylight, just the same, along with the groups of families, distant relatives, and cronies as they huddled, joking and laughing, on the clogged narrow sidewalks. After all, it was the end of the week once again. Time for ritualistic gatherings to be repeated as had been done for generations. And, as always, the preacher's booming words of faith and condemnation floated high over the familiar sounds of jammed streets. As usual, they were chock-full.

In the past there were horses and buggies, mules and wagons. Now there were cars of every make and model possible. A few new ones. A lot of old ones. Some delapidated beyond recognition. Then there were the others that should have been hauled off to the scrap heap years ago. The drivers, vying for attention, or just oblivious to good driving

habits, revved spark-knocking engines, popped tight clutches, slammed worn brakes, and squealed balding tires. But none of this could drown out the salvation sermon. The man of the cloth had the corner. And the message had to be delivered. It was his overriding passion. His self-appointed duty.

Then came the day the street corner was vacant. The tambourine had fallen silent. Gone were the shouts of hellfire and brimstone. The messenger was no more. Preacher Truelove had passed into the next world. And about that same time, the town seemed to die, too. Cohen's Store disappeared. Woolworth's moved out. The Jewell Box went. Two of the town's three theaters locked their doors. The billards hall gone. J. C. Penny and Belk's moved to the new mall on the outskirts of town. Eventually Sears followed. Hudson's Department Store closed. As for the Saturday go-to-town day, it withered and ultimately ceased to exist. Yet there was that one presence that remained forever stamped into the minds of all those who dared press close enough to feel the heat of the Reverend Mister Truelove. And the shadow of the preacher man lingered on.

Now as I stood across the street from where he once called on sinners to repent, the power of his invisible presence touched me. I didn't mean for it to happen. I hadn't even planned on driving through my hometown as I made my way across the country in search of those who had seen God. But as I drove toward Georgia, I decided to see what changes had occurred in my absence. Now I was caught up in the web of my own childhood memories. In my mind, there he was. The preacher was back on the street corner. In front of the Court House. Preaching. And, in my mind's eye, the leaves of his old Bible seemed to be blowing in the wind.

For a while I stood motionless in front of the building that had once housed one of the department stores. Occasionally over the years I had returned to my hometown for visits with my parents. On several occasions I tried

DANCING WITH GOD

moving back. It never worked. I had heard that one can never go home again. I believe it. Nothing is the same. The pieces just never fit together as remembered. And soon I was on my way again. Atlanta. Chicago. Washington. Seattle. A perpetual traveler. Now I was back in Shelby, but it would be only for a visit. It had been just a quick detour off I-85. It was for old times' sake, I reasoned, and could be good for my soul.

Just as in the past, the spirit of the preacher was there. He was more vivid in my mind's eye than ever. Beginning to meander up the sidewalk, I stepped into the street against the light. A car horn blew in warning, and foul curses greeted me home. More sympathetic drivers, traveling in the opposite direction, stopped politely to let me continue my crossing. I walked on in a different world. Of another time.

Stepping up onto the curb, I was relieved. The park benches! They were still there. "It was right here," I thought, "that a few old-timers sat and one or two even dozed a bit as the preacher delivered his warnings of the coming tribulations." Then I chuckled, not caring if anyone was watching, and saw myself as a kid of five or six. It was the first time I remember having the dickens scared out of me by that man yelling that hell was hot. That I was going to die. Going to burn. The devil was going to get me. Keep me forever. And only Jesus could save me. God's only son, who came into the world to die for the sins of the world. For my evil ways. That I may never die, but live with Him for eternity. Walk the streets of gold. Wear a crown of jewels. Live in a mansion in the sky. Forever!

So mesmerized had I been by the preacher, I couldn't take my eyes off of him. I had been too afraid to. I just knew that if I had turned around to see where I was going, I would have plowed face forward right into the devil himself. Instead, as my father towed me along, I kept twisting my head around and looking over my shoulder to keep him in sight as we quickly passed.

It had been a good day, a wonderful one, up until that point. I had been wearing my new shoes to prove it. But every two or three steps I had stumbled over raised cracks in the concrete sidewalk, trying to watch the holy man. That had not pleased my father. Each time I tripped, much to his dismay, I scuffed a toe of my new shoes. First one, then the other. Not having walked a block from the store where they had been bought, my two-toned oxfords were all skinned up—something my father threatened to do to me unless I paid attention to where I was going. He angrily jerked me along, my arm squeezed tighter in the firm grip of his carpenter's hand, to the point that I almost had to run just to keep from falling down. I wouldn't have hit the ground, however. My father had been too tall and I too small for that to happen. I would have been left dangling, my feet dragging the pavement, and the shoes would have been scuffed even more. But I would have paid dearly. My backside would have been bruised by my father's leather strap.

So, running as fast as my bony legs would carry me, I struggled to keep up. I was in

a frenzy and so was the preacher man. As he shouted at the top of his voice, my heart pounded harder out of fear. Fear of that man swinging the black book. And fear of an even closer danger: my father. That day I chose to do as my father pointedly demanded with his brand of persuasion, but the preacher never went away. He stayed, all through the years, just over my shoulder.

As I rose from one of the benches where I had sat to recollect, I noticed someone leaning against the Confederate monument across the green. Starting to walk in his direction, I realized the old man was gazing intently at me. Propped against the granite by his backside and resting his frail arm over the crook of his walking stick, he watched every step I made. That's the way the people of Shelby have always been, I thought, half muttering to myself. They've never been intimidated by a returned glance and—I laughed, remembering—they could and would always stare you down.

Since I had not seen many on the streets, much less spoken to anyone since I arrived, I decided to amble over and see what my inquisitive spectator had to say. Having grown up here and knowing the quirks of the area, I thought he might snub me. Then he would wander off down the street to the old café for a cup of coffee and a smoke with his cronies. More than likely, if he did, I would be the day's gossip. Of course the question would arise in the boisterous talk as to whether I was sane or just slightly off my rocker.

Instead of hobbling off as I approached, his eyes stayed locked on me right up to the moment I reached him. I spoke first.

"Howdy," I said.

He looked at me suspiciously for a time, then he gruffly barked, "Fair to middlin'. Last time I thought about it, anyway."

Encouraged, I continued. "What's going on around here?" I asked.

DANCING WITH GOD

"You wanna know what's goin' on 'round here?" he countered, seemingly annoyed. "In Shelby? Hell, ain't nothin' goin' on. Not any more'an I can tell. Used to—" He stopped, looked up and down the street, but he didn't finish his sentence. Finally, after a long pause, he said, "Looks ta me like tha place's 'bout as exciting as a one-horse town with a mule they think's a horse. May as well roll up tha streets. Far as I can tell, it's seen its days. Ain't the same, I can tell ya that. Used ta be stuff going on all tha time. Court takin' place rightshere in this building. People in an' out all tha time. Used ta go in thar and set and listen. 'Twas our ennertainment. Heared all kinda stuff. Learnt 'bout everbody's business.

"And thar was old E.H. Meannest man ever born. Funny sometimes, too. Warmed those courtroom benches hot. Left 'is kids an' 'ol lady home ta farm an' he'd come ta town. Thay was plummed scared ta death of 'im.

"But like as I said, he was a rascal that was funny. Tickle ya funny bone. Why he'd go in Cohen's, used ta be right in that buildin'. Well, E.H.'d go in tha store and buy hisself a quarter pocketknife and come back out and set down right in front a tha place an' start a whittlin'. 'Fore too long some old man'd come along and think he had ta have that knife 'cause it as so good at whittlin'.

"E.H., he'd a keep on whittlin'. Not sayin' a word. The old man'd keep pesterin' 'im to sell it to 'im. E.H., he'd shake 'is head no. Then, the old man'd offer 'im a dollar. E.H.'d shake 'is head and tell 'im that was tha best pocketknife he ever had in all 'is life. They went back and forth. Finally, when the old man got up to two dollars an' a half, E.H.'d sell.

"After tha old man'd leave, E.H.'d get up and go back in ta Cohen's and buy another quarter knife and come back out and set back down. 'Fore long somebody else'd come along. Want that knife. I see'd 'im sell five of tha knives in one day. And that was real money in them days."

Seeing that he was at least willing to talk, I prodded, "Lived here all your life?"

The old man gave me a harsh look. It was one of those expletive-filled snarls that floated out but was never audible. Okay, I thought, maybe it's time for me to move on. But I just stood there, having been momentarily thrown off guard. Recovering from the blow of his devestating expression, I smiled at him and hoped he would relent and warm back up. He did.

"Born an' growed up," he said, clicking his false teeth together. "Don't live here now. Got run clean outta the state years ago. Been running ever since. Stayed 'bout a good step ahead of tha devil and lived so long that I 'bout got 'im beat. Slowin' down some, but don't think he can catch me. Not now, anyways. He ain't fast enough ta do it, learnt that ta be fact over tha years."

We laughed lightly together. It was a Southern thing to do while trying to come up with something else to say to either friend or stranger. My intuition was telling me in the interim that here was an honest to goodness character. A little con, maybe, but, for sure, a straight talker. At his age, it was obvious he had nothing to lose by being anything else but straight.

So I popped another question. "Run out of town did you say?"

The man said nothing. Period. And I waited and waited. Silence. Obviously he talked about what he wanted to. And nothing else.

Just as it seemed we had nothing else to say, he tapped his stick on the toe of my shoe. I looked down and he spoke up. "What'cha lookin' fer over yonder? I see'd ya. Made me wonder."

Glancing back toward the park benches, I said, "Oh, that."

"Yeah. That! I see'd ya," he coaxed.

"A memory or two," I said.

"I'll take one, but gotta speak up. I'm 'bout ninety. Hearin' ain't too good," he said and bounced his cane off the concrete and caught it on the rebound. "Just being funny. What'cha got on ya mind over thar?"

"Nothing much. But there was this preacher when I was a kid—" and he interrupted me.

"Blazes to glory, son!" he snapped, "Hellfire Truelove, and the devil be damned and me along with 'im."

Before I could say more, the old man stuck out his age-spotted hand to shake mine. "Name's Tate. Old, ain't dead. Maybe am but don't know it." He grinned a wicked smile.

As I was about to speak, Tate grabbed my arm with as much strength as it seemed he could muster. Pulling himself up from against the statue, he leaned close and whispered in my ear, "Let's mozey on over thar and have a listen to the preacher again."

Stunned, I frowned and he saw it. Then he laughed and coughed a time or two. Sticking a cigarette between his thin, already puckered lips, he choked out, "Thought I was crazy thar. Now didn't ya?"

"Well . . ."

Pushing me into a walk, Tate added, "Ya see'd 'im over thar awhile ago! I can see, too. Ain't blind, yet. Ain't dead, neither. Just about. But got a little wind left and still breathing ta boot." He laughed at his own joke.

When he could speak without choking, he said, "Son, just old. Too old. Punishment, I bet'cha. Worse'n Truelove's kind. Take it any day over this. Maybe should'a took the preacher's words ta heart an' changed my ways ta his. But didn't. Anyways, what's tha difference? I'm still alive . . . well, breathin', and he's dead. He went ta his judgment and I got mine, I reckon. Somethang ta ponder, now ain't it?"

Strolling along, Tate hanging on to my arm and swinging his cane from side to side, I murmured back, "One way to look at it." Not knowing what else to say, I asked, "Where you headed?"

He said nothing, and I wasn't sure he had heard me. I started to ask again, but before I could, he asked point-blank, "Who are ya?" Raising the crook of his stick in my face, he waved the question away and added, "I mean, ya growed up here? What's tha family? Family name!"

When I hesitated a little too long for his liking, he questioned, "Son, ya listenin' or somethang got ya tongue?"

"No," I said, "just a little slow."

"Ya ain't old enough fer that, yet. Now me. I paid fer being slow and got little ta show fer my money. And shore 'nough got old 'long tha way. Actually, older'n old. Ain't too bad, though. A old fellar'n get away with more'n a young'un."

Chuckling, I told him my family name. He drifted away in thought. Within minutes, he came back, "Yep. Knowed some by tha name, but up in tha county. Over tha county line, too. Couldn't be no kin ta them. They was some mean 'uns, that's fer shore. Anyways, ya're too sissified fer that crowd."

Tate didn't seem to want to go any further on the family subject, so we dropped the talk for a half a block. As we neared the corner, I changed the direction of the conversation and asked, "Where you going?"

"Everwhar I want ta," he returned without even blinking.

Trying to find out why we were walking down the street, I asked kindly, "I mean, where are you going now?"

"With ya," he said, matter-of-factly, and I stumbled over a crack in the sidewalk.

Regaining my balance, I tried to catch his drift. "But I was walking along with you. Where are you going?"

"Mean we," he grunted, pointing at me and then himself. "We goin' ta take a ride up ta tha graveyard." He grinned and squeezed my arm just above the elbow.

I laughed. He didn't. He was dead serious. Recovering from the jolt he had given me, I said, "Hold on, Mr. Tate—"

"Tate!" he broke in. "Just plain Tate. My daddy was tha mister," he added, jutting his chin out from his thin, wrinkled neck to show he meant it.

"Okay, Mr. Tate—" I started again, but he cut me off.

"Don't hear good, do ya?" he shot back. "Name's Tate. Done told ya no mister to it."

Nodding, he warned, "Bad sign fer ya hearing ta go at ya age. Think I'd be a worrying, if'n I was in your shoes. Next thang ya'll have's a hearin' aid."

"Tate," I grudgingly complied.

"Good," he said laughingly.

With our little argument over, I came back to the matter of the cemetery. "Just for my knowing," I proceeded cautiously, "where is this cemetery you're interested in?"

"Ain't far," he said.

"How far is far?"

"Ain't far. Right over tha county line," he said, adding, "other side of Boiling Springs over thar."

Hoping not to offend the old man, I gently injected, "That's a ways from here. That'd take awhile to get there and back, and I'm sure there'd be people upset if we just took off." Trying to put him off, I suggested, "Maybe some other time when it'd be all right with your family."

"Got nobody ta tell. Just me. Always handled my own affairs, thank ya kindly. So now's just fine," he shot back.

Looking for a way to appease him, I suggested, "Don't think it'd be a good idea. Surely there's somebody who'd need to know where you're off to. Can you go along with me on that?"

Tate stiffened. He stretched as tall as he could. Pride was written all over his face. And for the first time, I knew beyond a doubt that the wiry character I had run into was going to have nothing less than his way. I shuddered to even consider what I had gotten myself into. Getting out of the mess I was in would take some real ingenuity, something that I was lacking. Yet he was not about to go away. Looking into his worn but alert eyes, I saw a youthful enthusiasm remained. Although he was fidgety, his determination was evident. He knew what he wanted, and I was the vehicle for him to have it. Inwardly, I squirmed.

Finally, I figured I'd stall for the time being. Actually nothing else came to mind. "Listen, Tate," I requested, "why don't you and I sit ourselves down on that bench over there. It's where the preacher used to do his thing. And we could have ourselves a good talk. You could tell me about your life." In desperation, I added, "I'm going around look-ing for people who've seen God. Maybe you have, too."

Tate livened up. His eyes shifted. He knocked a pebble from the walk with his wooden stick. And for a second he forgot about going to the cemetery, or so I thought. Then he pulled me over and he whispered in my ear, "That what ya want? Might as well. Got nothin' ta do and all tha time in tha world ta do it."

As we started toward the cement slab onto which the benches were bolted, he grinned widely and said, "After that we'll go up ta tha graveyard. Up at High Shoals. That's whar some of my people are up under. Hain't been ta tha place fur years an' years. Wudn't even able ta see my daddy an' my poor mama laid ta rest."

Sitting with him side by side, I was curious and asked, "If you're not living around here, just where do you live?"

Old Tate slouched on the bench. Aging joints cracked as he sought a comfortable position. Extending his legs out into the walkway as far as they would go, he then put one foot over the other. After more repositioning, he angled his head toward me and said, "I stay down over tha state line. Down yonder in South Carolina."

Puzzled, I ventured to ask, "You got people here?"

"Nope. Died off," he said with no further elaboration.

Searching for answers, I probed further, "You with somebody?"

"Nope. Jest decided ta roll in here and have me a look see. Find out if'n this place growed any since tha last time. And show off that I outlived all them devils and still here ta talk about it."

Baffled, I asked, "How'd you get here?"

"The road," he grinned, resetting his teeth.

"I know the road, but . . ." I paused.

He picked up where I left off. "Ya shore ask a lot of worthless questions ta look sorta smart. But I'll tell ya so as ta get it off'n ya mind," he snorted. "I hit the damn road. That's tha way ya get somewhar when ya want ta go. Always been that way. And God knows ya get ta whar ya want ta go or someplace else maybe more interestin'." Then he smiled sarcastically, adding, "Simple, now ain't it!"

My disbelief that this man at his age was traveling wherever he pleased showed off. Tate saw my amazement. He chuckled for a time, then perked up even more with, "Ya gotta lotta larn, son, a lotta larn. And age ain't got nothing ta do with it. Gotta get around ta know anythang. Don't come from settin' on your butt, neither. Gotta go, pure 'n' simple." With that comment, he leaned his cane against his leg and clapped a time or two, probably just to make sure I got the message.

Something else got my attention as well, and I brought it up. Reaching over his leg, I started to take hold of his cane, but he became very agitated. I held back, but asked, "You're pretty handy with that stick. You don't act like you need it by the way you throw it around. Got a story that goes with it?"

Tate picked it up and rubbed it. He smiled, then spoke, "Ya see'd that, now did ya? Ain't much of no story. Just handy. Ya got that, too. A man's gotta 'ave somethang, don't ya think?"

"I guess so, but it doesn't seem like you really need it for walking purposes."

"Use it fer walking just ta throw people off. This here's better'n carryin' a gun. Gotta have some pertection." He gazed at me, and as he did, a twitch appeared just under his left eye. Scratching at it, he said, "Keeps tha dogs off and can crack somebody's head if'n I have ta. But otherwise, get a long fine, thank ya."

We sat. Both of us watched what little activity there was going on in the heart of town. There was a reasonable amount of traffic, but shoppers were few. In my mind I was comparing what was going on to what was happening years earlier. As for Tate, I didn't have a clue where he was, whether he was in the now or in another era. A slight breeze brushed us and I decided to raise another question.

Cupping my hands together in my lap and looking straight up and through the tree limbs above us, I drew my words out slowly. "Say, over there on the corner, I said something about God. It looked like you had something to say." I waited. When he didn't speak up, I did. "Ever seen God?" I chanced to ask.

The same expression I had seen earlier returned. But he stayed still. In time he whispered, "Lived with tha devil once and see'd 'im several times after that." And he stopped. I held my fingers crossed in hopes he would go on, and finally he said, "Can't say I ever seed God."

My heart sank. I was sure he had, but here he was saying he hadn't. Yet there seemed to be words at the tip of his tongue. Licking his thin, pale lips, he said, "Nope, never truly seed God like lookin' at ya right now, but I shore did see 'is hand at work. Working hard! And saw what He can do in times of trouble, but that thar's a long story and ya ain't got tha time."

"Yes, oh, yes, I do," I excitedly exclaimed. "I got the time, if you'll tell about it," I pleaded.

"What about tha graveyard? Up yonder. High Shoals. Son, you ain't got tha time for no story!"

He had me good. For a cantankerous old codger, he was sharp. Quick, too. Tate didn't miss a trick. I knew there was only one thing to do. 'Fess up. My chips would have to fall wherever they happened to land. The rest would be up to him.

With apprehension, I started, "Tell you what. Let's talk awhile. Might be that later . . . well, we'll see."

Tate shifted. Cocking his hat back, he groaned, "Don't like ta stay in one place too long. Gotta move around."

"What about it?" I said, my hopes rising.

After straightening the sides of his crumpled pack of cigarettes, he dug into the opening to pull one out. It was bent but not broken. He caressed it back into shape. It seemed to take him forever to go through the ritual. Then he abruptly put it back into its package and said, "Gotta keep ya word. You said it. I didn't. Between you and ya maker. But I'm up ta tha ride. Now what'd'ya want ta know that ya think's so gawdderned important?"

"God!" I said.

Tate frowned. "Devil'll be after ya."

"I don't understand what you mean."

"Sonny boy, this here's tha fact. I see'd it time and time again. If'n God does somethang fer ya, tha devil'll try ta take it and attempt ta turn it plum around. Good thangs can be turned inta bad on tha spin of a dime." Tate waved at me, then proclaimed, "But ya knowed that anyhow.

"Now this here's just me talkin'." He laughed and went on. "Ta my way of thinkin', come ta me over tha live-long years, thar's somethang ya gotta do, no matter what. Ya gotta always be lookin' for tha Lord an' pay no attention ta tha devil. He wudn't 'ave a home if'n ya didn't let 'im in ta your'n. If'n everbody did that, he wudn't 'ave a home nowheres."

Tate then sat up straight, both feet on the ground, and twirled his stick between his outstretched palms. With his shoulders bent like a bow, he rolled his head from side to side. Several vertebrae popped. Finally, he said, "Got my idea of tha man upstairs, sonny." He glanced sideways at me to see if I was listening. When he was sure he had my ear, he said, "Live an' let live and let me work it out with my maker by myself 'cause down at tha end I gotta face Him fer myself. 'Cause ya and nobody else goin' ta be thar. Just goin' ta be Him and me.

"A lotta people," he went on, "a tryin' ta make people believe tha way thay want 'em ta and they awful mad 'cause thay can't do it. Like tha preacher that stood right here. I guessed he was mad. Not like crazy mad. Just mad, real mad. Nobody'd listen. I think he was mad at hisself, 'cause he wudn't shore 'bout it hisself. Wanted to make everbody believe a certain way and they wudn't.

"Always bothered me 'bout people tryin' ta make everbody believe their way. Scared me from doing it, 'cause someday I didn't want ta wake up ta larn I was wrong. So I told myself I gotta live and let live. Be nothin' on my conscious that way." He blew a sigh of relief.

Letting him take a breather, I sat for a long time without saying a word. Every once in a while he would reposition himself. I was convinced that the bench was eating into his posterior. He had no cushioning, as his body had not one ounce of fat. When I felt like he wouldn't mind talking again, I reopened the conversation.

"You must've gone through a lot to come to all that. How'd you do it?"

Tate became pensive. Then he said, "When ya live a life like I've had, thangs just naturally come ta ya if ya live long enough. Been thinkin' tha Lord'll go on and take me. Thought that a long time ago, but I'm a guessin' he's gotta little more ta do with me 'fore he's done. And I guess other thangs'll come to me while I'm a waitin'. Wish I knowed some of this stuff back when I was younger. Could shore 'nough used it then. Wudn't 'ave had to learnt some stuff tha hard ways like I did. Now I'm almost dead. But not all tha way," he cracked.

Reassuring him, I spoke up by saying, "If you're dead and I'm alive, I'd bet you'd still have a lot more to talk about than me. I'd like for you to go on and tell me about your life."

"Now don't take me wrong, son. I might be 'bout dead, but I ain't thar yet. But can't say I didn't warn ya 'bout all this being a long story. And I gotta go way back. It's one of them tall tales and all fired compli-ca-ted," he said, getting tongue-twisted on the last word.

Nevertheless, he started, "Reckon you heared 'bout hell. Well, son, that place, it ain't nowhar else but here. Right here! And I'm a meanin' it too 'cause I lived in it fer some time. Got real tared of it, but didn't know I could do nothin' 'bout it until tha hand of tha Lord come down." His eyes glazed over.

Taking a soiled, threadbare handkerchief from his back pocket, he opened it and rubbed it over his face. Then he said, "Go back a figuring, sometimes. Some get my age and that's 'bout all they can do . . . figuring, figuring, and a figuring. In my figuring, I weren't so mean, just bad.

"Now my daddy and a—well, my whole family and all my kinfolks, now thay was mean. Just plain an' simple mean—ever last one of 'em and there's a covey of 'em, too. Well, not anymore. None of 'em left. Near as I can figure, I'm the last one left 'cept nieces and nephews and thay don't mean nothin' to me.

"Son, my family never meant nothin' to me, either, always tryin' ta tell me what ta do and how ta live. Made hell look good. 'Cause thay couldn't even live what thay preached. Beats me why thay tried to preach ta me. And thay went ta church all tha time. But mean . . . that's the way thay was as far back as I can remember and I ain't lost all my mind yet. That's my problem, I remember.

"If you're sittin' where I'm sittin' and you're lookin' back, all in all it don't look too good. But the further back I step, I reckon I maybe could've been different sooner. But I was just ignorant. I guess I was scared thar was somebody'd who come and beat me, so I was going ta stand up fer myself. I learnt ta be that way. Had good teachers. My mean daddy fer one.

"My brothers, fer that matter the whole gawdderned family, thay t'weren't a group ta reckon with at all. Most of them would just as soon kill ya as ta look at ya. They all killed along tha way, every one of them, including my daddy. That was somethang I couldn't stomach.

"Most things 'bout my family was true . . . beatin's and killin's. I ain't too proud ta carry tha name. If'n ya don't know nothin' no different, ya just figure that's tha way tha world is and that's tha way life's s'possed ta be. Only thang left ta do is make the best of it. I did what I learnt . . . what I see'd done, what I had ta do ta get by. Did that till I learnt a better way."

Tate's mood changed. Something in him surfaced that he seemed hesitant to reveal. So we just sat silently watching the rhythm of the town beat on around us. I decided to let him proceed at his pace. Soon he leaned forward on his battered cane. I knew something was coming.

"Ya're going ta go with me ta High Shoals church! Yessir, that's what ya can do fer me. I ain't been there in years. It's 'bout time, 'cause I got ta know 'fore I leave this world that my daddy and mama is shore 'nough dead."

Tate turned. He seemed angry. His eyes were set straight ahead. Then he added, "I ain't leavin' this world till I know thay've done died and gone. I just gotta see fer myself . . . gotta see tha markers with tha names on 'em, 'cause if thay're dead, thay'd be buried right thar at tha church. If thay ain't thar, thay'd still be 'live which'ud be perty rare. Be old as Mathusla—"

"Methuselah?" I interrupted.

Tate ignored me and went on. "Anyways, I gotta know fer sure and you're tha one that'll go with me, 'cause nobody else'll do it . . . not at my age."

Breaking in, I quizzed him, "Let's see here. You got here from where you live. Why is it you didn't just go on up there?"

Tate's anger lifted and he laughed. "You smarter'n ya look, son." As his chuckles subsided, he said, "Roads're changed. Figure ya knowed tha way better'n me. And somethang 'bout ya just made me think about it more. Made me wanta go today."

The thought of taking the old man anywhere unnerved me. I hardly knew him. I didn't know anything except what he had already told me, which wasn't much. I didn't even know where he lived. On that, he had already made it clear that it was none of my business.

My heart beat hard in my chest as I tried to figure a way out. What if he dies along the way, I argued silently to myself. What if he's missed and someone calls the police?

But before I could tell him it would have to be another time, he was up and impatiently thumping my shoe with his stick. Realizing that he wouldn't take no for an answer, I reluctantly yielded and led him to my car.

As we drove down Lafayette Street and toward Boiling Springs, Tate started talking about his family. "My daddy must not 'ave thought I could grow up ta be a man by myself," he was saying, "so he took it on hisself ta make one outta me while I knowed I was still a boy. He told me, 'bout tha time I was thirteen, that he wanted ta take me into tha 'society.' That kinda made me proud in a way. Didn't know what tha 'society' meant, though. But it scared me, 'cause I'd already growed distrustful of him 'cause of his beatins and stuff. He was mean and would let me have it backhanded fer no reason but his own individual quirks. Fer all I knowed, whatever plans he had fer me, thay'd be some pain with 'em.

"Before long in his talking, he said I'd 'ave ta go with him ta larn 'bout tha society. Said I'd be at his side all tha time. And that was that. It weren't that he asked me ta go. It was settled in his mind, I was going.

"It was weeks or so 'fore anything came up 'bout tha society of his—that's what he called it. Tha 'society.' Later I learnt why he named it that. When I got older, I'd heared him telling folks 'round that didn't know better that he had ta go ta meetings of tha society of his 'cause they'd be gettin' ready to help some people 'cause they'd be poor.

DANCING WITH GOD

Funny how my mind worked back then. What I seed in tha county, everybody was poor. He never wanted ta spill tha beans 'bout tha real nature of what he was up ta, though. He weren't tha only one involved, neither. There was a whole bunch a men a part of tha 'society.'

"Anyways, one night he roused me right outta my sleep in tha middle of tha night. Scared tha livin' daylights outta me. Not my brother, though, who I had ta sleep with. He was already up an' movin' about. It was so dark I couldn't see a thang, just a shape in tha door. Took me a spell ta get my senses 'bout me and not think some spook was after me. By tha time I hit tha floor, I really got spooked, 'cause I then thought somebody'd died. I couldn't even talk, just stood in my drawers waitin' for him ta let me have it with tha dread. I knowed it was coming.

"I remember his words like thay was yesterday. He said real low, 'Get moving, boy. Get ya'self in a hurry. Scrape up your duds and get 'em on now.'

"Daddy weren't a man ta cross, and I knowed it. When he said do somethang, I jumped. He was mean and I knowed it. I guess he was trying ta be tha meanest in the county. Best I can recollect, that's where I learnt it . . . that part of him stuck in me. Still, there was others 'round that could outdo him. Maybe he was trying ta outdo them. Some

had a big name 'round for having him and anybody else beat. Yessir, them was hard times . . . tough just ta get by.

"That night I got myself in high gear and ran after him, jerking on my overalls fast as I could in tha dark 'cause he wouldn't let me light tha lamp. When we got outside it was muddy . . . rained most all day from summer thunderstorms. Mud was bad, but I was glad tha rain had stopped. Still, it was sticky . . . worked up a sweat walking up ta the barn where he had tha wagon hitched an' waitin'.

"We started rollin' and he hadn't even said one word 'bout nothing. I knowed better'n asking nothing. So we just bounced along. Thar weren't no talking. After a time we got close ta where he wanted ta be, 'cause he parked tha wagon and sat still . . . seemingly waiting for somethang. 'Fore too long I heard another wagon coming down tha hill toward us and there was another one 'hind it. After a little bit, another one pulled up. Ever last one of 'em was filled with men and almost grown men. Everbody talked low . . . so low I couldn't hardly make out what thay was sayin'. Inside, though, I knowed somethang was 'bout ta happen. All my insides churned 'round 'cause of what was going on.

"Daddy came back ta tha wagon and reached 'round under tha seat and pulled out a bunch of white cloth all folded up real neat like. It was real puzzlin' 'cause he said fer us ta put tha stuff on.

My brother must 'ave knowed all about it, 'cause he grabbed at tha top of tha stack and started sortin' it and drawing tha sheetlike thang right over his head. I just looked at him in tha dark and in a minute he figured I didn't know nothin' and he helped me. Didn't take no time fer me ta feel real funny all wrapped up in that cloth. Next he slid a thang right over my head and pushed it down and twisted it 'round. Thar was holes in it fer my eyes. When I looked 'round I see'd him fer tha first time in his getup. He looked just like a real honest ta goodness spook . . . a ghost.

"Then Daddy crawled up on tha seat and he looked tha same. Ever last man in tha gathering had done tha same thing, too. It was plain comical and I started a laughin'. That's when daddy slapped me 'cross my covered head real hard, and I stopped laughing then and thar. I wanted ta cry real bad. All he said was, 'This ain't no funny matter. Now get ya'self serious. Conduct yourself like a man and keep ya mouth shut or ya won't have no mouth ta shut or no teeth to eat with.'

"Daddy said he was ready ta tha men in tha next wagon over and we started rollin' again with everbody fallin' in line like thay was some order ta tha thing. Daddy tapped me on my head real hard with his knuckles, hurt like tha dickens, and told me I'd be seeing somethang important real soon.

"After a few minutes we turned down a road that took us 'cross a rise and down again. Each wagon pulled up side by side out from a little old house off by itself. Just like clockwork everbody fired up a bunch a torches. Lit everthang up.

"That's when all tha guns come out. There was more of 'em than you could shake a stick at. A man in the first wagon yelled out for Biggs ta come on outta tha shack. That man said somethang like, 'Biggs! Come on out. God's come calling. Now don't keep Him waiting no longer.'

"My ears . . . thay seemed ta be always burning, and that night thay shore did with that man shoutin' out like that and, in a short spell, hearing all tha coloreds screaming and squalling inside tha old house. Ever man in them wagons was standing tall and waving their fires and guns over their heads. I tried ta hide, I was so scared. But Daddy pulled me up by grabbing me 'round tha nap of my neck. As I stood 'tween my brother and Daddy, my brother shoved a little ol' single-shot rifle in my hand. That was tha same one I always went huntin' by myself with.

"Thangs was getting agitated like and somebody yelled out again fer Biggs ta come out. Thar was more screaming, sounded like women and kids, but nobody stirred much that I could see. Another man barreled out, 'Biggs! You heared. We know you ain't deef. Don't keep God waitin' no longer, 'cause it's Judgment Day.' And thar was mad in his voice.

"Thar was a long wait. Then somebody else spoke up and said all tha women and snot-nosed kids would 'ave lots of trouble if Biggs didn't come out and face up ta his medicine. More waitin'. Then somethang moved 'side the house and I heared a blast 'fore I knowed what was taking place. It was plum awful. It's still in my mind like'n it was yesterday." Tate dropped his head against the window of the car. His hat slid back, and he grabbed for it without even looking. Then he fell silent. We rode on.

Passing through the single traffic light in Boiling Springs, he roused himself. "Hey," he said, truly concerned, "ya sure ya know tha way?"

"Sure," I answered. "Going over about Cliffside. Then up toward Caroleen. Between Caroleen and Avondale?"

He grinned big enough for me to see his teeth. "Say howdy. Ya got it right. Ya can get us close, anyways."

"Don't leave me hanging," I pushed, urging him to go on with his story. Finally, after taking what I thought to be too much time, he started again.

"Well, sir," he said, "when somebody up an' fired off a shot, all hell an' her sisters broke loose. All tha men in them sheets was running like mad dogs 'round tha house whar tha gunshot come from. It looked just like fireflies going in ever direction. I just froze plum still standing all by myself on that wagon. Made my mind try ta thank 'bout other stuff, but it wudn't. I was shakin' 'bout outta my breeches and all tha while doin' some powerful prayin' that all them mules wouldn't rear up and head outta thar, taking me with 'em.

"In a little bit, I seed the lights comin' out of tha woods. Everbody was jerking at Biggs and kickin' 'im and punching at 'im. All his people had come outta the house all cryin' and pleadin' and squallin' at a high pitch. That got tha men even more rowdy'r'n ever before.

"First they tied Biggs ta a tree and a couple men started strapping him right on his bare back. It weren't long 'fore his blood started flying ever time he was hit. In the beginning he yelled out, but after a while he didn't move much. When everbody was worn out beating on him, they cut him loose and drug him out under a big limb and throwed a rope over it and put a loop in it and flung it over his neck. Everbody shouted and somebody said, "Prepare ta meet ya maker," and a couple men grabbed tha other end and pulled it so hard ole Biggs's feet come right off tha ground. When that happened, the rope got tied back 'round the tree.

"I didn't want ta look, but I did. Can't never forget Biggs's face. It got real blowed up lookin' and his eyes . . . thay bulged," and Tate wiped his own eyes. "Everbody roared 'cept his people who was still pleadin' fer tha Lord ta help 'em and pleading fer all tha men ta 'ave mercy. Nobody paid no attention.

"That's when my daddy spoke up to Biggs's people. He said, 'Ya best know ya place and stay in it. Biggs got too uppity. And we be a'bringin' 'im down. Ya too if ya ain't careful.'

"And all tha men laughed real loud, noddin' their heads back and forth. Then a bunch run over ta Biggs hangin' on tha rope and cut 'im loose. I heared the thump when he hit tha ground. Thought he was dead, but he was still alive.

"Next everbody dropped their torches and run back ta tha wagons. By tha time we got back out ta tha road, everbody was quiet . . . just talkin' low amongst ourselves. All tha wagons stopped all along side of each other. Daddy jumped off our wagon with the others and all tha sheets come off with tha hoods. That's when I recognized some of 'em and one of 'em was tha law. I knowed, 'cause he'd been out ta tha house a time or two and been up at tha store when I went with Daddy thar. And thar was tha preacher, too. Even in the low light, I knowed tha preacher no matter what. Give me tha worst fright of all. Figured 'im ta be good like he preached 'bout being. As for a lot of tha rest, I never knowed 'em hardly at all.

"Me! I was still shaking. Somethang was going on inside of me. 'Twas tha strangest feelin' I ever did 'ave. I felt roused up . . . like I was strong, and I was all broken up by tha way tha colored family was treated. And what thay did ta Biggs. Tore me up. Tha feelings raced back and forth in my whole body. I couldn't think straight with all tha strangeness.

DANCING WITH GOD

"When it was just us goin' down tha road by ourselves on tha way home, Daddy slapped me hard on the back and he said, 'Ya joined up now, boy. Can't be a talkin' 'bout this ta nobody . . . part of being a man. Ya see'd what happened tonight, ya let it out and somebody'll. . . . Remember Biggs!' That's all he said and never said another word 'bout it again.

"I only went out like that with Daddy just a time or two more. I didn't want ta be doing what thay was doing.

"I don't know 'bout heaven, but I got a pertty good idea of what hell is and it sure ain't what tha preachers say it is. Yessir, I knowed what hell was from when I was a young'un. Knowed then hell's right here. 'Cause tha devil rode that night, rode in that thar wagon with me, and rode in all them other'ns, too.

"Now I'm my age, there ain't a whole lot a difference 'tween where ya are and whar I'm at. Not that much difference. Everbody's all closer'n anyone wants ta admit. We're all right beside each other all tha time. Some thangs 'bout tha way we live're different, but we're still human beings. Mostly some thangs are tha same for all of us. Got that in common. But tha devil can ride up on ya awful close, if'n ya let 'im. It's somethang ever one of us decides.

"I would like fer everythang in tha way I was raised to be different, but that's all I knowed. Fer a long time. But somethang kept gnawling at me ta get out. Inside of me, somethang was sayin' that ain't tha way ta live.

"Death ain't no curse. And it ain't no cure-all. Larning what livin's all about's what's important. All tha answers in tha world's right here right now." He let his words fall to a whisper as we drove up to the church.

Although I had a lot of questions for him, Tate was out of the car and leaving me behind as soon as we arrived. I decided not to follow and let him have some time alone.

Off by himself, he silently walked the historic graveyard. This was his time. But he was careful not to allow me to see any marker he lingered over. It was a guess on my part, but I was sure he was trying to keep me from learning his family's identity. That was his business, I reasoned. I watched him, however, without being too obvious. And I couldn't help but notice him, from time to time, stomping about and pacing back and forth. More than once he retraced his steps over and over again.

Finally the old man took off. Zigzagging through the cemetery, he wove a careful path to keep from walking over graves as he went. Occasionally he staggered from taking too hard a step onto a stone and turning a giving ankle when he did. The rocks never slowed him. His mind seemed set on something else. Not once did he use that cane of his to aid his pace or to support his balance. It was just there, the crook in his hand and the shaft held in such a way so as to be pointing straight ahead. It was hard to ascertain if the stick was directing him or was merely his compass to get to where he knew he was going.

After passing through the most ancient part of the graveyard, with its fragile gravestones and faded inscriptions, he came to a halt at an old tree near the road. Running his hand over the tree's rough bark, he went on to pat it a couple of times before he leaned a shoulder against it. Instead of stopping there, he let his hand guide him as he let his body slide down along its base. There, under its twisted branches, he collapsed onto a protruding root. Without making another movement, he sat all by himself.

Seeing that he was in no hurry to go, and not knowing how much longer he would want to stay, I turned from him to make a round through the cemetery for myself. It was a fairly familiar place for me. Many times in the past I had walked these grounds. In most but not every case it had been to attend a funeral. And in no time I was able to locate the tombstones bearing the names of those I had either known or, in the least, been told about. Only over one did I linger. The tiny monument was small, and an effigy of a lamb sat atop it. It was a baby's lasting memorial. My sister's.

Margaret Carol was born on May 24, 1947, and died twenty-eight hours later. My mother, still hospitalized, had been too ill from the hard childbirth to be released to attend the funeral. If I was there, I couldn't possibly remember. I was only eleven months old at the time. However, my sister remained forever a part of the family. She was the member we never knew, except in death. But both my parents kept her memory alive. They would hold on to Margaret Carol as the daughter they longed to have, but fate dealt the hand that their family would consist of only two sons.

While lost in the recollection, weighing what it could possibly have been like to have had a sister to grow up with, a hand touched my shoulder. I jumped. It was Tate, and he was already talking before I could come out of the clouds.

"Seems this tha place ta be," he cracked. "Most my people's here. Mama and Daddy put under over yonder. Thay dead fer sure, 'less thay fooled tha undertaker. Knowed thay was, but had ta make sure ta have more peace 'bout myself. That part of my life's over this time 'round."

Then his expression changed. A cocked grin formed only on one side of his weathered face. His words were actually playful for a change. He said, "Ever heared 'bout hell? Ya know, like thay learnt ya in Sunday school. Well, tha sayin's that if'n a person dies and goes ta hell, then thay'll come back an' haint ya." He scratched his chin. After a pause, he said, "Don't know whar my daddy went 'cause he ain't never done that ta me." Tate laughed, and with a robust burst, he added, "Reckon thay ain't no hell 'cause if'n thay was my daddy wud've been thar and he shore 'nough wud've come after me. Showed himself in person, I'm a tellin' ya.

"So tha sayin's gotta be off or thay ain't no hell." He patted my shoulder.

Nodding, I looked at him. I had no words in response, and he didn't seem to be needing any. His eyes told me, however, that something for him had been settled.

As we walked toward the car, he started talking again. "Used ta 'ave big gatherin's 'round here. Other'n tha burying, that is. Old people just ate and ate. Food was everwhar. Then thay'd just go a walkin' 'round tha markers an' point an' try ta figure who was who's granddaddy and who was his daddy way on back as if'n that made any difference since they'd been dead for fifty or a hundurd years.

"And us kids would run and play. Had ta promise not ta step on any graves. Near as I could figure, they wanted ta show respect 'cause thay was 'fraid maybe a spook of some dead granddaddy or grandmama'd jump out and get somebody when thay'd be least expectin' it. Back then I was shore thay was crazier'n bedbugs in a old feather tick mattress, since I never see'd no spook."

Tate lowered his voice and said, "Maybe thay is and maybe thay ain't no such a thang. If'n thay is, then I figure thay tryin' ta better themselves wherever thay might be. And tryin' ta warn ya ta stay on tha lookout. But I'm a tellin' ya here and now, I still ain't goin' ta go walkin' on no graves. Not this man. Lived this long not doin' it, ain't goin' ta start now. Ain't no sense temptin' 'em. Just in case!"

Passing a row of gravestones bearing the same last name as mine, Tate pointed to one, then another. And he cocked an eye at me. "See here," he said, suspiciously. "Told you thar'd be a whole section. Maybe way back some of your relations?"

"Kept it to myself," I admitted, "'cause about every cemetery from here to the sea holds a relative or two of mine. A few more than others. Some are up at Union. Others over at Bethel. Then there's Sunset Cemetery. Corinth, Sunshine, Bostic, Cleveland Memorial Gardens. And it goes on and on. But about coming here! I figured if I didn't say anything, you would let me off the hook."

"Get outta bringin' me?" he blared. And he went on without waiting for me to answer. He knew he already had some of what he needed to know. "Son, ya smarter than ya look. Sorry it didn't work. We here, ain't we?"

"Yep," I said, "and I got a pretty good number of my people buried here, too. Even my sister. Right over there. Was a baby when she died. Never knew her. Feel like my growing up would've been a little different had she lived."

"Got tha feelin's fer ya. Awful livin' an' not knowin'. Terrible thang." He seemed to be apologizing. But he was not finished. "Tha awfulest thang, though, is knowing and it bein' sour. Ya know what I mean! Sometimes I think it's better lettin' tha man upstairs take care of thangs his way. I believe he knows what he's doing better'n we do. Better'n me, fer shore. That's just tha way I gotta believe, anyhow. Thangs make more sense thata way. Ta my way of thinkin', that is."

I agreed with him. Then I confessed that many more of my relatives had been laid to rest here and there throughout the cemetery.

"Figured that, too," he said. "But I got this ta tell ya. Some of 'em here it's better ya never knowed 'em. Daddy used to run with a few of 'em. And that being tha case, thay was bad ta tha bone like my daddy. If thay a part of ya family line, lots of 'em lived real mean. Others right honorable folks. Of tha same family. Beats me how that happens. Did in my family, too. Some trash, others respectable-like. Never figured how that kinda thang could happen."

After we got back into the car, Tate left his door open. Leaving one foot on the ground, he slouched with an elbow on the console. "Tell ya somethang," he said. As a young'un I heared my mama scream as my daddy beat her. He beat her a lot. That's just tha way it was. Daddy took ta beatin' us when he wudn't beatin' her. Got ta whar that was just natural fer us kids. Never knowed no different. Terrible, now that I can look back without being so mad."

Then he paused. When he didn't pick up where he had left off, I looked over at him. Water had welled up in his eyes and he was digging in his back pocket again. Stretching out the stained handkerchief again, he half folded it. Although I glanced away so as not to cause him any embarrassment, I could tell he was wiping his eyes. After another minute or two, he coughed into the rag and was ready to resume talking.

"Gotta tell ya, there are some thangs I ain't proud of. Growin' up ta be sorta like my daddy was one of 'em. 'Cause when I got grown, I got ta likin' this little gal. She took a likin' ta me, too. So what did we do? Get hitched. Best thang ever happened ta me up ta that time. But my daddy was in me and I started a beatin' on her. Way it was s'posed ta be. I learnt it. Knowed ya woman had ta respect ya. Ya could be tha man, that way."

Catching his breath and clearing his throat, he continued. "She never had a hankerin' fer tha beatins. Never liked me hittin' on her. Thought I was larnin' her how ta be a proper . . . respectful wife."

"Didn't take long fer her ta figure she wanted somethang else than that way of livin'. So she up an' left me. 'Cause I had so much of my daddy in me, if'n I could a found whar she took off ta, I'd a followed her. Best I didn't. Probably would a kilt her. Daddy said he'd a helped me. But all I knowed was she was gone.

"Had relations outta state or on tha other side of tha state, and she hid out. Never saw her again. Never knowed what happened ta her. And after tha hand of tha Lord touched me, shore wud've liked ta 'ave asked her ta forgive me. But never got tha chance. Wharever she is, in this world or tha other'n, I think she knows. Figure she does, anyhow. If'n it's any consolation ta her, I lived with it all these years. I learnt tha hard way and that way shore 'nough ain't perty." And with that remark Tate took a hand to his leg and lifted it into the car.

Slamming the door, he added, "Time ta go. 'Bout had all I can take of this here place. Seed enough and don't reckon I'll ever 'ave ta come back. Even if'n I live a whole lot longer and plan on doin' that. Gotta bunch of thangs ta be doin' before I get that call." He laughed heartily. And I joined him, but I had one question more on the subject and was longing to ask it.

Gaining the courage, I threw it at him. "Tate," I said, "after your wife left and time passed, did you ever get married again?"

He stopped laughing. "Coulda been a whole bunch of times."

As I pulled out of the parking lot, I chuckled. He didn't. "Once or more?" I chimed.

Gruffly he moaned, "Son! Ain't none of ya business." And he brought the subject to an abrupt halt. Somewhat miffed, I pushed down on the accelerator and the car picked up speed. After going over the speed limit, I backed off to make sure I didn't get a speeding ticket. And another one for the safety inspection that had just expired the day before.

Either because of what I had aroused in him with my question or my having taken a different route back to Shelby, Tate said little. Instead, he busied himself scanning the countryside. He and I both were traveling familiar ground. I wondered what was going through his mind as we rode along.

At about the halfway point, I spoke up and said, "You've just got to tell me about your brush with the hand of God. You've talked about it, but you never explained it. Bet it would be mighty interesting," and I leaned toward him to make my request even more urgent.

Tate turned from his rapidly changing view. Now he was looking dead ahead. Still he said nothing. This time I didn't push. If he wanted to tell me, he would. If he didn't, no matter how hard I pressed, he wouldn't. By now, I knew him well enough to know he said and did exactly what he wanted. Nothing more and nothing less. There was no game about it.

When he turned back to explore the horizon, I guessed there was nothing he wanted to say. He surprised me. After putting the handkerchief he'd been holding all this time back into the pocket of his trousers and adjusting his hat, he began.

"Daddy and Grandpa always a goin' out on tha trips fer tha 'society,'" Tate said. "Daddy'd gotten sorta doubtful 'bout me all throughout my growin' up years, 'cause I didn't like none of that kinda business. But once in a while, he voiced it in such a way that I knowed I better go with 'em. This was one of them times. And I was a grown man, but I knowed I didn't 'ave no choice. Sometimes it was just that way. So I go along with 'em on it. Both real sorry I did, an' glad, too, 'cause this'n was different than I ever seed before or aft.

"Wagons was gone. Cars 'ad come along. Thar was a whole string of 'em all traveling together down tha highway. 'Bout dusky dark. We was in the lead. Grandpa, Daddy, me, and one of my brothers. And then we come into this little old town. Maybe thar was one stoplight. Don't remember others, if'n thar was any.

"Son, my daddy was drivin' and he cussed and said he wudn't stop for no stoplight. And he went right on through it and it was redder'n blood. Nobody behind us did either, 'cause I turned ta watch. That's when it happened. Daddy hit somethang, and he and Grandpa cussed and laughed in tha same breath. My brother bounced from what we run over and jerked hisself up on the back of Daddy's seat. We was in the back. And he swore real loud and pounded Daddy's shoulder real hard. He went ta praising him like he had won a jackpot or somethang. But a funny kinda strange feelin' come over me. All of a sudden like.

"Real fast like, I turned to see what we'd hit, but I seed nothin' outta tha ordinary. So I flung myself around ta get a look outta tha little back window. All I seed was cars bouncing ever time thay got ta a certain place in tha road. And then everybody started blowing tha horns an' grabbing fer tha hoods ta cover thar heads. 'Fore long we all had 'em on and all tha men in tha cars had their arms out tha windows and shaking their fists. It was like everbody got mad real fast. Still I didn't know what 'ad taken place. But inside of me, I didn't feel real good. Somethang just had run through me. Kinda sickly like. Whatever it was that took place, I knowed it was plum awful."

Catching a breath, Tate went on. "'Bout a mile outta town, Daddy pulled over and all tha cars did tha same. Thar was a whole line of us, all off ta tha side of tha little narrow road. It looked like a big meetin' was takin' place, but this time everbody had thar guns with 'em when thay come crawlin' outta all them cars. Had them hoods still on, too. And everbody was all talkin' at tha same time."

Tate was so agitated, he paused. In his excited state, he patted one pocket, then another. He was looking for something. Finally, he must have found it. With a finger and thumb going into his coat, he pulled out that crumpled pack of cigarettes. Rumaging in it, he realized there wasn't even one left, having finished the last one at the cemetery. Wadding it up, he pitched it onto the floor and grumbled to himself. Then he went back to where he had left off.

"I was still in tha dark 'bout all tha fuss," Tate wheezed. "All I knowed was my brother kept telling my daddy, 'Ya got 'im. Ya done it good. God bless.'

"And my daddy shouted at 'im time and again, 'Don't let me never hear ya use His name in vain. I learnt ya better'n that. Tha commandment.' And we all piled outta tha car like all tha other'ns. But Daddy was kinda shaken real bad. He was tryin' ta grin, but he was a sweatin' like a stuck pig.

"When thay all got together, thar was a lotta talk. And tha laughin' went down. Thay was a figurin' what ta do. That's when I learnt what happened. Seems Daddy'd run over a old colored man tryin' to get across tha street. And Daddy up and run that light and I knowed he kilt 'im or he was shore 'nough dead after all tha cars done tha same thang an' run right over 'im.

"I knowed it had ta be somethang awful seein's how I got tha strangeness like'n I did." Tate bowed his head. Raising it back up and seemingly growing bigger as he did, he regained his strength. Soon, he was talking again.

"Sonny boy, I never felt like that before. It made me sick ta my stomach. I went over ta tha ditch and throwed up, right in front'a all them men. Somebody said I was tha weaklin'. I heared 'im. And everbody hollered at me ta be a man. But I just wanted ta run away and crawl in a hole. 'Cause up till that time I never see'd nobody kilt. Thay hurt some thay wanted to larn a thang er two. Though not so fer as takin' a life. Not when I was 'round, anyways.

"So my daddy comes over ta me and tells me ta straighten up in front'a all his buddies. Told me it didn't make 'im look so good. Seein's how he couldn't take care of 'is own family, how could he lead tha 'society.' And Grandpa was right behind him.

"Finally everbody decided ta go another way and leave off from whar they was goin'. And tha word was fer everbody ta clear out in all different directions. So everbody got ta goin' back ta their cars and leavin' fast as thay could.

"But I said I wudn't be a goin'. I was walkin' back if'n I had too. Daddy was somethang awful mad at me. But he knowed I meant it. That's when tha law walked up. He was in one of tha cars 'cause he was part of tha 'society.' My friend E.H. followed up 'hind him. Thay really got carried away with me. And tha law pulled 'is gun and demanded I get in tha car so everbody could get outta there 'fore more trouble came. But I wudn't do it and he cocked tha hammer. I was ready fer 'im ta kill me. And I knowed he was fully capable."

By now, I was so wrapped up in Tate's story, I had slowed well below the speed limit. I was afraid if I got back to Shelby before he finished, he would just up and jump out without telling me the ending. I was not going to let that happen, so I injected, "What happened next?"

Tate grinned and said, "Tha hand of tha Lord reached down."

"This I've got to hear. Go on," I pleaded.

He did. "E.H. begged the lawman ta hold back. That I'd get in tha car and we'd all leave together. But I said I meant it. That I wudn't go and that was final. Everbody knowed I was a lot like my daddy, and when I said it, that was it. So tha lawman pulled tha trigger." Tate stopped.

"What?" I said. "What!"

Tate acted like he was going to go on, but instead he hesitated. Then he went on to say, "Bet ya real hungry. Wudda liked ta 'ave bought ya a meal. After doin' all this fer me, but—" And he stopped again.

"That's okay," I admitted. "We'll get something in town. Now I'd like for you to tell me more."

"Well, son," he said, "tha rest is history. But if'n ya gotta know, I tell ya this much. That gun wudn't go off. Was a dud bullet. That's when E.H. stepped in ta say fer 'im ta let me go. That that was some sorta curse on tha operation. Said thar'd be hell ta pay.

"Never figured 'im ta step in like that an' cross tha law. Could'a got hisself kilt off then an' thar. Tha lawman wudda done it ta 'im an' never blinked a sorry eye 'bout it. But E.H. was mean an' everbody knowed it. An' when he stood up fer somethang, everbody lent a ear.

"Me an' E.H. run together fer a dozen or more years. Run liquor over several counties. Tha law was in on it, too. Had moonshiners under his protection in them days. An' ta keep makin' it, them shiners had ta give some ta tha law. An' me an' E.H. was tha pick-ups. We'd load it up an' run it ta members of tha 'society.' Had what was called tha terri-tory. Then thay'd do tha sellin' and keep some fer thar part and thay'd settle with tha law fer his cut.

"E.H. was older'n me, but we gotta be fast friends like. Sorta looked up ta 'im in them days. Guess he was goin' ta pay me back, 'cause he knowed he could count on me in troubled times, an' I knowed tha same 'bout 'im. Up ta that time I honest ta goodness never knowed E.H. ta 'ave nothin' but a bad bone in 'im. Reckon he had some good in 'im after all. Did that day, anyways. But I knowed tha law wudn't goin' ta go just by E.H.'s word.

"So E.H. and tha law had theirselves a talkin'. Took some goin' back and forth, 'cause tha law got real scared I'd go runnin' my mouth an' cause 'im trouble. Ruin his standin'. Wudn't know what deal them two cut, but thay came together on it.

"When he got back ta me, he told me that I better get clean outta tha state 'cause if'n I ever come back he'd be lookin' fer me. And he'd kill me dead.

"I gave 'im my solemn word, 'cause I knowed he'd do it on some dark night. I'd end up under a mountain rock whar nobody'd know whar I disappeared ta. Ta seal my oath fer shore, I made tha sign ta him.

"And that evenin', right then and there, everbody got in them cars and pulled off. My daddy and my grandpa and my brother. And I started walkin' and never looked back. Never come back ta see any of my family. 'Cause tha man upstairs saved my life and I fig-ured I'd change my ways. Never ta be like 'em again. And I ain't. Left all that behind.

"But," Tate sighed, "I snuck back 'cause thay was somethang I had ta do."

Immediately, my mind whirled with thoughts of Tate going back to manhandle that lawman of his. I dreaded what he would say next. But I quizzed him anyway.

"What was so important that you would risk your life?" I asked.

"Didn't think I was goin' ta risk my life. That tha man watchin' over me like he'd done would take care of me. So a couple days later I went back ta that little old town and inquired 'bout tha family of tha colored man. S'prised some of tha people thar and made me a suspicious sort. But thay told me and I went ta thar house. Said I knowed their pappy, which I didn't. And that I owed 'im some money fer a job he'd done. Scared 'em ta death, 'cause thay figured I was up ta somethang.

"Anyways, I give 'em ten dollars, which was a lotta money in them days. Said thay deserved it 'cause he wudn't 'round ta collect. Told 'em I was sorry 'bout their loss. Then thay wanted me ta eat with 'em, but I told 'em I had ta go. But thanked 'em anyways.

"And that's tha story of how tha hand a God reached down ta touch me. Changed

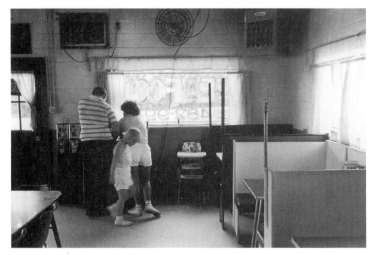

my life. Caused me ta take ta goin' here an' thar and workin' at this an' that. Been everwhar. Seed tha other sea on tha other side of tha country. Did some loggin' up in Warshington. Helped ta build some houses along tha way. Just did this an' that and learnt I could take care of myself."

Pointing his finger straight up, he added, "Learnt that it just wudn't me lookin' out fer me. That man up thar was doin' a lot of it fer me. Devil tried trailing me fer a while. Got inta some scrapes here an' yonder. But 'cause of tha man upstairs, everthang always worked out and I started payin' a lot closer 'tention ta who I was hangin' out with and whar I was hangin' out. That's when thangs really a started changing. And, ya know, I got a perty good life, all 'n all. And here I'm at still goin'. And outlived 'em all. Probably wud've been kilt or kilt somebody else if'n I'd stayed and I'd never 'ave gotten to know anythang no different. Why I say ya gotta go ta know if'n this place or that'n's whar ya wanta be settlin'. If'n it ain't, ya just move on. It'll keep ya alive and blossomin'."

"You really think that was God?" I asked as I signaled to turn off U.S. 74 and onto Marion Street. We were just outside of Shelby.

"Now a lawman don't carry no dud bullets," Tate cracked. "Not even in them days. Besides, I see'd tha devil in 'im. Told ya that I'd see'd tha devil a time er two. That was one of them times. And tha Lord was thar, too. And put 'is hand ta work. Never figured why He'd do it fer me, but He did and that makes me terribly grateful. Tried ta make it up ta Him along tha way. Don't think I succeeded ta a great degree, but I done my best. And still tryin'. Least I can do."

"Believe you have," I whispered. "Probably done more than most," I added. Then I asked, "Have you ever done much praying since then? Just interested," I explained.

Tate snapped back, "Never done it then. Never felt tha need since. Ta my way of thinkin', tha Lord had 'is eye out fer me when I was bad an' livin' like I was. So I figured when I was tryin' ta live better'n my raisin', He was still thar. I knowed it too by what He'd done fer me in them times of real trouble. Besides I never wanted ta take Him off His more troublin' problems. He had other'ns like me or worst still, an' I figured I'd give Him free reign to take care of 'em. I knowed 'is work ta be cut out fer Him."

Then he laughed and added, "Must be a hard job being tha Lord. Harder'n tha road I hoed in this life."

He and I chuckled a little together, then I asked, "Like to get something to eat? You've got to be mighty hungry."

As we slowed at the traffic light a block from the courthouse, Tate beamed. "Sorta late now, I reckon," he said. "Ya can just drop me on tha square anywhar."

"Oh, no," I protested. "I'm up to buying you a dinner."

"If'n I had tha time ta eat, I'd be a buyin'," he said. "But seein' tha time, I gotta be leavin' ya right now. Maybe thar'll be another time. Ya'll be seein' me and I'll be a seein' ya. Now I gotta be goin'."

As I argued, he interrupted, "Ya gotten go an' be ornery. Plain fact is I got plans. Somebody's pickin' me up." He pulled a wristwatch with half the band missing from his pants pocket. "Time got away from me. She'll—" He caught himself, saying no more.

I couldn't resist. "What's this you say? She?"

"None of ya business," he barked. "Pure impertinent."

His door was open before I could come to a complete stop in front of what was once the old Cohen's store. Just before slamming the door closed, he stuck his head inside and said, "Real pleasure doin' business with ya. 'Preciate tha ride. Tha talk," and he pushed the door shut without the lock completely catching. By the time I had reached over and reshut it, he was speeding across the street to get to the courthouse side. He was going against the light. I laughed and pulled slowly away. A part of me wanted to wait and get a glimpse of his lady friend. But I didn't.

No sooner had I started picking up speed and I was stopping again. The traffic light at Warren Street caught me. As I tapped the steering wheel in impatience, I absently glanced to my left out of a force of habit. Without thinking I spoke out loud, "Forever the preacher's corner." It was as if his ghost would not let me pass without acknowledging his invisible presence. Of course he wasn't there, just those empty park benches that echoed a distant past. Nevertheless I visualized once again the Bible-toting preacher man with his face awash in sweat and his voice yelling out, "Heaven or hell?"

The old preacher's question lingered only for a moment or two, and my mind shifted without any effort back to Tate. Then I was shaken by the blast of a car horn blowing me back into the present. The light had changed during my drifting. Automatically I looked up at the light just to make sure it was now green. It was, and I waved a polite "thank you" to the driver behind me and let off the brakes. As I started accelerating, I couldn't help but to take one last look at the corner. The preacher's corner. I laughed and whispered to myself, "And now Tate's."

4. FLOYD JUSTICE

TOCCOA, GEORGIA

Gently caressing his old Gibson guitar like it was a priceless jewel, Dr. Jim Chastain strummed out the notes of an old Eddy Arnold goldie. Edging up to the mike beside the gas-burning heater that took up half of his den, he belted out a stanza of the song. Stopping, he smiled big and laughed, making light of his singing. But there was one thing about him—he took his music seriously despite his downplaying his abilities. He loved the art form so much that the den of his home could have passed as a recording studio. A number of banjos and guitars angled back on stands in the living room. Others were safely tucked away in cases on the sofa.

Had he made other choices in his youth, the doctor could have just as easily ended up on the stage. As a natural-born storyteller, as someone who could carry a tune, he could have been a singing Will Rogers. He was that good. Yet, on this particular day, I hardly wanted to hear him. I was more than a little peeved.

My old friend had sent word for me to come to Toccoa. I had told him of my search, and he was trying to help me out again. It was the doctor who had come to my aid a few years earlier, joining me in my race across the country to meet Leandis, about whom I had written in my book *Shadowcatchers*. Now he was there for me once more with an acquaintance of his who would talk about his encounter with God. That promise fueled my imagination. Ordinarily I might have made excuses. But on the power of the suggestion of my mentor of seventeen years, I rushed four hundred miles for the visit. Never once did it cross my mind that I would be sitting back, far out in the country, listening to a tear-jerking ballad and wondering why my trip had become so botched. But that was exactly what I was doing, and I was not too pleased about it, either. To make matters worse, my displeasure didn't seem to faze my friend in the least. He was on to the next verse, the amplifier turned a notch louder just to make sure I heard every word. Jim was in seventh heaven.

Me? I was in the pits. He knew it and his smile grew wider on every high note he hit. My sulking didn't deter him; his attention stayed firmly focused on his music.

It wasn't that Jim hadn't tried to set me up for my interview. For a half hour he had tried to convince the man to meet with me, but his efforts had not been successful. There had been a change of heart. Now the man wasn't going to talk at all.

"You've got to look at where you are," Jim had said, trying to console me. Then, picking up the old guitar and letting go of his own disappointment, he clicked on the amp and lost himself in song.

In my heart I knew he had tried, but I couldn't control my own gloom. Small towns are small towns, I reasoned. They have a way about them. Word spreads fast. If one person knows something, everyone knows, very quickly. The repercussions can be felt for a very long time. And that was apparently what had happened. But the "why" lingered in my mind until I realized that the "why" of anything cannot always be answered. I told myself that over and over as I reconciled the fact that my trip had gone bust.

Then the words "Nothing is ever as it seems" rolled out from the recesses of my brain. I knew that to be true, but accepting it was a different matter. I tried, nevertheless.

After Jim sang another song or two, I stopped harboring any ill thoughts toward the man I didn't know, and never would, and got into the swing of Jim's music. In time I was back enjoying his singing as I always had. I even tried to sing along.

After starting another song, and well into the first verse, Jim stopped abruptly. "Hey," he said, "if you had been here a few weeks ago, you'd have had a real tale."

"What's that?" I answered back, nonchalantly.

"Old boy was up on the river fishing. Just slipped and fell in. Disappeared. Got sucked right under and never came back up. Had it on the TV during the news," he went on. "There was an old couple on the other side of the river who saw it. One of them ran to call the rescue squad."

"Did he come back up?" I asked, my interest picking up.

"Nope. When the rescue squad got there, they started dragging the river."

"Did they ever find him?"

"Oh, yeah."

"How long did it take them to find the body?" I asked, knowing that sometimes drowned bodies aren't found for days.

"'Bout two or three hours till they pulled him up," Jim said.

Thinking about the tragedy, I whispered, "Sad. Bet, though, that guy would've had a thing or two to say about God." Going right into a question without stopping, I added, "Did he have any family?"

"Some kids. Think he was divorced. He's from Toccoa here." Then he added, "That was some story. The newspeople showed up. Guess they heard it on the scanner. Had a real thing going on up there. Too bad you weren't here for it. Maybe you can do a follow-up and take it from where everyone else left off."

Interesting idea, I thought, but immediately dismissed the notion. That would be more like rehashing old news. That certainly wasn't the purpose of my trip. Then again, I quarreled with myself, nothing is as it seems. But dropping it seemed the thing to do, and I did.

Plucking a string or two on his guitar, Jim spoke up. "Let's go get some old boys together and play some music."

"Play some music," I laughed. "It's more like listen to some. But, hey, I'm game. You know how I love music. Any of them any good?"

"You never know. You just never know. According to what night it is and how they're feeling."

With that I sipped my last swallow of coffee and went to the sink to rinse the cup. Out of a force of habit I turned off the coffeemaker that was always on day and night at Jim's place. Closing the door behind us, he said, "Get in. I'll drive," and we were off to round up some music makers.

Night had settled over the county. The winding, twisting roads of the hill country became tangled in my mind and left me wondering if Jim knew where we were headed. My biggest question was whether he could find his way home. If it was up to me, I doubted I could nose my way back.

With a turn to the right, one to the left, and a drop down a long curving hill, Jim finally signaled one last maneuver. Just on the far side of where the slope bottomed out was James Justice's. Hardly recognizable as a driveway, the narrow, rutted dirt road seemed to evaporate right into the side of a mountain. As the little Honda rolled in and out of each mud hole, the headlights vaulted up and down. With every bounce, and there was one right after the other, I could see a house coming up out of the distance. With some doing, we managed to creep up to James's home at the end of the lane, which had turned to mud from the latest rains. Because of the place's magnificent seclusion I felt we had made our way into an enchanted hideout known only to a select few.

Dogs barked incessantly, warning their master of our approach. As we got out, I watched with an ever-vigilant eye for any canine that might be sneaking up from behind to nip at the uninvited intruders. Instead, I found a nervous cocker spaniel confronting me, head to head, on the front porch at the top of the stairs. The cocker's partner stood by his side. Together they seemed ever the menacing duo. But the aging and greatly rotund bulldog merely sniffed and settled back down on its own miniature couch, which had been designed and manufactured for a child's room.

Shuffling to the door, James yelled at his cocker to quiet down and invited us to come on in. With the walking stick he had to use because of a recent stroke, he poked open the screen door. Once we were inside, he hung the stick over his unusable hand and pressed his good one toward us for a hearty shake of greeting. Surprised at the unannounced visit, he nevertheless beamed at seeing his old friend Dr. Chastain. And, in turn, the doctor introduced me to James and his wife, Edna.

"Doc, it's good to see you, but whatever are you doing out here?" James questioned.

Jim answered right up. "Let's get some old boys together and play some music."

"Sounds good to me," James responded. "When?"

"Now's as good a time as any. Can we use the game room?" Jim asked. He turned to me and explained that James owned a thirty-by-forty-foot-square building at the edge of the highway. Until recently James had run a billiards hall and had charged for day fishing on the tiny lake beside the structure. On weekends he had a live band inside and made a little money from admissions and refreshments. Because of his stroke, he had to close it down and even had to stop selling a few used cars now and then. He complained that his doctor had to inform the Department of Motor Vehicles of his disability. The department had recalled his license because of it and had taken away his privilege of driving. He knew that he couldn't drive anyway, but just going through the process had diminished his self-esteem. Losing his license had compounded the blow he felt from having the stroke. Both had taken away his sense of mobility and independence.

"Yeah, you can use it. Get everybody together and we'll open up."

"What about Floyd? Think he'll come?" Jim asked, referring to James's brother. "Want to go with us to get him? I don't know where he lives, anyway. Besides, I think Steve would like to talk to him about the accident."

Taken aback by his seemingly spontaneous comment, I shot a puzzled glance at my friend, questioning him. He shrugged it off like water rolling down a greasy back, leaving me wondering what he could have hatching in his mind.

"Sure, I'll go with you. I reckon he'll come, if he's home," James answered. "You know how he likes to make music." Then he warned, "It takes me a while to get around. I'm just a little slow. But if you'll help me, we'll go." James began to get ready, knowing the doctor would wait for him.

Leaving Edna with the dogs, the three of us headed out on the round-up. Again the blacktop two-lane angled first one way then the other as the road curved up and over and around the gentle mountain terrain. Shortly we were on the outskirts of Toccoa. Once on the far side of the small town, we found our way to Floyd's mobile home. Blowing the horn a time or two, still the common way of doing things in the country, Jim waited for a response. None came. All of us sat tight. He blew the horn again. We waited.

Then James started working his way out of the car, speaking as he did. "He's here 'cause that's his car, but he ain't going to come out. He don't know this car's yours. Don't know whose it is. Don't care for the business we might have with him. I'll have to show him it's me. I'll go get him."

Straining with each step to move, James haltingly inched his way toward the fence protecting the entrance to Floyd's trailer. Pushing on the gate, as best he could despite the debilitating affliction, he hesitated. He didn't see the angry dog, nor did we, but a vicious growl coming from the corner of the enclosure brought instant alarm. "Floyd, it's me, James," he yelled instead of proceeding one step farther.

In a lightning flash the door of the metal home jerked open. "I didn't know who was here. Didn't recognize the car," Floyd apologized.

With the overgrowth obscuring just about all of the mobile home and even threatening to overtake the gate, I was still unable to see the man with whom James was talking. It didn't take Floyd long, however, to decide he had nothing better to do than make some music with the boys. Slamming the door to his home, he was at the gate and pushing through it as if he were on his way to a fire. Only when Floyd slowed down to take James's arm did I get my first full view of the man who had been reluctant to welcome people he didn't immediately recognize.

Floyd was a bear of a man. Yet he didn't seem to have an ounce of fat on his tall frame. But he did have hair. A lot of it. So much, in fact, that very little of his face was visible. Even part of that was framed by thick plastic glasses the same color as his shoulder-length jet-black hair. His enormous but slightly graying beard fell nearly to his broad chest. A very wide mustache fully covered his upper lip. Only his nose and a part of his forehead remained hairless. His eyes, however, were striking. And not even the lenses of his essential glasses could hide the kindness that emanated from them. I liked him instantly.

"The FBI's looking for you," Jim said to Floyd once we were all in the car and heading out to find more good old boys and pick up guitars at Jim's place. Then, hassling him about his beard, he added, "That's why you grew that thing, wudn't it?"

Pulling up on the seat from where he sat crammed with me in the back of the Honda, Floyd was quick to say, "One of my kids is nineteen and never knowed me without it. And my last old lady, she ain't never see'd me without it. We was married twenty-one years and she ain't never seed my face. I could shave and dress up and scare ya to death, I guess."

We all howled. Then, as if to say his beard had nothing to with the kind of person he was, he added, "I'll tell ya what! I ain't goin' to do nothing to interfere with nobody's business and harm nobody." Again we laughed and settled back to hear the roar of the tires on the road and watch the wiper blades swiping the fresh rain from the windshield.

Leaning over and taking his eyes momentarily from the highway, Jim said to me, "Floyd's a real fisherman."

With great enthusiasm Floyd responded, "I caught nearly five hundred one time. I try to catch 'em everday, if I can. If I miss a day, I try to catch more the next. James got about sixteen bags in that freezer. He's got a freezerful."

"Yeah, he likes his fishing," Jim laughed.

Floyd continued, "I got seven reel and rod in the backseat of my car and I got six in the boot. I got thirteen.

"Old boy said one time, 'You goin' fishing?'

"I said, 'Well, when you see me, I'm coming back or going, either one, according to where the river's at.'

"Salt and grease and a pan's all you take with you. You don't take no food. Little old bitty brim, 'bout that long's good, if you fry 'em real hard where the bones fry up and eat 'em head and all. If you fry 'em good and crisp, they're good. Tasty fish. Oh, I scale 'em and clean 'em. I can cook any meal, a full meal, anythang you want."

"What else have you been into?" I asked, trying to get into the conversation.

"I been in two or three different shootin's," Floyd admitted. "Man goin' ta harm me, I'm goin' ta get 'im. And I shot a old boy down here on the road. But he shot at me twice and I shot 'im with a twenty-gauge shotgun. Didn't shoot him where . . . I winged him. I hit pretty good. I didn't mean to shoot the guy. He shot at me, shot my trailer. And I just shot 'im in the left arm. Called the ambulance, called the sheriff. They checked me out and all. But the ambulance got 'im before the sheriff got there, and I left.

"The neighbors told the sheriff and I told. Had a little old hearing thang. The boy was on parole and wasn't 'posed to have no firearms. Come in my yard, pulled a pistol on me. I could've shot 'im in the face.

"This other guy . . . we was ridin' up the road after the shootin', and he said, 'You the first man . . . just shot a man down there and you stop and pick a cat up and take it to the vet.' He said, 'Man, I can't handle this. Look! I can handle a lot of thangs. I been through a lot of stuff. We just left where they loaded that boy up and took 'im to the hospital and we stop where a little kitten's been run over.'

"See, I just stopped and picked it up, got it in the truck with me, and took it on out to a vet and the old boy said, 'Man, I can't handle it. You shot that guy and you stop and pick a cat up and take it to the hospital and stay an hour and a half and you weren't even worried 'bout that guy. You worrying 'bout this cat.'

"I just turned around to him. I said, 'This cat didn't bother me.'

"He said, 'Man, I can't handle it.'

"He called his wife out there to the vet to come get him."

Having picked up Floyd, Jim drove us all back to his house first so that he could gather up his musical instruments needed for the hastily arranged jam. As James looked on, not able to help because of his physical condition, Floyd, Jim, and I carried guitars, banjos, amplifiers, cords, and microphones out to the car. Quickly Jim decided that one vehicle was not going to have enough room for all of us and everything he wanted to take back to James's place. Besides, he was going to pick up another friend, a former performing musician, now a retired chiropractor, who had been Jim's mentor. So he asked if I would drive my truck, load some of his stuff in it, and let Floyd ride with me. When he saw me nodding a yes, he began helping James into the car the two of them would be riding in. Floyd and I piled into mine and we headed off.

As we navigated the narrow roads, Floyd reached back in time to his childhood. Soon his voice was drowning out the road noise. "I've had hard times, man, and I don't fuss about it." Then, he proclaimed, "I'm here," as if to say that no matter what, that was the most important thing. He never let on that there was any more to it than that.

Then, he went on, "I been through a lot of thangs. I'm not saying thangs don't bother me, but what I say is bottom line . . . if you're going ta stay here you've gotta get up and go on. Not that I don't worry 'bout stuff. Man, I do. I worry a lot 'bout everthang, but I don't go on out here and show it. I'm not goin' ta let it get me. That's what I think."

Before I knew it, he was telling me things he probably had kept to himself for most of his life. "See," he continued, "I'm one . . . ain't but one of ten people that we knowed of in the world back in 1965 that's got eyes like mine. I can't see out of but one eye at a time. I can use either one of 'em anytime I want to and never have to shut the other one. But both of them don't work together. I can switch 'em and you never know it."

It was hard for me to understand what he was telling me. I had never heard of such a thing before, but he had grabbed my attention and I was eager to hear more. And the way he was explaining it made it humorous. If his had not been a serious condition, I would have laughed with him because, if for no other reason, his laughter was contagious. Yet I held back for fear of offending him.

He talked on. "I messed a guy up, guy that first checked my eyes. You've had eye tests? You see the greens and reds. I told that guy that I see two greens. Now I see two reds.

"He said, 'You don't see five of 'em?'

"I like to ruint that guy in Gainesville. They brought another guy in. See, my eyes was crossed. I couldn't even see. Crossed all the way in. I got ta where I couldn't see back when I was eleven. I had to strain to see. My eyes was crossed. And they operated on 'em. They took both of 'em out and cut on 'em and worked on 'em and fixed 'em where they'd be straight. And they give me that test. You know, they said, 'You see five dots?'

"I said, 'All I see is two reds or two greeens. Two reds up on top.'

"He said, 'No. You don't see that 'cause that thang combines 'em. They're sort a like the Olympic symbol.'

"'I don't see them together. Either I can see the two reds or two greens.' I messed those doctors up."

I asked curiously, "How do you switch them?"

"I'm looking outta the right. Now I'm looking outta the left. Right. Left. It's weird. I didn't never know it. It don't bother me. I can shoot a rifle. Both eyes still open. It's funny. Both're supposed to focus. Mine don't focus together in the middle. It's like if I had one eye it'd be the same difference. It's the funniest thang. They's somethang wrong in there."

He laughed and I laughed with him. "Sure didn't cause you to miss that old boy you shot," I said, hardly able to talk.

"Nope," he roared. "Told you it never hurt me shooting a rifle."

As we neared his brother's old ramshackle music hall, Floyd's mind was back on music. "I used to do about four or five benefits a year," he said. "Some little kid needed a kidney or somethang, and we'd play twelve hours straight. Wouldn't cost nobody a dime. There's no charge. Everbody'd come in if they wanted to give a dollar—if they wanted to—and they'd bring stuff and I'd have a big auction. All money raised would go to that little kid."

Wrinkling his brow, he said, "Some of these people, it's hard for them to get to the hospital and back. That's what ya do it for. It's work just for the people to get there and back. And it takes money.

"This guy from Salem, he plays a banjo. He's a fine guy, used to play with the Carolina Mountain Boys. I can get the Georgia Mountain Boys to go play. Get the Smoky Mountain Hillbillies outta Franklin. And anybody loves bluegrass. The young'uns gettin' ta where they like it. I know the elderly people do. Older people . . . mountain music.

"I'll do anythang I can. It's to help somebody. And I'll do it, too. Oh, I know I'll do it."

As soon as Jim, his chiropractor friend, and James drove up, Floyd ran to help his brother out of the car. Then he asked if he could borrow James's car to go up the road to see if some of his other friends would come on down. His brother threw him the keys, and he was gone.

Before long, Jim was searching for electrical outlets. Old Christmas lights were plugged in and then unplugged and plugged back in in an effort to find overhead lights and juice for the electrical guitars and amplifiers. By the time he had finished, there were wires running everywhere, so many of them that it was easy to trip and turn over one of the many microphones. Finally, everything seemed to work and he was plucking out a tune up on the platform that he shared with a full-sized bed.

"What's this for?" he asked James, referring to the antique bed.

"Oh," James laughed, "you want to spend the night, there it is. Sometimes somebody can't or shouldn't go home. Well, they can sleep it off right there. Got everything in here. Bathroom back there," he said, pointing over the pool table commanding the largest portion of the nattily arranged room.

He waved to the back, and we saw the weathered door to the outside swing freely back and forth with the wind. Over our chitchat we could hear the glass bulbs of the Christmas lights from parties long past clinking in the breeze. Only rusting nails held them barely suspended near the old building's sagging ceiling. But they seemed secure enough, and soon our minds turned to other things.

In the lull we heard a car rattle to a hard stop. It was Floyd, and he was in such a rush that he frightened the napping geese at the edge of the nearby pond. They squawked, fluttered, and in a noisy panic, made for the safety of the water. Within minutes Floyd was bounding through the door, his friends barreling in in single file behind him. It was like a family reunion, but a rather unusual one, where for everyone all that counted seemed to be the music.

Nothing made any sense. No songs or familiar tunes could be detected with all the

tuning going on. It didn't take long, however, before a chord or two became discernible. Yet something remarkable happened. It was a study in contrasts. There were two cultures. One white. One black. One country and bluegrass. The other, jazz. If a music battle was brewing, it didn't take long for it to be won. The white old-timers who loved country music had to take a backseat to the jazz of Floyd's black friends. And Floyd was right in the middle, singing along.

"Oh, try me," they sang. "Try me-e-e. And your love will always be . . . oh-h I need you. I need you." Then they went, "Walk with me. Talk with me. And let me know that love will be all right."

On and on it went. Hour after hour passed. All of us, except the four black men and Floyd, draped ourselves on the musty, overstuffed chairs and sofas worn past their prime. Not being able to play, I settled back and enjoyed the show. Some of those who could pick seemed peeved they were never given the opportunity to pluck out their country sounds. Yet no rancor surfaced beyond a few exaggerated facial expressions.

Sometime up in the early morning everyone "was given out." It had been a full night. The sights and sounds had been entertaining, to say the least. Now it was time to break up the party and head home. James and Edna were clearly showing their fatigue. Jim

needed to get his friend home. Floyd's friends feared not being able to get up for work within a few hours. I was in need of coffee. Only Floyd was still wound tighter than a rubber band. He was wide awake alert and ready for more.

When the music had finally died, Jim started gathering his gear together. Then he thought of a better idea. He got James's permission to just leave the gear and return for it sometime the following day. His excuse was the rain—it could ruin a guitar in nothing flat. I was pleased with his decision, and a cup of coffee in town at the all-night café beckoned me.

It was decided that Floyd would again ride with me. Jim would take James, Edna, and his friend home and meet us at the café. I had no problem with the plan.

I thought about Jim on the way to Toccoa. For him, music was as important as it was to the old-timers. But he was different. Not only did he love the music, he made sure his older friends were remembered. Yet he did it in such a way so as not to make them feel they were being taken care of. His approach was sincere. He gathered them together to do something they loved. For every one of them it was still the music. Any song that Dr. Jim Chastain wrote carefully reflected that. He even gave one the title "Still the Music." Once I told him that it would surely be on the charts one day. Although he had clearly written it out of love, he seemed to like my comment.

Soon I was to learn, however, that our getting together to play music had been more of a ploy. He had wanted me to meet Floyd. I was to became aware of this only later when he met us at the café.

When Floyd and I arrived, the place was crowded. People were talking over each other. It was hard to hear even one's self. Even at that hour, singles, couples, families were coming and going. Tables that were not taken were piled high with dishes. Before they could be cleared, other customers would fill the booths and wait for the bussers to take away the dirty plates. Waitresses bustled back and forth, sometimes with meals in their hands, sometimes with sloshing coffeepots. One hand held decaf, the other regular.

In the middle of this frenzy, Floyd and I joined what could only be described as a circus. Many of those in the restaurant were regulars. To one side a man sorted his mail, which seemed like a month's worth. Bills went in one stack, flyers and advertisements went into another, and throw-aways from the bills went onto the seat.

In the booth nearest the door, a car deal was going on. One man was counting out hundred-dollar bills, the other was signing a title over to the man with the money. Outside two older women drove up. Both, dressed to party, stared into the fully windowed café, as if they were casing the joint. Finally, one of them emerged from the car, came in, and made her way to the restroom at the back. Within minutes she was back out the door, in the car, and the two drove off.

Other booths were filled with young lovers nudging each other, parents with tired, sleepy-eyed kids jumping up and down on the plastic-covered, barely padded seat, and here and there were frowning people who just plain didn't seem to like each other. Wedged into all of the ruckus was Floyd and me.

Talking above the fray, I asked, "You from here?"

Floyd answered, "See, I was raised in the country. Raised in a two-story house above Hiawasee, Georgia. Didn't see no television or power till I was eleven years old. And that ain't been that long ago," he said, thinking back. Stopping for a thought to pass through his mind, or to count the years, he went on. "Forty years ago. Everbody thinks now you s'posed to have conveniences. Well, it might'a ruint me when I found tha convenience." And he laughed at his own joke as we were finally being served our coffee. A good third of a cup ended up splattering across the table and into my seat. Without a second thought the waitress was at the next table. Everyone seemed to be de-

DANCING WITH GOD

manding the brew at the same time. We were most assuredly at the community gathering center.

Having overcome my hostility over the spill, I asked Floyd, "You married?"

He was quick to answer. "I wish. I don't know what happened. That's what I still don't know. Wudn't no argument with me. And she was good ta me. She'd do thangs for me. You know, anything. We just like . . . I don't know what happened. That's what hurts me so much."

A sadness filled his half-hidden eyes. Then he said, "She left me and went off and stayed a year and a half. And one day she come back. Sent a guy over here, nephew or something, and said she'd like to just drop by and see me. But that was that. No sense in starting it back up.

"I believe the mornings get me more than anything else. When you wake up, it's very lonely. I could have somebody down here with me or . . . and you think about it again like what's going to happen that evenin'. You got ta go through that datin'. I . . . I can't explain it.

"I'm just old-fashioned. I can get along with anybody, but I don't mess with nobody. I go on about my own way. Don't harm no human being and go on about my business."

Seeing that it was hard for him to talk about such matters made me change the conversation. So I asked, "You got any kids?"

"Got three kids. One's thirty. One's twenty-eight and I got one that's nineteen. Got a grandbaby that's ten years old. When it comes to my kids—I take care of my kids. That's the bottom line. I don't matter when it comes to them. I'm not one of these out-front people, though. But it seems like I'm on the top of loving more. Seems like I know where the love—but I don't go 'round everday and love 'em and hug 'em. I love my kids to death.

"I don't know. I don't go to anybody. I don't talk to nobody. I don't tell nobody my troubles. I just don't do it. Seems like I can handle it. I talked to you more today than . . . I don't talk to nobody."

"And he don't," Jim said, sliding in beside me, "but what he should've done is have my coffee waiting for me. You all knew I was on my way."

We both grinned and Floyd said, "You ain't done no work for it yet."

After a few chuckles I thought about work and asked Floyd, "What kind of work do you do, besides your benefits?"

"Work?" Jim said. "He fishes. That's what he does." Hitting Floyd's arm with a sharp tap, he asked, "Did you tell 'bout what they pulled out of the river?"

I wasn't sure what the doctor was getting at, but from the way he raised his eyebrows higher than I had ever seen them go before, I was curious. Floyd knew instantly. Shaking his head back and forth, he laughed nervously. Then between his teeth, he said, "The way they told it, I believe it was two hours and forty—they said two hours and a half. Somebody else said two hours and forty . . . I don't even know."

Speaking up, I asked, "Doctor, is this about that news story you talked about?"

"Yeah," he said, "but Floyd needs to tell you about it. He knows more than I do. He was there." With a quick nod toward Floyd, Jim roared, "Tell 'im about it, Floyd."

What was to come blew me away. It was nothing I could have prepared for. My imagination just could not have climbed that high.

Stretching, Floyd growled, acting as if there wasn't much worth talking about. "Guess I've been the biggest catch up there. I knowed I'd stayed under there fifty year, sixty year, or something like that."

Jim roared. "Go on," he said. "Tell us about it."

"I just slipped off a rock and went in the river. Trout fishing," Floyd said. Then he went on as if it were happening to him all over again. "The water! It just took me back under there, back under the rock probably fifteen or twenty feet." His voice rose to a higher pitch as he described his encounter with death. "You've got to get back out—it's pulling toward you. Bubbles coming in all the time. No way out!

"I was really afraid after two or three times trying to get out. I said, 'Hell, I'm going to lose all my air pocket. I ain't going nowhere else. I mean . . . you know . . . this." And he lost his words to his laughter.

"I mean, it's funny now. I can chuckle 'bout it now, but the deal was, man, you . . . it aged me some. I know that." His words mixed with his laughter again. When he caught his breath, he added, "I think about it all the time. I've been through a lot of things. Man, I've been through shootins and I used to be rough. Nothin' didn't bother me. But now it keeps comin' back . . . being in that river. It keeps comin' back and thangs keep bothering me about it. I keep wondering why . . ." His words died. There was a long pause, and at the same time it seemed that the whole café went into an eerie coma with Floyd's silence. As if coming out of a deep sleep, he went on. "I keep wondering why I got outta there. You know, I mean, I'm glad ta be breathing and glad, you know, but the reason for it, I don't know. They got me out, but still it bothers me. It does. It bothers me."

Floyd, retelling the horrors of nearly drowning, was back. Back in the river, that is. His glassy eyes told me that. They seemed set. He was looking far beyond the windows he was gazing out of. Finally, he started again. "All that time . . ." His words fell off, only to come back up within a second or two. "Two hours and more," he said. "Somebody said two hours and forty minutes. Others said two hours and thirty. That ten minutes. It ain't . . . it wouldn't mean any difference. It wouldn't matter if it's just ten minutes. After the first minute or two, it's just a continuation thang.

"Now I thought of some stuff under there. They said I was under there two hours and forty minutes, but I knowed I was under there a hundred year.

"It was like I was goin' ta die, then again it was like I was . . . I mean it was like I was going to be around a little bit longer. Didn't never give up, I don't think. Well, I know I didn't."

Excitedly I said, "You could've stayed under until you died since you couldn't fight your way out because of the current."

"I'd a fought myself to death first. But see, I could hold my head up to breathe. There was an air pocket. It was mossy like. I knowed when I felt that moss it wasn't completely under the water.

"When I went under, that water, man, just doubled me back . . . pulled me back up under there. I thought I was going down the river, but it got dark. I know a little bit 'bout dark and I thought, 'I'm gone.'

"So, I got to huntin' . . . you want to go up. Water! Naturally I was holding my breath. You want to go up, get your head up. I had to keep my head bowed. And you'll find air, if you can before you die.

"To put my feet on the ground, there was a wedgelike thang. I couldn't tell where the water went on through at 'cause it wasn't rolling back on me. Understand! It wasn't like real pressure, but when you move out of where I was at, it was pressure. It had to be going through some more rocks or . . . well, I don't know. I got in a still spot. But it's dark under there. No light! Well, you could see faint . . . it's not a light, but it was . . . it's lighter than dark. More like a thick screen.

"Where I was, they blasted two rocks out up there about seven years ago 'cause there was a hole in there so big the water just went rough and round so much. They liked to 'ave never got a boy out of there one time. He came out dead, though.

"Listen to this," Floyd demanded. "My daddy told me when I was a kid and he took me fishing 'bout the same place, 'There's some holes up here that'll suck you under and nobody'll never find you.' He said, 'Don't never step on slick rocks. You'll fall in and the river'll suck you under. Watch out for the rocks. Don't get in there. They've been a lot a people drowned up here.'

"When I was under there he told me right then. I could hear the words just like the day he said it. Said it right then. He's been dead since 1990."

"Your daddy came to you while you were up under the rock?" I asked.

"He just spoke it."

"It's a wonder you didn't lose your mind all the time you were under there and your daddy coming to you and chastising you for slipping on the rocks."

"Well, if I was all right to start with, I would've." He broke into a ripping wave of laughter, and Jim and I joined him.

"Floyd," I asked, "what did you think about during all that time?"

"I thought about family and stuff and all . . . most thangs I'd a done, people, you know. Tried to figure whether I'd a done things right or wrong or whether . . ." His words trailed off. Then he added, "Why should it a happened like this. It wasn't a reason why I should die. I didn't think about why I should die. If you going to die, you don't think why it should be me. I don't question death 'cause it's just somethang you going to do. But why like that . . . having fun and just made a mistake." Again he stopped long enough to laugh and get his coffee cup refilled.

When he spoke I thought he would be back on the river. Instead, he said, "I don't ever drink much coffee. I guess tonight's different. Got to have another cup. And another. For some reason or another."

"Lucky there was somebody to go for help," I said, "but they were dragging the river for a body. How'd they get you?"

"Big hooks with tape around them with . . . like Styrofoam floats," Floyd said. "It goes back under there. They goin' ta get you out. That winch on that truck'll break you in two. If you was hung, it'd pull your leg off. You going with it. That thang cracked my ribs. I didn't want to go out . . . I didn't know what had me."

"What went through your mind when it caught you?"

"Thought a monster done got me after all this. I tried to hold back. It got me and I went with it. I said, 'Hell, now somethang else's got a hold of me.'

"That was the most scary thang right there. I said, 'The devil got me now. He's done reached in here, he's fixing to pull me.

"The way they had it, they drug me from under that rock. When they come over that rock, I come on and I come outta there. When I come out and knowed what was happening, I got a hold of that thang. I wudn't goin' ta turn it loose. It was around me, but I wudn't goin' ta turn it loose no more.

"Everbody thought I was dead and they were going to pull somethang out of there. Going ta pull a son of a gun outta there. Man, I was moving when I come out. I couldn't stand or nothing.

"I come outta that river, man, and hey, everbody's going, 'He's alive!' They all went crazy as a bat and still dragging me. If he hadn't cut the motor off, he'd a pulled me through that snatch box and killed me.

"They thought it was a ghost come outta there. Oh, they was running and all. 'He's alive! He's alive!' I could hear it, 'He's alive! He's alive!' They couldn't believe it.

"I said, 'Get this damn—' I believe I cussed, I'm not sure. I mean, Lord have mercy, man! I didn't know where I was going. I—I—that's what got me, that last five, ten seconds . . . you don't know where you're going. When I come out to that light, that's when I got . . . you couldn't turn me loose from it then. I tell you what, I seen the light. I opened my eyes before I started out. I kept 'em closed most of the time when I was down under there 'cause there wasn't no use keepin' 'em open. You done figured out reality.

"I come outta that water, man, and when I come out on top and got that breath, I was kicking everwhere. I got loose from that thang and I went 'bout from here ta that red little van yonder and went across another rock and come out on the other side. I started toward my car and they was all . . . I said, 'I ain't talkin' ta nobody. Man, I gotta go.' They was all running after me, making the awfulest faces, just wantin' ta know . . . I got up and stood around, walked around a minute before I knew where I was. Mud all over me. I mean, look, I guess I eat some of it, I don't know.

"I didn't talk to 'em. I wudn't goin' ta stand there and talk to 'em. 'I'm out of here.' I was goin' ta get away from there. Man, Lord, I—I . . .

"I got my hat. This is the hat." Floyd took off his cap and turned it one way and then the other to show it off. For him it was a trophy. Then he went on without slowing down, "That lady got my hat. It's the same old hat. I'm goin' ta wear this son of a gun, boy. My rod, I don't know where it went. I got more, though."

"Do you know what happened to the fish you had caught?" I asked. Jim and I laughed.

But Floyd was serious. "They were still on me. Hooked to me." Then he laughed. "That's one day I didn't get my eight. I started to go back fishing. But I come on home.

"Soon as I got home . . . I was tired. I was tired, I was wore out. Drove home and didn't even think about it. That's funny to me. I thought about it later and I—what in the world! And I had to think, was I up there? I went to sleep that night. Woke up the next morning, I thought . . . soon as I woke up, it's been on my mind. But I ain't lost a bit of sleep over it." Floyd turned to watch all the commotion in the café. From his body language I sensed that he had finished his story. After all, he had relived it all over again for me. Now it seemed he was ready to move on to other things—anything, but enough of the river.

Bottoming out our cups, all three of us waved the waitress away as she approached to give us yet another refill.

"Time to go home and hit the sack," Jim commanded. And we all agreed.

"I'll take Floyd home and meet you at your place," I said to Jim, and nodded "Let's go" to Floyd.

Once at Floyd's, he invited me in. He had something to show me. Inside it was obvious that it was a bachelor's pad. Things were in disarray and he apologized for the monstrous stack of dishes covering the kitchen cabinets and filling the sink. "It's just me here," he said, "and I let things get a little out of hand."

Motioning me down the narrow hallway of his trailer, he said, "When I got this mobile home, it was broken in the middle and I fixed it myself. Did it up pretty good," he added, boasting of his work. But that was not what he wanted to show me. In one of the bedrooms was a huge bass instrument.

"It's the real thang. Not electric. Don't see much of these anymore." He smiled proudly. "Had it made to order."

"Is that what they called a 'doghouse bass'?" I asked.

"That's what it is, but it's hard to carry around. Nowadays everbody uses electrics—seems like it anyway. Have to have a truck to haul this around. Used to have to tie it to the top of a car when the band traveled around."

Moving back into the cluttered living room, I asked Floyd, "What do you reckon that river thing was all about? I mean, it's a miracle you made it. Anybody else would've been dead. What do you think?"

Contemplating this for a time, he slowly started talking, "In a sense, I don't know what for. What's the . . . where is the thang wrote down at . . . He's got the scale. Who rules? I know who does!"

Both of us sat for a while, neither saying a word. Finally he said, "It's changed me. I'm walking a little lighter."

Taking a deep breath, he said, *"He was there. He was. To the last minute. I know. He's the One, no matter what you get into. I felt Him there. I knew I wasn't goin' ta die. I'd be here a little longer.*

"I respect people that goes to church and I respect churches." His words fell to a whisper, and I could barely hear him. "But I still . . . I know that's not the only place where God is. I'm not a Christian, I know I ain't, but I always feel Him. He's always in me. Ain't no people goin' ta be around me talking against Him. And I'm not saying that 'cause I'm talkin' to you. But that river thang! It's always there. Ever minute." Then, catching himself, he shook his head back and forth saying, "I wouldn't say ever . . . well—" He stopped for a moment, thought about it, and nodded up and down. "I *would* say that. Ever minute!"

His words hung over the box of a room like a mist after a spring rain. Neither of us dared utter another word, and a silence grew in the vacuum. It was as though nothing else could be said. So, with the dawn quickly rolling into morning, I bade Floyd a friend's good-bye. It was hard, because I could feel his pull as if to say, "Stay a little longer."

All the way back to Jim's, I couldn't shake Floyd's 'river thang,' as he had called it. Try as I might, it was just impossible to fathom what he had gone through. At the door, just before leaving, I had asked him one last question. "Do you think there was some reason you lived?" I had mumbled.

His answer rode with me in the drizzling half-light. He had said, "It's not all plain now. It's hard enough just to try to live thangs." Then, as I hit the bottom step on my way out, he added, "I was out walking awhile ago, just walking in this rain. You appreciate thangs."

When I walked in at Jim's, nothing seemed any different than when I had come in earlier from my long trip down. The coffeepot was on. He was in his usual chair. A guitar was on his lap and he was picking a favorite tune. I flopped down into what was becoming "my" chair, and he smiled. I grinned back, and for a tense second we both could've burst into laughter for no other reason except exhaustion. We didn't and the moment passed. Just as I closed my eyes to relax and unwind, he jolted me wide awake.

"Want to go get some breakfast?" he teased, beginning to stand and put his guitar down at the same time. Walking across the room, he laughed wickedly. "Close the door behind ya."

5. GERMAINE CURLEY

The road to Empire, Louisiana, was lonely. For long, desolate stretches there was only the uneven pavement. The highway seemed endless, the road never quite rising high enough above the pancake-flat terrain to reach the horizon. Squeezed tight on either side by earthen levees, silent guardians from the Gulf of Mexico on the right and the Mississippi River on the left, the concrete path seemed about to be swallowed by the parted waters.

Yet the road rolled on over the narrow spit of land in the false light of the rapidly approaching darkness. Thank goodness it wasn't hurricane season. Many times in the past, monstrous storms, seemingly possessing a navigation intelligence all their own, took to the highway and rode it straight up to New Orleans. In their wake, the road at times all but vanished, sucked under by the massive flooding left in their passing. Lest anyone should ever forget to heed the warnings, the road is the only way in and out. It is a lifeline on shaky ground. The route of salvation.

Salvation. Or rather, the way to salvation was what I was hoping to discover as I dropped off of Interstate 10, fought traffic through New Orleans, crossed the Mississippi River, and traveled south into Plaquemines Parish. There were people here, living communally, who said they knew the divine plan for the universe. They called themselves the Christos family. It was in the early 1980s when they moved into the Delta and occupied the dilapidated century-old island fortress of Fort Jackson. Immediately they set about repairing the aging structure in order to make it inhabitable. It was to be their spiritual home base. When I first visited them in 1982 as part of a *National Geographic* photographic coverage of the Delta, they were plowing full steam ahead with their plans of rebuilding the place. But there was one thing the "family" could not do: They could not free themselves of the vicious welter of constantly attacking mosquitoes. The infestation was probably the reason the fort had been abandoned in the first place.

Now, years later, I was returning, not to spy on their progress, but to ask them about God, something I could never do while working for *Geographic.* This was a subject I could not explore while there. On my present journey, I had no constraints. I was free—to learn, listen, and record. The Christos family could possibly shed light on matters of the soul. I was open to the prospects, anyway. All adventures, I had learned from Native American spiritual elders, were roads back to one's self. Like artists capturing within the confines of a canvas what is beyond its borders, those on the fringes can bring to light what the mainstream cannot see, much less comprehend. And, in my thinking, this tiny sect could produce another key to unlocking some of the spiritual mysteries of life.

My search stalled almost immediately. After finally finding a room at one of the very few, and mostly full, motels around Empire, I was told by a clerk that the leader of the group had died, and his followers had scattered. Like the absorbing blackness of night, I fell into a twilight of despair. Akin to a traveler on a road who would soon run into the sea, I seemed to be at a dead end. But I determined not give up without a fight. Something had brought me here, I reasoned. And whatever it was, that *something* was still here.

All night long I wrestled with the one question that plagued my weary mind: Why am I here, then, if not for the Christos family? With every roll of my body, the thin sheets slid as if on slippery oil over the plastic-covered mattress. Soon the cheap cloth was wadded up into a ball. And so was I. Sleep was out of the question. In a fit of desperation, I turned on the light, made a few notes, and then ventured out into the humidity to get a can of soda. During the walk across the still parking lot, a thought came to me. I would start from scratch, I told myself, and begin posing the God question to strangers.

Upon returning to my room, I took one swallow of the dark carbonated drink, then set it on the nightstand to begin its fizzing flight into undrinkable flatness. Contented with my plan, I was ready to sleep. I was just about overtaken with drowsiness before I could unravel the yellowing fabric and crawl between the covers. Only the brightness of the south Louisiana sun glaring through that one section of the drapes that could not be closed could wake me. And in the morning it did. It wasn't the revving truck engines. It was the brilliant light.

After showering and dressing, I ventured out into the parking lot. Although it was early, the motel was all but empty from the full house it had been the night before. Only a couple of cars and a pickup or two remained. Meandering over to the office, I went inside to search out the free coffee most motels provide for guests. I was not disappointed. After pouring myself a cup, I spoke a "Good morning" to the clerk. She smiled in returning the greeting. As I started for the door, I hesitated. The clerk noticed immediately and asked, "Can I help you with anything?"

Instead of answering I just stood there. My thoughts were on God, and I was battling with myself as to whether I should ask her if she knew anyone who'd been touched by the divine. As I tossed the idea back and forth, she waited in anticipation for my response. Then I blurted out, "Do you know anybody who's seen God—ah . . . ah, who knows God?"

The clerk was mystified for a moment. Her expression told me that my remark was not something she was used to hearing, much less having to answer. After thinking, the woman yielded, "My mother's seen some strange things in her life. Bet she'd talk to you about it. She's seen, I think, her brother at her window. Then, later, she found out he had died about the same time he appeared to her. You could talk to her."

Now I was getting somewhere, I thought. So I asked, "Do you think she would talk to me about it?"

"Oh, yes. I think she'd be happy to. Well, to anybody, for that matter."

Excitedly, I said, "Maybe you could take me to her."

"She doesn't live here," she quickly replied.

My disappointment overcame me. It was obvious she could see what I was feeling from my expression, so before I could respond, she added, "I can tell you how to get there."

"Please do. I'd like to meet her. She'd probably have a lot of stories."

Then she started to give me directions. The mother was in a nursing home up in central Louisiana, a few hours away. Actually, three or four hours. I was tired of traveling, and I wanted a more immediate result. It seemed I was back at a dead end.

Finally, seeing my frustration and knowing from the look on my face that going to visit her mother would be too much of an undertaking, she suggested that there was someone who could tell me everything I needed to know about anyone and everyone living in the parish. Yes, she would be helpful.

"You could tell me who it is," I said, "and if it's not far, I'll go to her."

"See Germaine. She knows everything. Besides, she'd have to know God. She couldn't have done the things for people around here without some kind of connection like that, if you know what I mean. And goodness, what she's gone through."

"Germaine," I said, thoughtfully. "I know a Germaine who lives here. She runs the Delta Marina."

"That's her. Germaine Curley," she said.

The clerk kept right on talking, but I couldn't concentrate on her words. I was thinking of Germaine. There was no one else quite like her. I had never forgotten her, although we had not stayed in close touch. She had befriended me when I needed a friend back in 1979. I had suggested a story on Louisiana's Vietnamese fishermen to *National Geographic* through Black Star, my picture agency. *Geographic*'s director of photography had been out of town, and the idea went directly to one of the magazine's editors. He immediately gave me an assignment to do the story.

Those were troubled times for the Vietnamese living in the United States. Because they had chosen Empire as their base, the tiny community had become the center of conflict between longtime white American shrimpers and the struggling immigrants. There was the inevitable clash between two cultures. There were language barriers. There were laws of the waters the Vietnamese did not know, and even when they did, they had difficulty understanding and practicing them. Then there were the unwritten rules of American seafaring etiquette long since established by the locals. At the same time, some unscrupulous seamen preyed on the unwitting Vietnamese by selling them boats that were far from seaworthy. A few of the boats had been downright dangerous to take into the open waters of the Gulf.

Finally, there had been displays of open hostilities. Some of the Vietnamese had been shot at. One or two of their ramshackle death traps had actually been set on fire. It had not been a good time to be in the area working on that particular story. Although the problems came about because of a few, and only a few people, tempers in all the camps had been at the point of exploding. An all-out war could have easily erupted over the least provocation. And into the very heart of this, I waltzed. The old adage was true: Fools walk in where angels fear to tread.

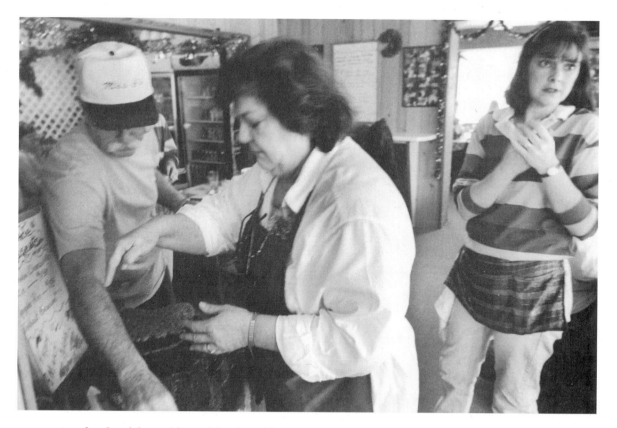

her head from side to side, she added, "I didn't get to work there very often. I was one of the people that wrote a check and sent people there. When I was out among the people, I would come across so many who were in need and I'd always say, 'Okay, I'm going to make arrangements for you to get to Caring Hands and see what we can do to help you out.'

"Then, I was hit with the heart problem. I was only fifty-seven at the time." Germaine rolled her head over and looked at me, her eyes appearing to grow dark. There was not the normal gaiety in her tone. But she didn't hesitate. She was taking me to the depths of her close call. "I was coming home from a doctor's visit," she recalled, "and luckily I had my granddaughter Alise with me. And God was definitely in that car, too.

"I passed out." I could sense that she was visualizing what could have happened: Dying, with her granddaughter in the car, in an accident off the side of the road, or worse, involving another car and other people. I knew the way she thought. She couldn't bear to be the cause of someone else's suffering.

"I was driving," she went on. "I was in Port Sulphur. I had just seen Dr. Knox drive by going in the opposite direction. It was closing time and he was headed home. I had taken my granddaughter out to lunch and shopping that day after my appointment with Dr. Knox earlier that morning. She and I were on our way back to Empire. It was

Martin Luther King Day—January 18, 1993. And I—I mean my heart started flipping and I passed out and I came to, luckily, still on the highway. And I said, 'Alise, I'm in serious trouble.'"

As she talked, I could just hear her telling her granddaughter, "Alise, I'm in serious trouble," and I could just see her kindly face, trying to be calm, and certainly coaxing Alise to be aware that something was wrong. But even then, she wouldn't say it in a way that would alarm her granddaughter. She was using the same tone on me now. Like it had been no big deal, but she knew it had been.

Germaine went on, her words carefully chosen. "We were very fortunate. I saw cars at Knox's office, though I knew he had just pulled away from there. So I turned in there. I don't know how I did it. I don't know how. My heart rate was a hundred and ninety-two beats per minute and stayed that way for eight hours.

"They were scared to move me. They were scared to do anything. I stayed in Port Sulphur, lying in the doctor's office. They thought they could stabilize me but couldn't. So finally, after four hours, they put me in an ambulance and we headed north for the hospital in New Orleans. I stayed in that bed, in ICU, just thumping. And I mean I could feel it. It just . . . wouldn't come down. The medication they were giving me wasn't affecting me at all. At about four-thirty in the morning, the cardiologist came in and said, 'Mrs. Curley, we are having such serious problems trying to get your heart rate down. It's got me puzzled. I don't know what to do.' And he walked out of the room."

Germaine didn't go into details about her fear then or what was really going through her mind now, but I was sure I could see her in that hospital with her arms crossed over her chest, waiting patiently for them to do something. Definitely she didn't scream or show any panic. Not outwardly, anyway.

"At five-thirty, my son walked in the room." Her words reflected the relief she must have felt. "And directly the nurse ran in the room, 'cause I was being monitored outside, and she was all aflutter. She said, 'What happened? What happened? Your heart rate is now down to one-fifty.'

"They tease me till this day," she chuckled, "that Kelly, my son, did it. He had an effect. He's always been special, okay, he really has. Kelly walked in and my heart rate dropped to around one-fifty. I can't remember exactly. The children all tease us because they say Baby Jesus arrived and my heart rate stabilized." Germaine laughed heartily.

When her laughing subsided, she went on. "Before I was sent home, I had the angiogram. All of this, oh, frightened me. Lord, God, I was in such a state. My children were all so anxious about me.

"First they tried to give me a stress test and I passed out. I mean I went out like a light"—she snapped her fingers, and her words flowed on— "just after I was on the treadmill maybe a minute, minute and a half. So they knew my heart was in bad shape. They ordered an angiogram for the next morning and discovered three blockages and that I had to have—" she stopped, then she told me— "I had what they call the widowmaker . . . where the blockage is so near the heart that it . . . it explodes the heart."

Sighing, she admitted, "I was overweight then. Even more overweight than now. Anyway, they wanted me to lose weight, and they wanted me to rest and so forth before this operation.

"The operation was scheduled for March. I was to lose some ten, twenty pounds, whatever I could lose. And I did. I was pretty good about that." I knew she wasn't one to stretch the truth. Her body language confirmed it. She had her hands crossed over her heart. But she didn't stop for long. "I was also very good about resting. Once they scared me with the widowmaker bit, I knew I needed to do something about the stress I was under. And I did. I slowed up on everything. And did a whole lot of praying. My husband, Pat, and I, we just took to saying our Rosary together. We talked a whole lot.

"Then along came another scare. God definitely touched me again. They sent me home with a drug, and on about my third or fourth dosage, I had a horrible reaction to it. I was sitting on the couch and I looked up at Pat and I said, 'I'm dying, Pat.' And I said, 'I love you,' and, 'Good-bye,' and I went.

"He had the good sense to check my pulse. I had a pretty strong one, but I felt like I was slipping. He got the ambulance there right away, and all the paramedics came and I was in a sweat. I was wet to the point you could wring out my pajamas. I was barely conscious. I was just coming in and out, in and out, and then my heartbeat went crazy. My God, I didn't know a person could do that. So back to the hospital again. I got that all cleared up, and then I was sent home again.

"The operation went off without a hitch. The only thing that I can tell you that . . . I was in stress about was that I was losing a very dear, wonderful person at the same time who I believe was a saint here on earth, and that was my aunt Jane. She discovered she had cancer, and within six weeks that was it. She was gone. She died while I was in the hospital. I didn't want the operation because of that.

"I was very distraught, having to . . . I walked out of her room in the ICU and into the hospital for me to get operated on. I knew I was seeing her for the last time. Most beautiful person. And because I couldn't be at her funeral, I wrote a letter and Kathleen, my daughter, read it from the altar."

Germaine couldn't go on. Talking about her aunt brought back too many memories. But instead of dwelling on them, or maybe to cover her emotions, she stood up and leaned against the door. Her eyes moved slowly over the restaurant as it continued to fill with customers. She appeared anxious, yet she sat back down. There was more she wanted to say before she had to get back to work.

Slowly, Germaine began again. "Because of all the parish problems," she said, "and with my health in such a state, my husband pleaded with me to get out of politics. He begged me. He told me, 'We're moving away from here. You make up your own mind what you're going to do.' Then he shocked me when he said, 'You can stay here if you want, that's fine, but I'm going . . . with you or without you. I love you too much to see you letting these people kill you like this.' That was not like him. He'd almost always gone along with whatever I wanted."

"And that was that!" I laughed, slapping the table. "You moved to Picayune, Mississippi."

Germaine tapped the table, almost mimicking me. "I knew, for the first time in our marriage, he meant it and he'd do it."

"And so?" I teased.

"We moved here," she said, getting up to leave. As she did, she apologized, "Now there's work to do." And she was off working the tables, speaking on a first-name basis with those younger then herself and putting a Mr. or a Mrs. on those older. Finally she disappeared from my view altogether.

After Germaine was gone, her husband, Pat, came around to keep me company, perhaps because he had been given instructions to do so. Nevertheless, he was eager to fill me in on the success of their restaurant.

"The first day here was the slowest day," he said proudly. "At eight in the morning, she started cooking the Creole. People started coming from out of the woods. It was unbelievable. Business tripled since we took over. People in town can't get over all the cars parked here."

Pat was almost jubilant in remembering. "Took only about a month for business to do that. 'Bout a month," he said, nodding happily. "At first it was just strictly seafood. Then she started cooking spaghetti and meatballs once a week. Every Friday it's Étouffée. She put up a sign that said, 'Étouffée and Fettuccine.' Some people even asked, 'What is fettuccine?' Now they pack in here. They just love it.

"She was talking to the district attorney, who had come in to eat and said, 'Got to teach these folks how to eat.' So that's what she's doing.

"She does everything. She does all the homemade desserts. We send her home at two o'clock to rest everyday, and she goes home at two o'clock and starts making desserts. Oh, she may rest about an hour or so, but if we're busy, she'll come back. Lot of times she'll call and ask if we're busy and we say, 'No!' She's got to have a little rest once in a while."

Pat and I talked until he was called back to the kitchen. The burden of serving such a crowd had become too much, so he was needed to help lighten the load. As soon as he ended our conversation he was up and diving into the rush. Within minutes he raced out the side door. Since I was free to wander, I meandered through the crunch of tables and traced his steps. When I found him he was absorbed in steaming crawfish—pounds of them. Over and over again he'd toss more into the steamer. When they were done, out they'd come and more would go in. It was a full-time job just to keep up with the dozens of orders. So I left him shoveling the crustaceans for the duration of the lunch period.

When the business slowed, Germaine took to looking for me. Ready to get out of the noise and find a quiet place to unwind and talk, she waved me out the door.

"Follow me," she said as she headed out. As we made our way past empty tables cluttered with mounds of dirty dishes, she bellowed, "We live just down the street. Won't take us but a minute to get there. It's the only place we can really talk in peace and quiet."

Before Germaine could get within three feet of the door, a member of her wait staff rushed up to her and pulled her to a stop. Immediately Germaine's arm went around the waitress's waist, and the young woman pressed close. Her mouth was up to Germaine's

DANCING WITH GOD

ear, and Germaine tilted her head to hear the waitress's soft words. For a time they huddled. It seemed secrets were being passed.

When Germaine released her benevolent hug, I started for the door again. "Not so fast," she called. "It's going to be a little while before I can go. There's something I need to tend to, so," she chuckled, "have one of the girls get you a fresh cup of coffee. Won't be long. Sorry," she said, moving toward a table by the window where an older woman was sitting alone.

As I looked about for a place to sit that was out of the way of those still eating and the young women cleaning tables, I saw Germaine pull up a chair beside the lady who had asked to talk to her. As if by some power beyond her, Germaine naturally took the woman's hand in hers. There was a worn look on the woman's face. Germaine immediately sensed her pain, relaxing her motherly clasp of hands, and wrapped an arm around the woman's shoulder. From the expression on Germaine's face I could see that she knew the lady had a problem.

In time the lady made every indication of leaving, but still she talked on. And she continued to do so as Germaine walked her to the door. Then the lady was gone.

Seeing me from a distance, Germaine nodded and beckoned me to follow. As we made our way to the cars, she took me by the arm and whispered, "You saw that woman?"

I nodded.

"I've never seen her before in my life. Not before today. She's never come into the restaurant before. Do you know what she said to me?"

"No," I quickly responded.

Germaine let go of my arm and propped against the car fender. Catching her breath, she went on. "She said to me, 'I just knew you were the kind of person who could help.'"

Listening to her, I got the idea the woman wanted something. So I popped out with, "Did she want a freebie?"

"Oh-h," Germaine sighed. "Oh, nothing for herself. Oh, no! It was for someone else, not for her. That little woman found out about a mother who is dying of cancer. So is the mother's daughter. And they have nothing. They're about to lose their home, and they don't have anywhere to go. They don't even have food.

"All this woman wanted to know was if I could do anything to help them. She'd already done everything she could, and now she's trying to find people who could chip in to help. See, that woman doesn't have anything herself. What little resources she had, she's exhausted even that. Now she's trying to find anybody who can do just a little something. She's so concerned, it's just tearing her up to see these poor people suffering. She knows the mother's going to die, and she's wanting to help make her as comfortable as possible. The last thing in the world she wants to see happen is for her to be hungry and to have no place to live. So, all she's wanting to know was if there was anything I could do. Anything at all."

"Germaine," I asked, "how did she know about you?"

For a minute she remained silent. Then, with a squeeze of my hand, she said, "I don't know. I guess it's because I'm here. I seem to draw these people. I don't look for them, they find me." In a soft murmur, she added, "It's what I'm here for. And they come in."

Even before she finished talking, I was thinking to myself, It's little wonder Germaine had that heart attack. There are so many in so much need, her heart just broke.

"But," she repeated, her words calling me back, "that's why I'm here. God's taken care of me because He has more for me to do."

Neither of us said anything more. We got into our cars and I followed her to her little rented house alongside the busy boulevard. As we entered, her last words seemed somehow to be still floating in the air. Without saying anything, Germaine pointed. I followed her directions. She was telling me to take the big, overstuffed arm chair, while she sprawled out on the sofa. There we sat quietly for a time.

Breaking the silence, Germaine spoke up first, saying, "It's been hard on me here in Picayune. In Empire I knew more of what God wanted me to do. But here . . ." Germaine sat up, her elbows resting on her knees. She was thinking. Then she motioned up at the two or three Bibles neatly tucked between other books in the bookcase across the room. "I don't read the Bible enough," she said, giving no reason for the statement. Then she was gazing into space again.

Somehow I sensed she was overcome with a sense of guilt. I couldn't imagine why, and she didn't explain. Maybe she wasn't reading the Bible enough, I thought, but surely she could see that she was following her Catholic teachings by living them.

While caught up in my own reasonings as to why she felt as she did, she pulled me back into her reality by saying, "I was depressed for a long time after my heart surgery and, perhaps in some way, I may still be. But I'm not near as bad as I used to be, when my attention span was so altered I couldn't concentrate to read. I couldn't sleep at night. I wanted to stay in bed all the time. And all those symptoms. I honestly prayed myself out of that. I really did.

"I got to thinking, 'Now, I can't live like this. This is not living. This is dying. And I think that I'm a strong enough person . . .' and that's another thing about me. I know that I have a strong character, and I will pick myself up when I'm down. Nobody else has to do it for me. That's why I know that God's in me, because I can do that on my own, because my faith is that deep in Him . . . that I know that I'm going to get better, that I know this is going to change, that I know good is going to come, that I know I'm going to be better. I'm going to be all right."

"I know you are," I uttered, trying to console her. She'd been through a lot, and I was hoping to let her know there were those of us who cared for her well-being. "Try not to be too hard on yourself," I pleaded.

"You can't get away from God," she retorted. "No, you can't. There's no way. He's always with me. I just don't recognize Him all the time. He's not forsaken me.

"I feel comfortable about God being in me, because I like doing good things and I think that's the way God is . . . that He does only good things. We may question what He does sometimes—we say, 'Why do bad things happen to good people?' But there's a reason for everything, and He can't be blamed for my brother dying of cancer or my sister having this or that or Jimmy's stepson dying of cystic fibrosis. I think those things are not of God. I don't think he gives us diseases. It's not His fault that we get a disease. I don't believe that, but all things happen for a reason. I do believe that. And you grow if you allow yourself. You can grow from those casualties in your life . . . those low times in your life."

"I guess that's why people pray," I said.

Germaine wrinkled her brow and sat quietly. Then she responded, "It is, but I've had dry periods where I couldn't pray. I've had dry periods where I couldn't even think about my God. I can only tell you that in the back of mind I knew that I was going to be healed again, and that my praying would become easy again, and that everything would fall back into place because of my strength.

"Now I pray a lot. I talk . . . really. I don't pray when I'm alone so much as I just . . . I can be talking to you and praying at the same time. I feel comfortable talking to God in prayer rather than saying the Rosary, the act of contrition, the Hail Mary, the Our Father. I find that very repetitive and I get lost in it after a while. The first couple of decats, I'm okay, but after that I just enjoy talking.

"My form of prayer is, 'Forgive me.' That's my first entrance into prayer. I'm just always asking forgiveness for the things that I didn't do today, for the people I didn't tend to, for the insensitivity that I had today toward people's needs. I just generally ask for forgiveness of my sins and also ask that 'Should I die at any' "—she stopped, correcting herself—" 'whenever I die, please know that at this point in time I'm asking for forgiveness of those sins that I may have on my soul when I die. I want you to know that I repent all my sins.'

"It sounds silly, but in sincerity I mean it from the bottom of my heart that I don't want to go to hell by no means and I believe in heaven. I honestly believe in heaven. And I feel like . . . I'm comfortable in prayer."

"Germaine," I stated, "your prayers must get answered. You said you believe in angels. You wouldn't say that unless you had some reason."

Germaine knew what I was saying, so she yielded, "I *know* there are angels! I believe in them. I've had times when angels were with me. When I was six years old, I had my tonsils removed and I was sent home. In the middle of the night I was bleeding to death . . . a hemorrhage. And I remember angels being around me. Just like moving." Germaine waved her arms in the air above her head and spread her hands wide with fingers outstretched. So striking were her movements, I could almost see the angels who had visited her long ago. It was as if they were in the room and swirling around her.

"On three other occasions angels saved us—saved me once and saved Pat and me twice. Some psychics would call it premonition, I guess. I feel like angels tell me things. Once I was told not to open a particular door. To get away. I'll tell you the story," she volunteered.

"My mother was the postmaster in Empire in those days," she started. "She held that job for forty-two years. And she wouldn't allow any of her family to have mailboxes. There weren't enough to go around, and for her, the public came first. She didn't want anybody to think she was favoring us. She was stern about it. Besides, we'd have taken twenty boxes among us.

"You've got to understand the post office was in the grocery store. When you came into the store, there were the mailboxes to one side. Then behind them was her office. It was really so small I don't know if you could even call it an office. No one could get into that little room except through this one door. So to take care of us she had built shelves that sort of looked like a bookcase with dividers. Every one of us had our own slot, but there were no doors covering the compartments. We weren't worthy of a locked mailbox, in other words! My uncles and my aunts and everybody would come through the store and go into that office and get their mail.

"Well, one Sunday afternoon Pat said to me, 'Did you pick up the mail yesterday?'

"And I said, 'No.'

"Then he said, 'Well, let's walk over and get it.'

"I had my own key to the store, of course. We all did. Since the post office was in the store, we had to have a way to get in to get our mail. After unlocking the store, we made our way to that little office and . . ." She paused.

She was there, in her mind, in Empire and on the way to the store. Emotions of the time were flooding back on her. After a moment or two and a short hard breath, she continued. "The hair on the back of my neck stood up. The angels told me, 'Get out of here!'

"That was a frightening thing. It was a strange sensation of . . . I don't know . . .

tension and urgency. I said, 'Pat, let's get out of here!' And Pat has always recognized my third sense, sixth sense, seventh sense, or whatever. And we got out of that store.

"He said, 'What in the world!'

"I said, 'Something made me get out of there. Something told me to get out!'

"Because we had entered through the back door and come back out the same way, we rushed around to the front. There was a car there. That didn't set with me, because it was a Sunday afternoon. The store was closed. And no one had ever parked there like that before.

"I said, 'Let's go home.' As soon as I could get to the phone, I called Mama. I said, 'Mama, I don't know, but something's not right at the post office. I was going to get the mail, but when I started to unlock the door to your office, something told me to get out. And that's what Pat and I did. Then there was a strange car out front. I think something's going on over there.'"

Germaine was excited. The way she was talking it was as if she wasn't just retelling the story, it was happening then and there. And she went on.

"Mama just says, 'Oh, well, somebody might be just walking around by the canal or something.'

"I knew better. Back in those days, everybody knew everybody, knew their cars, too. But I didn't know who that one belonged to. Anyway, I asked myself, What would a car be doing at the store on a Sunday afternoon?

"My mama got a big surprise the next morning. As usual, she goes and opens her little post office. And it had been robbed!" Germaine laughed with an element of anxiety she must have felt because of the experience she had lived through. Her laughter was certainly not to make it all seem like a joking matter.

I was caught up in her story, and I wanted to know more. "Were the angels right?" I asked. "Was there something more to their warning?"

Again Germaine laughed. "I'd say so. They caught the robber and he brazenly admitted that he heard us on the other side of the door. He thought it was funny, and he had to let us know that he had a forty-five-caliber with him. And he was just waiting for us to open that door. He said, 'You would've been gone if you'd opened it. I'd have blown you away.'"

"And you thought angels told you to get out?" I asked.

"Now, why did I feel the sense of danger?" she boomed. "I feel an angel told me . . . my guardian angel. I've had it happen other times. That's why I believe we all have guardian angels." She looked at me. I felt she was checking to see if I believed as she did.

From my expression she relaxed. She knew what my response would be. So she didn't ask for an answer, but I threw a question at her. "What was the other time?" I asked.

"Pat and I were on our way to Thibodaux to a fund-raiser," she started, "and we stopped in a little town to get us a soft drink. We each got a Coke. He said, 'Come on, let's go.'

"I said, 'No! Wait a minute!'

"And he said, 'What do you mean, wait a minute?'

"I said, 'Just wait a little while. I got a feeling about something.'

"So we waited. It wasn't that he wanted to, but he's learned not to question these feelings I get." Germaine really laughed hard.

I laughed with her this time. I could just picture Pat looking around for angels after she said she had those feelings again. Then I asked, "Were your angels right? Was there a reason you were supposed to wait?"

"We would've been in an accident," she said. "It's like this. We got back into our car and took off. Just a little way down the road there was a collision. It had just happened, and it involved about five cars. Some of the people had really been hurt. If we'd been just seconds earlier, we would've been in that accident." She stopped, raising a finger into the air.

I thought she was pointing to heaven, but then she let me know she had something else to add.

"There's another time the angels saved me," she said, adding, "and this was just recently. I was coming from Empire by myself and I very nearly fell asleep . . . well, I fell asleep at the wheel," she admitted. Then she continued, "I was in a hair of going over an embankment . . . one of the little bridge crossing things. When I came to, I was right at the edge. If I had continued, I'd have been gone. What woke me up? What did it?"

"Do you think God is speaking to you through the angels?" I asked sincerely.

"There are some who say God speaks to them. For me, I don't stand around waiting for answers from Him. I don't think God strikes you. You know, these people who say that 'God told me I had to become a priest, I was called.' I often wonder to myself, 'What sensation do you get when God speaks to you?' Maybe I've never been still long enough for Him to speak to me and tell me personally, 'This is what I want you to do.' "

"What about the angels?" I asked. "Sounds like they told you what not to do," I said, and we both laughed.

Germaine leaned back on the sofa. Then she admitted, "I know we get messages. That's what I believe. I do believe that, 'cause we still have things to do. I don't think God's done with me, yet. I've said it time and again, He's got things for me to do." She stopped and closed her eyes.

She was tired, and it was time for me to go, but there was something about the way she was grasping the arm of the sofa that caused me to pause. She needed to rest, but I sensed there was something more. Our conversation may have been drawing to a close, but she wasn't going to end it until she had her final say. Being tired had nothing to do with it.

So I waited. Soon a smile came over her face, not that one wasn't always there. This one was just a little different, the kind of different that made me know I'd be glad I hadn't just up and left. After flashing me with a joyous, all-over-the-face smile, she spoke up.

"Some say they've seen God," she said. "For me, I have to say, 'No, I haven't.' But I was brought up to *feel* God all the time. And all of my life, I've felt His presence. I feel the sense of God in me."

When she paused, I asked, "Have you ever wondered what God looks like?"

"What God looks like?" she smiled. "I know, and this is just me," she said, folding her arms across her chest. "He's just two big beautiful arms that will encircle you and hug you and hold you and . . . and He has no face and He has no body. He's just two giant-sized puffy beautiful arms. And with those arms He can hold you and cuddle you. And enclosed in them you feel absolutely safe and comfortable. And it's love that radiates out of this big puffiness. This beautiful softness. That's how I see God!"

6. WILLIAM J. McFARLANE

His laughter came in bursts, at first building slowly, then exploding in uncontrollable eruptions. One minute he would be staring out the window on his side of the car; the next he would be roaring in laughter, slapping his knees, clapping his hands together, and rolling his head forward and back. Then, he would fall silent again. Calmly he would allow his body to slump over to rest against the door, and his head would tilt sideways to touch the glass. He would appear to be in meditation.

Then, all of a sudden, he appeared agitated, all wound up, as if an internal volcano were rumbling. The sounds began as moans at first, like the low guttural hum of a monk beginning an ancient chant. But without warning his thundering waves of ecstatic, nerve-tingling laughter flowed forth. Soul wrenching. Alarming. Almost wicked. Strangely funny. And even joyous. It was so intoxicating, in fact, that his laughter demanded laughter as a response. And mine spewed out of me like a geyser. It was instantaneous and absolutely impossible to bring under control, even after he had gone silent.

When it seemed that the storm had finally passed, just my thinking of his laughing so hard would cause me to cough out another chuckle or two. I couldn't help it, even with my chest hurting from the bruising it had just gone through. But about the time I was ready to say, "Thank God," and enjoy some relief, his on-again, off-again hum would begin. And I braced myself for what I knew was coming. My giggles were already rising to the surface to meet his bursts.

Keeping my mind on my driving was just about the hardest thing I had ever done. I chastised myself for doubting my intuition, as I seriously contemplated putting him out somewhere alongside the road. But I rode on. I didn't have it in me to leave him on the side of the road.

It had been on a whim that I stopped to pick him up. After leaving Germaine's, I traveled across Louisiana and part of Texas on my westward journey without talking to a single person about God or anything else. All I did was order food and coffee. But take on hitchers? That was something I never, but never, did, no matter how desperate for company I was. Although I had often had the urge to give someone a lift, I refused to be pressured by that desire to show compassion for a fellow traveler who didn't have the means to find other modes of transportation. My reasoning? The state of this country. We've been told there is evil out there, and it blares out of the devilish tube every day on the evening news.

So now I was stuck. Fear raced through me and I trembled. Fortunately he had put his pack behind the front seat, so he couldn't go for a gun without my knowing it. And with the lightweight clothes he was wearing, I would have been able to see one had he been carrying it on his body. Nevertheless, he made me very nervous. But the laughter saved me. His laughter. It started all over again. Then again. And again. It seemed endless.

He had been on the ramp leading onto the interstate. I had exited the four-lane for gas and an overcooked hamburger. An unhealthy choice, the news reports seemed to forever bark, yet it had been extremely satisfying. After taking care of the necessities, I eased through the intersection and pressed down on the accelerator, hoping for a clear shot back onto the roadway. And there he was: alone, pleading, asking only for a chance to get a little farther down the road and a few miles closer to an unheralded destination.

He had on a baseball cap, graying hair protruding from beneath the band. His hair was a little too long for my taste. And it would've gone over his ears and covered his collar a tad had it not been for the wind sweeping it up to flap like a bird's feathers. Then there was the scraggly beard. Had it been any thinner, he wouldn't have had one at all.

The only thing that could be said, in good conscience, to praise it was that it was blacker than his hair. Of course there was the mustache. It was a wonder, turning under with the curve of his upper lip to completely hide it and making him appear toothless.

His attire left no doubt he was a road man. Long-sleeved shirt, with the ends of the sleeves rolled exactly twice. Blue jeans. Sneakers. A worn old bag sat behind him, probably holding all his earthly belongings. Or so I reasoned. This, my warning bells tolled, was the kind of person you should not stop for.

But there he had stood. On the western side of San Antonio. Weather looked like rain. The forecaster on the radio had just said, "Sixty percent chance of rain and sometimes heavy thunderstorms." It was there, right then, in a split second, something spoke to me. Told me, "Pull over! Pick him up." And shock of all shocks, I found myself slamming on the brakes just as my speed was topping out and the ramp and the road were rapidly becoming one. And next would have come the precarious merging into the overbearing and unyielding traffic. That's when I stopped, just short of passing him by. As he reached for the door handle, I had a powerful urge to floor it, to take off and leave him. He would never know who I was. Never see me again. But I didn't, and he bounced in, happy as a lark.

He was too pleased for my comfort. He had been hitching from Alabama, trying to get over El Paso way. Even from San Antonio, that would still be a long way. Something inside of me groaned because I was headed that way, too. Part of me was thrilled to have someone to talk to, but another part was concerned that it might be a ride I'd never forget.

So, as I gunned the gas, I studied him as best I could out of the corner of my eye. I didn't want to be too obvious. He was about medium height, thin, looked like he'd been on the road way too long. It seemed obvious that he was a drifter. But he was friendly and started talking immediately. Just talking away. His name was William. His skin was dark, and he had dark eyes. I never would've guessed what his background was, not just from his outward appearance, but I had worked with Native Americans for many years, and he looked as if he could've been a member of one of the many Indian nations I'd worked with across the country.

His name was William J., he said. William J. McFarlane. For a time he let it go at that. Then, coming back to the name, he said, "I got to tell you. I've got that 'J' in my name. And you're going to have to know what it means sooner or later," but he didn't elaborate.

I waited. And waited. My curiosity was getting the best of me, so I just up and asked him what the "J" stood for.

He didn't seem to want to tell me. He just said, "Let's let it go as William J." This made me more edgy than I already was.

His laughing fits continued. I tried not to laugh when he did, but there was no way I could avoid it. As always, once he was over his laughing spell, he would revert back to his talkative self. Within an hour I had learned a lot about him. He'd been in Vietnam and had suffered from post-traumatic shock syndrome.

"I've had nightmares. Nightmares and nightmares. Oh, the dreams," he said. Then, with terror in his voice, he said, "To this day, I still wake up fighting. Sometimes I'm running and running. I was captured and got away. And in the dreams I'm trying to escape, but the guards are always after me.

"It's real!" he yelled out. "I'm telling you, it's real. You don't believe me, I know it. I can see it on your face, like on everybody's face I tell. But it's real!"

Turning to look at him, I started to speak, but he screamed, "Hey, watch where you're going! Don't kill us here. I've been through too much to die like this. Watch the road, man."

Immediately, I followed his command, needing no more convincing to do as he told me. My thought was that he was just a little more than unstable. And he might be prone to acting out in that instability. I didn't want to take any undue chances. It wasn't that I thought he was dangerous—far from that, I came to realize after the amount of time we had spent together. He was just easily panicked. He really did value living, because he knew death. It haunted him. Ate at him. Tortured him day and night. And in spite of it, he still wanted to live. So I did as he asked, and he returned to normal. When he did, I felt secure enough to talk.

"It's not that I know what you've been through—" I started, but he immediately interrupted before I could go on.

"No, you don't," he said with a forcefulness that caught me off guard. "Look," he said, and pulled up his shirt. "See that?"

The scar was about the ugliest thing I had ever seen. It started right at the place where the collarbones came together and in a jagged fashion continued all the way to his belt and disappeared beneath his pants. Then he traced another one with his finger. I couldn't see where it started, but it must have been on his back. It came across his belly, just below the rib cage, and continued all the way to the other side. The line took a dip and his flesh caved in and several streaks jutted out, forming something similar to a sunburst.

I was simply speechless. When I didn't say anything, he said, "That's what I gave for my country. It's my cross. Looks like a cross, doesn't it? That's what I call it. And I carry it every day of my life. They laid me open. Cut me apart. And laid me open. Gave me a cross."

Just as he finished, he went into one of his rounds of laughter. This time I didn't join him. I couldn't. There was nothing to laugh about. I wondered how I could say anything to him after seeing his "cross," as he called it.

After traveling in silence for a while, he whispered, "I nearly got blown apart. Almost died. Probably should have, and they thought I was going to. But I tricked them and lived.

"I know what you're thinking. That's no sunburst. That's lightning bolts, and I felt every crack of the firestorm that caused this. Still do. It's what the dreams are about." He propped his head against the window. His bottom lip quivered, but he wouldn't allow himself to cry. He wanted to, it seemed, but he wasn't about to show any sign of weakness.

We rode on. The Texas storm clouds had caught up with us, and the first drops of rain began falling. As the skies darkened, I turned on my headlights. Occasionally, I hit the wipers to sweep off the water. Then I turned the switch on to intermittent. Within minutes I had to have them on constantly.

William J. sat back in thought. I could sense he was building up for another laugh. Nevertheless, I started talking and he listened. It was at that point, that, quite by accident, I found out that carrying on a conversation stalled his deep dive and held it at bay. The longer the discussions with shorter pauses, the less the lapses into that mystified world of his.

"William J.," I said, "I started to tell you that I was in Vietnam, too. But—" He cut me short.

"What!" he shouted. "You were? And you let me go on about stuff that you knew about! I got to tell you," he said, turning more serious than ever, "no self-respecting Vietnam vet would've ever done that. If you were for real, you'd have spoke up just as soon as I got in your car. But now you say you were in Nam. Must've been Air Force. Couldn't have been Army. Not Marines. Oh, maybe Navy? So what was it and where were you in Nam?"

William J. was adamant. He wanted details. In that way he was no different from other Vietnam vets I'd met. It was important for them to pinpoint precise locations, times, and dates. One thing I knew: I had to spell it all out or he would start venting. So I had to go on and explain. With William J. there was no way out of it. "Well," I started, "I wasn't in any of the branches."

"Oh, don't tell me," he spouted. "You were with the embassy . . . no, no . . . I know. You were a newsman. Yes. That's what you were. Oh, my God. I'm riding with a damn newsman. Well, I got news for you—I've a mind to just get out. You're a newsman! Of all the things I've gotten myself in to. I'm with a newsman. A newsman!"

"Hold on," I pleaded. "What's wrong with being a newsman?" I asked. I didn't wait for an answer. "I'm not really a newsman. Never was. I did magazine stories back then. Now I do something else. Really. I travel around and try to figure out the meaning of life and learn it from other people. Now that's not being a newsman, is it?"

William J. calmed down some. But I could feel his eyes digging into the side of my head. He was riled, and I wondered what his next reaction would be. His mind did shift occasionally. Where it would lead him on this one was the big question. I didn't have to wait long for the answer.

"Newsman." He winced when he said it, then repeated it. "Newsman, I've got to tell you—"

"I told you I'm not a newsman," I corrected, but he didn't seem to be swayed.

"Newsman, I've got to tell you, I've seen some good ones and I've had to deal with some bad ones. Only a few did I ever come to respect. And those I'd have died for. They were real. But the bad ones, well, let's just say that it's a wonder they weren't fragged. If you were there, like you said you were, you know what I'm talking about."

"Oh, yes." I shook my head in acknowledgment. "That's getting taken out by one of your own troops."

"And it happened. Sergeants. Lieutenants. Majors. Right in the back of the head." And he went, "Bang! Dead. Reported as killed by the enemy and buried in Arlington with honors. But dead, just the same, and not leading from the rear another squad into an ambush." I could hear the anguish in his voice.

"You know what you're talking about," I said, trying to defuse him a little. But he was riding.

"It was an ambush, all right," he announced. "You saw what it did to me."

"Wait," I protested. "What's this got to do with newsmen?"

"Lieutenant wanted to look good. The newsman wanted to come along on a patrol. Too many chances were taken and we fell into a trap. I told you what it did to me, but I left out the worst part. It's in the nightmares. Thank God they don't come around as much as they used to. But I can close my eyes and see it all like it's happening right now."

"You don't have to tell me," I comforted. "Just leave it." But he seemed bound and determined to let me in on his horror.

"The explosion happened all at once. No warning. And I was flying. I didn't feel it when I hit the ground. First my chest and stomach were on fire, then I didn't feel anything. But all I could think about was trying to find my buddy. I crawled around and around. He was nowhere. And there were more shells dropping. I couldn't make sense out of it. I didn't know where it was coming from, and there was nowhere to run. Just scared to move, but I had to find my buddy. He was my best friend.

"Then it was just like I crawled right over him, but he wasn't moving. So I grabbed at him and pulled on him. Finally I just heaved him up and over onto me. Then I hugged him, 'cause I knew, oh hell, I didn't want to think about it. But I knew he was dead. So I couldn't even look at him. I just looked up at the sky. And he still didn't move. That's when I looked at him, and, God, the nightmare. It was hell. I was holding my best buddy and he—he, he didn't have a . . . a head. A body, but no head. Right there I lost my mind. I went crazy. And I've not been right in the head since.

"I went to screaming, 'Come get me. Damn Vietcong, come on. Get me. Take me. Kill me. I'm dead anyway.' They had to gag me, 'cause I was giving our position away. Guess what? They had our position, if it *was* the Vietcong. Know what I mean? Could've been our own army. I never knew. And what's more I didn't care right then. I just wanted to die, too."

William J. coughed, strangled on his own saliva. For a minute he couldn't talk. He tried, but his voice failed him. He coughed again. After hacking two or three times, his words came back. "For the past twenty-five years everybody's tried saving me from myself. I've got news for them: they're twenty-five years too late. Somebody should've done something to stop that thing before it got like it was. But, no. The government did their thing. And it got bigger and bigger and worse and worse. There was no winning that. Too much money involved. And I lost my mind while everyone just whistled like nothing was wrong. Well, I feel sorry for the people who got us there. They've got a lot of paying to do. My buddy paid with his life, but they'll be paying from now on. Forever."

Catching his breath, William J. started laughing. And he laughed and laughed and clapped his hands. But there was no joy this time. Only sorrow. And a strange combination of sounds and movements coming together to create a bizarre rhythm. It was the tragic music of a fellow traveler in pain.

Then, suddenly, he was out of it, talking as though nothing had happened. "Where are you taking me, anyway?"

"What do you mean?" I said in surprise.

"You're going somewhere, aren't you? Well, where? I want to get to El Paso, and you've never told me where you're going," he quizzed.

Stunned by his instantaneous reversal, I stammered, "Going to New Mexico, I guess. And that means I've got to go through El—" I stopped, but it was too late. I had given myself away. I had wanted to be able to weasel out of letting him ride along just in case, but now I had boxed myself in. And he picked up on it.

"Goood. That's good. That's the direction I'm going. Man," he said, "this is great. See, most of the time I don't get a lift this far. Usually it's for an hour, two at the most. But this is just great. Something's favoring me today. We'll be in El Paso late tonight."

That's when I stopped him cold. "Hold on," I spoke up. And he shot me an evil eye if ever there was one.

"I knew it couldn't be true!" he shouted. "I know, I know. You've just thought of something you've got to do and you'll be having to go another direction."

It was time for me to laugh. And he grinned, too. Then I told him, "I've been traveling a long time today. Actually, I didn't think I'd go past Stockton. Stay over there and head on out in the morning."

"Oh," he said, beaming. "That'll be okay, too."

"As a matter of fact," I offered, "I could pop for a room for you tonight. Be on me." But he wouldn't hear of it.

"No. Cannot do. I don't take charity. But Stockton tonight'll work out great. And I can handle myself. You do what you've got to do. You'll just have to be on your own. See, I've been moving around on my own for a long time, and I think I can do it for another night or two. That's just the way it'll have to be. Hope it doesn't hurt your feelings too much."

Nodding in agreement, I turned my full attention to the road. That is, I fell into thought and said nothing more. William J. dropped against the door and before too long he was dozing. The quiet was strangely comforting.

After another hour or so, I developed an urge for coffee, and my truck seemed to be craving its gas. At the next exit, I pulled off the interstate and up to the first station I came to. With my tapping of the brakes William J. was awake, a little groggy, but awake.

"This can't be Stockton," he said. "I know how to calculate, and according to my math, this just can't be Stockton. But it is coffee. I can smell it."

In less than fifteen minutes we were back on the road. Both William J. and I struggled to hold on to our coffee, sip it, and do all of that without spilling any on ourselves or the seats. We succeeded, and for the next half hour we savored every drop of our brew. We didn't bother with conversation until our cups were nearly empty. It was William J. who spoke first.

He said, "For tomorrow I've been thinking of a little side trip. If that's okay with you. Won't take long."

"Where would that be, seeing as I'm driving," I chuckled.

"You'll just have to wait and see."

I decided to drop the side-trip thing and ask another question. "Tell me, just how long have you been a drifter?"

"Never," he shot back, not elaborating.

"Never? What do you mean?" I asked. "That's what you're doing now. Looks like you've been on the road a long time."

"Yes, I have. Been on the road a long time. That's my career. But I'm not a drifter. I just decide where I want to go and I get there. Then, after a while, I decide to go on to a better place. Or a different one. That's not drifting. I know where I want to go. And you'll just have to think of me in a different way. That's all I've got to say about it, except that I'm free and there's not a soul going to get me to stop. I go wherever I want to. This is still a free country. No?"

"Excuse me," I apologized. "I guess I'll have to think about that awhile."

"And while we're on the subject, tell me something," he said. "What are you on the road for?"

"Working on a writing project. Going around and looking for people who have seen God or anything they thought was divine."

"You're doing that? In that case, have I got information for you. But I'm not talking. Not now. Maybe sometime. Not now."

Feeling that he and I had developed some rapport, I whispered, "There's something I'd like to know. Maybe it's too personal. But . . ."

"Got to be up front. What is it?" he beckoned.

"Well, I don't really know how to ask this. You understand. I don't want to offend you, but there are things you do. And it's getting to me. Well, you . . . you . . . you laugh a lot. Wonder if you could let me in on what's so funny?"

"What's wrong with that?" he asked. "That a crime?"

"No," I quickly replied. "It's just that . . ." I dropped it.

William J. clammed up. He didn't say a word for the longest while. Then, suddenly, he blurted out. "Can't talk about it now. I don't even know you. Got to know someone pretty good to talk about that. You could use it against me. And there'd be some pretty angry people if you did." That's all he would say, and I didn't press further.

Except for a little talk here and there, we rode in silence until we approached Stockton. That's when William J. said, "I guess I'll get out at your motel. That way I'll know where to catch up with you in the morning."

"No, you can't do that," I returned. "I'll take care of the rooms."

"Oh yeah, man. Look who's talking and look who's walking," he demanded. "I got to warn you that I'm the master of my fate. And I'm directing me in this film." William J. laughed and added, "You're right. You can't be no newsman. You don't ask the questions right and you sure don't know how to twist people around with your words. But newsman's still a good name for you. That's a keeper. It's got a strong echo effect."

"Echo effect. Don't think I've heard that one before."

"Made it up." William J. beamed. "I hear things and they just come out. Sometimes it's just one word and it just echoes over and over in your head. The mind takes over—

it's powerful, you know—and repeats it. Wham. It sticks. And everybody who hears it re-members. It's planted and there's not a thing anybody can do to turn it off. It's there. Going 'newsman, newsman, newsman.'"

Curious, I asked, "How did you develop this?"

"A gift," he snapped, delighted that I would ask.

He had me going, and he knew it. His sideways smile gave him away, but I was falling for it anyway. Sometimes I'm a sucker for traps, even when I know I'm going to be tripped up. So, throwing caution to the wind, I asked, "How's that?"

"How's that what?"

"The gift," I said, growing a little agitated, "how'd you come by the gift?"

William J. winked and leaned over to say, "Given to me in Nam. When I got blown apart and my buddy ended up in pieces. But I don't want to talk about it. Some other time." Then he changed the subject by adding, "That looks like a good motel over there. What about your room for the night?"

I had no choice but to follow his advice, since it was what I was going to do anyway. As I pulled up under the motel canopy, I told him I was signing him up for a room, too. But he immediately became upset.

"Hey, man, I told you I'd see you in the morning. That's just the way I am," he in-toned sternly.

"Well," I said, reluctantly, "bunk in with me, then."

His voice went deep and he spoke very slowly. "You don't want to do that. No way. You might not make it through the night."

"What? How so?"

"Flashback," he warned, "and there'd be no tomorrow for you. I'd take you out and not even know it. Those things make me crazy. And I wouldn't want to hurt you. So let me

go in peace. How 'bout it?"

William J. and I both got out of my truck at the same time. As I made for the front entrance, he saluted and chuckled. "In the morning, newsman," he said, and he walked away.

While registering, I breathed a sigh of relief. William J. was gone. And I truly believed I'd never see him again. It had been an experience just riding across Texas with him. Now I was the one who was free.

After moving my truck to a parking space in front of my room, I carried all my gear inside. There was no need to eat, as William J. and I had done that an hour earlier, not long after finishing our coffee. But I did go for a soft drink and a candy bar to go with an old rerun on TV. Then, dozing off a time or two, I finally turned off the set and the lights and crawled under the covers.

Sleep was impossible. I rolled and tossed. Got up for water. Staggered to adjust the air-conditioning unit. Covered my head. Uncovered my whole body. Went to the bathroom. Looked at the clock. Turned the television back on. Shut it off. Then, began to doze, always just at the edge of sleep. William J. was in my thoughts. He and what he had gone through wouldn't leave me alone. Not even for forty winks.

When the sun came up, I was already wide awake. Not feeling too good, but wide awake. After showering and dressing, I decided to check out, get some coffee, and hit the road. My rider crossed my mind, but William J. was just a passing thought. I was sure he was gone, probably in El Paso by now and sleeping late. I was badly mistaken.

When I opened the door of my room, William J. was the very first thing I saw. There he was, his hair wet, leaning against the front fender of the pickup. His face was a little distorted because of his wincing from the brightness of the sun. And he was grinning. Big.

I couldn't move. I was stunned. He saw my disbelief and snapped to attention and saluted.

"All present and accounted for, sir," he shouted. But he didn't stop there. "Newsman, sir, how'd you sleep, sir? Fine, I hope, newsman, sir! Newsman, sir, your day is planned, sir. Everything taken care of, sir.

"Thank you for asking, newsman, sir. I slept good and ready to go. Sir." Then he dropped the salute.

"What did you do all night?" I asked, not knowing what else to say.

"Slept," he came back.

Stammering, I asked, "W-where?"

"Where's anyone supposed to sleep?" he answered with a question of his own.

"Where?" I quizzed.

"In a bed," he answered and added, "but I believe you should know that. And just to make sure you don't ask again, I'll tell you I don't give all my secrets away. Next question. If you've got any more!"

I stood still, unable to get a word out. Then he moved toward me and grabbed my bags to help me load the truck. It wasn't until I had unlocked my door and flipped the electric door locks to let him in that I regained my senses. Like it or not, William J. and I would be a duo for at least another day.

He was in a talkative mood this morning. "I've got my coffee. You'll have to get yours. That place right over there's got some and it's fresh. They just made a new pot. I saw them do it," he said. "The way I see it, we'll get back on 10, westbound, for a few more miles, then take U.S. 67 south and hit 90. We'll go west through Alpine until we get to Marfa. Then it's 67 again all the way to Presidio." Laughing, but not in one of his fits, he proposed, "If you're up to it, after all that, we'll go on into Ruidosa. It's where my grandmother crossed the border. It's only a little detour. We'll still get to El Paso some-time, but, hey, everybody's got to be someplace. And you'll like it. I guarantee it."

It was an adventure, I told myself, so I agreed. But I didn't have to tell him. He saw it in my eyes and reached over for a handshake to seal the deal.

Finding U.S. 67 was easy and we made the exit with no problem. Soon the interstate was well behind us and the two-lane stretched out straight in front of us. For almost fifty miles we wouldn't see another person or car. It was just William J. and me.

For some time we just soaked up the scenery. There wasn't much to look at, but we stared at it anyway. Then William J. started talking.

"I've given it some thought," he said, breaking the silence. "You wanted to know about the 'J.' That's a funny story—"

Interrupting him, I spoke up. "You don't have to. I figured it was personal."

"It is. But we've become friends, and I don't hold out on friends. Life's too short." He sneezed, then continued. "My mother. She's the one who wanted me to have a name in Spanish. Her mother came across the Rio Grande there at Ruidosa. Don't ask me what my grandfather was doing down there. He was originally from Montana. Never heard the details of that one. The family kept quiet about it. But that's another story.

"Anyways, my father put the name William on me. But they went 'round and 'round about my middle name. But you know how people are. Even though in Spanish it's pro-nounced Hay-zus, everybody started saying Jesus. So I became William Jesus. Talk about heavy. Then when Uncle tapped me—"

"Wait," I broke in. "Uncle?"

"Uncle Sam. You've heard of him. The government. Uncle'll find you no matter what. I tried to dodge him as long as I could, but he got me, put me through basic, and shipped my ass to Nam. I had to fight for him while the politicians sat back, collected their big salaries, drove fine cars, lived in high-dollar houses, and made the decisions that killed my buddy. Now you know who Uncle is.

"But back to my name. In Nam it was hell. Every other G.I. was saying Jesus this and

DANCING WITH GOD

Jesus that. And I was always answering. Thought they were talking to me. At first, they thought I was answering just to be joking. You know, like when someone says, 'God,' and someone else says, 'Yes?'"

William Jesus and I laughed hard. Then he picked up his story. "My mother loved that name. She told me when I got older that she gave it to me because she wanted me to stay connected to the Spanish part of my family.

"Still, I don't tell just anybody. It's a personal thing with me. Secretly though, I have to admit that there might be more to the story than that."

"What do you mean?" I asked.

"It's strange," he whispered. "My mother loved the Virgin. You know, the Virgin Mary. Mother of God. She was very religious." Leaning closer, as if others may have be listening, he added, "I'm not too sure about this, but I think my mother thought she and the Virgin had something in common."

"What are you saying?" I asked, more interested than ever.

"The Virgin gave birth to Jesus. Do you get it?"

"No." I shot him a hard glance.

"Do I have to draw it out for you?"

"Jesus was virgin-born."

"You got it! My mother thought she was a virgin," he said soberly.

"Not in this day and age!" I exclaimed. "Everybody knows how babies get here."

"Not my mother. And that's the honest to God truth. I don't believe she ever knew *that* was how. Now, she wasn't stupid. But when I was born, she was ignorant. Didn't have much education and was really young. And sometimes everybody just thinks someone else told you about those things. So I think that's the real reason I got that name. Besides, her name was Maria, which is Spanish for Mary. Now chew on that load for a while."

Thinking about what he must have gone through all his life, I tried to console him. "I'll tell you this much," I said, "William Jesus does have that echo effect, as you call it. Don't think I'll ever forget you or your name. It's kind of got a ring to it."

"Are you making fun of my name?" he barked with a halfway laugh.

"No, definitely not," I assured him. We laughed again.

As we moved farther south, William Jesus was quick to give directions to make sure I didn't miss any of the turns. His intent was to get to Ruidosa. And in traveling with him, I realized that when he had something on his mind, he was bound and determined to get to where he was going. Had I decided to go on to El Paso by taking U.S. 90 on through Marfa and by passing Presidio, he would have flung himself out of the truck and hitched on by himself. But that was not something I planned. Oddly enough, I was growing a little fond of traveling with him. If nothing else, he was making my journey more in-

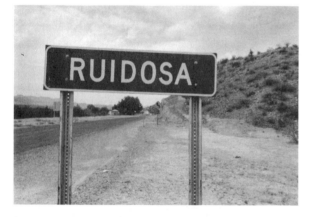

teresting. And I had in the past found what I was looking for in places I just happened to end up. Someone even told me once that when I stop looking, that's when I'll find it.

There wasn't much to Presidio, as towns go. The terrain flattened out and the little community seemed about as low as the land. But to William Jesus he wouldn't have been any happier had he been rolling into San Francisco. For him it was a reconnecting, a time for

pleasant memories, which replaced harsh thoughts of war and the explosions of the flashbacks in the middle of the night a long way from and a long time since Vietnam.

"Did you live here long?" I asked.

"Never did," he murmured. "My mother brought me here once and told me stories, but that was a long time ago. Was just a kid. And she was having a good time just being here. That made it better, 'cause she was never really happy. Can't remember a time she ever was, except when we came here," he said with sadness in his voice. "I think her

DANCING WITH GOD

mother's buried up on a hill around here or over toward Ruidosa. She told me once that her mother's grave had a statue of the Virgin on it. But don't ask me to show it to you. That part, the place, I can't remember."

Only a handful of adobe houses, a store, a bar, and an abandoned church made up the village of Ruidosa. If we blinked we would've missed it, but William Jesus was absorbed. Then we were on our way back. One way in and one way out—there was only the one hard-surfaced road. We could have tried the farm road, but in the village we had been told that taking it would be dangerous. It was dirt and gravel and had no services. None. All the way back to U.S. 90 west of Marfa. If anything had happened to the truck, we would've been stranded. William Jesus probably could've handled it, for he was the fearless traveler. Me? I'd just stick to the blacktop and forgo the extra adventure. Being with him was enough excitement for me.

About halfway back to Presidio, William Jesus exclaimed, "Look up there. Stop! There's a cemetery. Park there. Let's go up there for a look." And I obliged.

Taking his time, he walked through the graveyard. Then, bending down at one of the markers, he said, "That's like my mother talked about. The Virgin. Maybe this is my grandmother's grave. Maybe it's not, but that's what the statue must've looked like."

He was at a grave with a very carefully crafted Virgin Mary standing as a guardian. She was beautiful and William Jesus took his time admiring her. Then he started talking. Not to me. Maybe to the statue. Or maybe to some invisible something. I couldn't tell. Yet he was deep in conversation. His words were too low for me to make out what he was saying, and I would not have wanted to invade his privacy.

Just when I thought he had finished, William Jesus started laughing. So much so that he lost his balance, and from his stooped position both knees went to the ground. But that didn't stop his bellowing. It went on for another five to ten minutes, all the time kneeling in front of the Virgin. Finally he quieted and crossed himself several times. Then he was up and stretching. The first thing out of his mouth was "Let's go. Now it's El Paso," and he was eager to move on, having nothing more to say.

We didn't say a word to each other all the way back to Presidio. For that matter, we hardly said two words between us once we hit U.S. 67 and headed for Marfa. William Jesus drifted in his world, and I wondered what kind of internal world he really had. Before I knew it, the miles had rushed by and we were in the town of Marfa and turning left onto U.S. 90.

"Time to eat," I proclaimed, pulling into a decent-looking hamburger joint. William Jesus didn't move. His eyes were open, but they seemed to be glassed over. My first thought was that he had died on me, and I nearly panicked. The eyes can be open, wide open, and a person could be dead, I reasoned. As I pulled the handle on my door, I tried

rustling him by saying, "Let's eat!" But he just sat there. In desperation I got out, went to his side, and opened his door. When I did, he moved. And I could finally breathe.

"What? What? What's up, man?" he asked in a daze.

"Eat!"

"Yeah. Oh, yeah. Good idea. But where?" He struggled to come to his senses.

"Right here. Right now. You've been out of it. And we're already at an eating joint," I laughed.

Rubbing his face with both hands, he threw a long leg out of the car and onto the ground. He tried getting up, but he couldn't. For a minute, he tugged hard to rise, then realized he hadn't unbuckled his seatbelt. He fussed, throwing a curse at the belt. Finally he was untangled, pushing the door shut and following me in. Still we said little to each other, and that's the way it was all through the meal of charred burgers. The pit stop was boring, and soon we were driving west, both of us cradling our carryout coffees.

William Jesus finally spoke. "I'm glad you talked me into going to Ruidosa," he said without a laugh or even a hint of a smile. "You did the right thing," he added. "That was good."

Was he serious? I didn't know how to react. So I just drove on for a time, trying to find some way to respond.

My pause must've been too long for William Jesus, and his impatience got to him. He clapped his hands, and I thought he was going to go into his laughing mode, but instead he teased, "Hey, newsman, you got to lighten up. You take everything too serious. Man, you're too stiff yourself. Can't you ever laugh at yourself? I know you can't laugh at me, even when I'm joking, and that's what I was doing. Laugh at me, once in a while." He clicked his tongue as if calling a dog. Then he lowered his voice. "Hey, but don't do it too often. It might make me a little nervous after a while." Then he burst out laughing.

He had my number. He knew I didn't know how to take him most of the time, and he was well aware that I was more than slightly cautious with him. He was alert and acutely aware of just about everything going on around him.

"Okay, okay," I chuckled. "You pegged me. And I betcha I do better."

Then he retorted, "Hey, man, makes no difference to me. It's your life. Your future. You just gotta be your own person. Don't mind me. You gotta be. 'To be or not to be, that's the question,' wouldn't you say?

"Look at me. Wouldn't you have to admit that I'm just being me?" he asked, beaming. "And that's all I'm ever going to be.

"Now get serious! Think about it. That's all that's important in this world, anyway. And that comes straight from God. Absolutely directly from God. And that's the truth."

"God?"

But William Jesus didn't respond. His mind had shot from the conversation to something going on in front of us. "Oh!" he bellowed, "Oh! It can't be. It can't!"

Then, after rolling down his window, he stuck his head out and into the sixty-five-mile-an-hour wind. His hat went flying off, sailing away into the Texas sky. Not caring about that, he yelled, "Jesus, Joseph, Mary. The . . . it's the Virgin!"

His words were half understandable, half garbled, but I caught enough to make out what he was saying. It didn't make sense, because I still hadn't seen what he had. I was

searching the horizon one minute and trying to keep an eye on him the next, and attempting to drive as well. My fear was that he was hallucinating and would bound out the window without a notice.

"What? Tell me!" I shouted out. "What is it?"

William Jesus came in from the wind and sat straight. I thought it was over, whatever it was. But, no! He was still pointing and saying, "Jesus, Joseph, Mary. Stop. Right up there."

"Why? Tell me—"

But he cut me short. "Oh, God. It's the Virgin. Stop. It's the Virgin. She's here and I was just talking to her back at the graves. She heard me, like she always does. Now, here. Stop," he proclaimed in all seriousness.

Braking as best as I could with excitement rising, I pulled off the side of the road. As I did, I saw what he was talking about. It was a woman, all right. She was covered from head to toe, wrapped in cloth. And she was riding a donkey, just as pretty as you please. I hadn't seen her until that moment, for she had blended in so well with the ocher color of the soil. She was well off the road with its speeding cars and impossible freight-hauling eighteen-wheelers. She was hugging some railroad tracks that were running parallel to the highway, and she was paying no one any mind. Apparently she had somewhere to go, because she and her donkey were moving at a good clip.

William Jesus hung out the window and marveled, but he never said a word to her. It wouldn't have made any difference. Her gaze stayed straight ahead, and her donkey kept its stride. She bounced up and down, having fallen comfortably into the rhythm. The steady beat produced by the heavy-ladened little legs of the burro made sure that she only saw the ground. The poor creature looked as if it would sink, along with its burden, at any moment, right into the ground. But he never slowed. He kept right on moving. Step after step.

"I'd like to ride with her," William Jesus declared. "Think that donkey could carry both of us?" But he answered his own question. "No, no. No way. But just look at that. The Virgin. Here. It's a miracle."

And the woman and the donkey kept right on going while we sat parked. William Jesus was still marveling at the sight as they pulled way ahead of us. They obviously had no time to spare.

As he blabbered on, I wondered where she had come from and where in the world she could be going out here, a long way from Marfa and a measurable distance from the withering village of Valentine.

What kind of trip is she on? I questioned silently. Was that donkey her only transportation?

Nobody had to hit me on the head to convince me she wasn't going to let us in own her secrets, that was for sure. So William Jesus and I were left to come up with our own theories. That was a dangerous thing. We could read anything we wanted into it. And that's just what William Jesus was doing. His talking was nonstop.

"Go slow when we pass," he pleaded as I shifted gears and accelerated. "Let me get another real good look. This I might never see again."

As we edged up alongside of her again, we crept along, the truck moving only as fast as it could on idle, and slowly passed. William Jesus roared, "The Virgin. That's her. Oh, Mary, full of grace," he intoned. "Thank you. Thank you. Now I'm blessed. And you're blessed above all women. And men," he added. Then I heard him whisper, "Speak to the Father for me. Thank Him for coming to me in Nam."

With the woman dropping farther and farther behind us and finally disappearing out of sight, William Jesus fell silent, his expression one of joyous rapture. He believed he had truly had a visitation. No one could've ever made him believe otherwise. For me, I didn't know. I did see a woman on a donkey.

Now, I had no idea of what to expect from William Jesus. So I waited him out.

After having gone only about five miles, with my speed steadily climbing back up to the fullest extent of the posted limit, William Jesus went to swaying. The low hum was back. I knew what was coming, but all of my attempts to draw him into conversation proved fruitless. He was speeding into one of his departures. Soon he was gone, and the laughs started. He was bent over into them. I drove on very carefully, ever vigilant of his actions.

Even before he stopped laughing and long before he settled into a quiet calm, he was talking to me. "God does that every so often," he said, as reverentially as he could between chuckles.

"What's that?" I asked with nervous caution.

"He shows me. Reminds me. So I don't forget," he stammered out.

Now he was back to the real world. No more laughing. But he was serious.

"You've seen me," he declared. "You've seen who I am. I can tell that you don't judge me. Don't hold anything against me. And I can tell you the rest."

"Wait a minute!" I raised my hand.

William Jesus was adamant, and his face showed it. He was prepared to take me the rest of the way with him, but I didn't know if I wanted to go. It could be deeper than I cared to sink, or higher than I wanted to rise, whichever might be the case. But he didn't seem to care what I thought. He was taking me whether I wanted to go or not.

Then he dragged me in. "I laugh. You know it. Well, I do," he explained. "That's because . . . I can't cry. So I laugh. I see my buddy with his head off and I want to cry, but I laugh. Then when I get into it, I hear things. It's always that voice. The one that was in Nam."

"Is that when it started?" I asked as politely as I could.

"That's when. I was going to die holding my buddy. But the voice came from behind me. It told me I wouldn't die. And I wanted to cry 'cause I was scared, but I started laughing. It was a joke. That voice. Telling me I was going to live when I knew I was going to die. But the voice said no. That's when I laughed at the joke. And, oh, did I hurt. All I could see was red. Blood was everywhere. The shells hitting all around. Fire. Screaming. I knew I was in hell but still breathing. Didn't know if I was really alive or already dead. Nightmare! Nowhere to go, no way to run. Pain, dying, death. I felt everything, and even though there was nothing in me to hurt, I did. And then that voice."

William Jesus was shaking, and I didn't know how to comfort him, as there was no way to know what he was feeling. Yet, during my short assignment as a correspondent in Vietnam, I had seen a lot of soldiers blown apart. And I had seen the body bags stuffed, unceremoniously, with the corpses of soldiers who had died in one firefight or another. But I had not been stranded at a fire support base when it was overrun or on a patrol caught in an ambush. So I didn't know what he was feeling now or when it had actually taken place. And it didn't matter that it was then or now. For William Jesus it was going on right now, and had been since the day it had taken place. So to try to comfort him would have been absurdly out of the question.

All I could find to say was "The voice?"

"The voice." William Jesus shook his head. "It was God. Or somebody close to him that he sent. And he knew what he was talking about."

"How so?"

"I'm here. I didn't die. My buddy did, but the voice said that my buddy was okay. He was going to be with Him. And that made me laugh even more, out of joy. And every time I think of my buddy, I want to cry, but I laugh. And I hear the voice, my buddy's gone to be with Him, and I laugh more.

"I know it's nuts," he laughed, "but—" He paused. "Sure, I'm nuts, crazy, but I'm okay, too. Now that's crazy for you."

"Crazy's a judgment," I said, without really knowing what I was talking about. Then I asked, "Is that all the voice said—or says?"

"Oh, no," he blurted out. "A lot more. It's hard to understand, but there's more. The voice told me that the dying was to wake up the world."

"What's that about?" I asked.

"Said the dying—the GIs, the ARVN, the Vietcong, the villagers . . . everybody . . . both sides—was to send a message to the world. The voice said, 'Stop the killing,' and everybody was dying to save the world from this ever happening again. Said that the politicians were wrong. Had wrong motives. That the people who make and buy and sell the weapons were wrong. They were dealing in death. That they were blinded by money. But they had no excuses. And someday they would see. But they would have to settle the debts they had even when they opened their eyes."

William Jesus dropped his head as if to fall into his own quiet thoughts. Then he raised up and repositioned himself. After he did, he added, "Know what's so out of joint? My buddy didn't know he was dying for the world. He just died trying to live to get through the day. And that hurts me so much. Oh, how that hurts. And look at me. I didn't die. So why did I live? Not to save the world, 'cause I don't know how to do that. I didn't stop that crazy Gulf War thing the politicians tried to say was noble when really it was just for oil. Then there's the corporations, all the governments, even the churches that are filled with people who are nuts for power. And the world's going right along in its craziness.

"But the voice I hear," William Jesus went on, "tells me never to be a slave to anyone again. Tells me to be free and live that way. Says to keep moving, and that's what I do. I stay on the road. Says never to worry about anything." Then he said in the most sober tone he had ever mustered during our drive, "Says to love myself and that if I do I'll be loving Him. And to love everybody and everything and in doing that I'll always be walking with Him. Now that's beautiful if I could just do all that. But it's beautiful, anyway, and when I start forgetting then something like the Virgin shows up to remind me."

Rain was falling when he got to El Paso. William Jesus told me where to get off the interstate so he could get out. He lectured me about stopping alongside the highway. It was just too dangerous. He pointed out that he'd seen too many stopped cars rear-ended by drivers simply drifting out of their lane and into the emergency lane without realizing the car that had pulled over had stopped. Many die that way, he said.

So I followed his advice and, once off the ramp, pulled into the lot of a convenience store. That was where he wanted out. He would have nothing doing that I should hold his hand all the way to where he was going. I hated to have to yield to his demands, but with William Jesus, no one had a choice once he had made up his mind. He could take care of himself, he insisted, although a lot of people had tried to straighten him out. Then he said that those trying weren't even able to handle their own lives, so how could they deal with someone else's?

As I pulled to a stop, I offered to get him a cup of coffee. But, no, he would not have that. And then he ran into the store. I sat alone for a minute, thinking. I was going to miss him. Actually his unpredictability had become his asset. He had been an adventure. Without him, well, my trip wouldn't be the same. Rather, I mused, it would be too quiet and really lonely.

Then I dropped the gear into drive and started to pull away, but he came running out with a cup of coffee in his hand. The hot liquid was spilling over his tanned fingers. He was waving to me with his other hand. I stopped, only to learn that the coffee was for me.

"There's something else," he yelled. "First, this is for you. Got to stay awake." Then he lectured, "I've got to tell you. You want to know about God, then go to the top. The voice talks to me, it can talk to you, too."

"Well," I begged off, "I figure the best way to learn about someone is to talk to someone who is close to the one I want to know about. How's that?"

He and I laughed. But he wasn't ready to let me go just like that. "Then you've got to find people who can tell you about living. You know, it's not just about God. It's living. That's what the voice tells me. Live. Live. Live. Freedom. Live it."

After handing me the coffee through the window, he tapped my shoulder. That had been the first time we had touched, even in joking, except when we first shook hands. I wanted to jump out and hug him, but thought he would have been revolted by the sentimental display of affection. So I thanked him for the coffee instead. He liked that.

Then he slammed his fist down hard on top of the truck. "Peace." He grinned. I hesitated for a second, and he said, "Go on. Get going. You got miles to go before you sleep." Leaning into the window, in a mumble so low I could barely hear him, he whispered, "I'll remember you." And he made like he was pushing my truck away as if it had stalled in an intersection.

I took my foot off the brake, and the truck started rolling. Just as I revved it for my start up the ramp to the interstate, I looked back for one last glimpse of William Jesus. He appeared to be waving, but his hand was held in an unusual positon. Glancing quickly back and forth from him to the road and to him again, all the while rushing on, I could see in the blur of speed that his thumb was up and his first two fingers were slightly bent. The two remaining were turned downward, almost touching his palm. Then the symbolism hit me. This wasn't a waving of good-bye at all. He was blessing me. And he was laughing his head off.

7. GWEN SCOTT

She was going out to feed the ants. Feed the ants! With fists full of crumbs, she went out the door that opened onto the patio and on out into her little backyard. Protected by a tall privacy fence, the snug enclosure looked like more of the New Mexico desert that stretched outward in every direction from her Albuquerque subdivision all the way to the horizon. But Gwen saw something more. This was her healing garden, and she was quick to point out the different indigenous plants and herbs. I saw only one thing. Brown—brown weeds, brown stones, brown dirt, brown everything, even brown ants. To Gwen, however, this little square of sunbaked brown was a flourishing garden. A place of re-creation, of restoration, and a sanctuary for even the smallest of creatures. This refuge included the ants, which she was about to feed.

With a long, stretching stride, she stepped off the concrete-slab patio and onto one of the cinder blocks she had carefully laid out in the form of a large circle. Within this hoop, two rows of blocks had been placed perpendicular to each other. At the point where the two lines intersected, Gwen had meticulously positioned a silver reflective sphere. Even a trained eye would have found this to have been placed as close to the middle of the ring as humanly possible without very exacting instruments. And this was where she was determined to be.

With both feet firmly planted on one of the numerous man-made stones, she raised both arms outward and up. As she released the crumbs, a slight breeze kicked up and carried the nourishing morsels on the wind for a few brief seconds. Then they fell. When they did, Gwen was pleased. The bits and pieces of bread had very lightly covered fully a half of the enclosure. What she couldn't do, the warm dry breath of the desert had.

But she was not content. Her work was not complete. Now she was back on the patio, bending over and carefully placing bottle caps onto the palms of her hands. They were filled with water. Then, she did a balancing act across the stepping stones and into the circle again. Delicately she put a cap here. And there. Then to one side. And finally to the other. When she stood up, she was beaming.

"Ants need to eat and drink," she said with a smile, adding, "and the desert can be harsh. They have a purpose. They're part of the universe, too, just as much as we are. And we're supposed to be good stewards. So I try to look out for them."

As Gwen pushed on the door to go back into the house, she laughed. "Doing that means they don't have a reason to come into my house to scrounge for anything. They've got theirs now. I've got mine. And mine they can leave alone." She made her statement loud enough that all the ants, even the ones deep in the ground, could hear it. I think she raised her voice on purpose, so the little creatures would be sure to have no excuses.

As if they paid any attention, I thought to myself and laughed out loud.

Gwen looked questioningly at me. She said nothing but seemed to be waiting for my response to her gaze. When she sensed that I was not going to be forthcoming, she laughed, too. Obviously it was her way of poking fun at herself. Of making light of her actions. I got really tickled and laughed hard with her. Not at her. We both chuckled long after we had come in out of the blazing sun. But in that very short period of time in the garden with her, I had begun to realize that she really did care, even for the ants. And that was no joking matter. She saw them as a vital part of creation. That was, for her, something not to be taken lightly or even lightheartedly. She took that very seriously.

Gwen was unusual, in the best way possible. It wasn't so much in what she said, and she did have a lot to say, but it was in what she did. She was always doing. Always for others. If she had a fault, it was that she cared too much. If that was possible! But on that she would argue. She would be quick to say that the problem was that people didn't care enough and that there was so much to be done. Again, what needed to be done would be

"I want to know if you've seen God," I all but whispered.

"Is that all?" she shouted, pursuing it no further.

Momentarily left alone, I thought, How strange! And it was. Here I was in Albuquerque. In Gwen's home. Just her and me. All because of the letter she had sent after reading my books *Wisdomkeepers, Wisdom's Daughters,* and *Shadowcatchers*.

She told me sending that letter had been a first for her. "Never, but never, have I ever written to an author," she said. "I don't know what it was that made me do it." But do it she did.

She had written to tell me she had moved to New Mexico to further study herbs and plant medicines. Then she said, "I began my journey with Chief Two Trees."

Chief Two Trees! My work with Native Americans had started with the same Cherokee medicine man. My interest had been stirred by the contents of her letter. I read on to find that she was involved with some of the people of the Acoma Pueblo. She thought I would be interested in going to Acoma and invited me out for a visit.

Instead of writing, I had decided to call, and my wife and I accepted her invitation. During our time in Albuquerque with Gwen, she had taken us to Acoma Pueblo. We walked with her along the dirt streets of the old city, and she introduced us to some of her friends. She took us into the home of special friend Norma Jean Juanico, an Acoma tribal member and renowned traditionalist potter who had been selected by Acoma's spiritual elders to make the sacred pots for the pueblo's annual religious ceremonies.

Then, Bellimino, chanter of the old songs, led us off the plateau and down the narrow two-lane blacktop. Yet, the farther away we traveled, Acoma loomed higher over the stark terrain and grew bigger and bigger on the precipice of the horizon. The aging

for those who were in need. So many with so little. To her, those in need were
portant, maybe more so, than those who had bought into the system of w
power. That was an illusion, and she would not hesitate to say so. She did sa
chance she got, making the opportunities, if she had to, and taking liberties wl
otherwise existed. Yet she was never the zealot or fanatic—just a fireball. Sl
come into the world to be complacent or just to sit. One look at her accompl
would show that. They were dizzying to consider.

No matter what Gwen did, she put everything she had into it. When she
her bachelor's degree, she graduated magna cum laude. Then she went on for l
ter's. Again, it was with distinction. Magna cum laude. A few years later she bec
first female news anchor for the ABC station in Philadelphia. She went on to be :
as a Neiman Scholar in journalism at Harvard. By the time she joined Cable Nev
work, as anchor for CNN's *International Hour,* she had already been a sec
school English teacher, a college professor, a TV reporter, and a producer. She wc
on to receive two Emmys and be a member of the CNN *International Hour* tea
won the New York Television and Film Critics Award for Best News Hour in An
The Atlanta Society of Journalists would also honor her with its award for Bes
Show. Yet Gwen left all that behind her to move to New Mexico in a quest to explo
inner spiritual rumblings.

Although making the move as part of her personal journey, she had not sl
down. She just could not sit idle. She had to be involved. Her new tasks would be tc
over the weekend assignment desk for an Albuquerque television station, to go back
the classroom teaching on-camera techniques to would-be documentary video
ducers, and to produce and star in the one-minute *The Herb Lady* television spots
turing herbs and medicinal plants. Still, she would find time for her art. On any g
day she could be found passionately dabbing and splashing oils and acrylics on car
after canvas.

So now it was little wonder that she had already been still too long. Her exuber
energy was showing in the way her hands were constantly in motion.

It was no surprise to me when she bounced up, bounded out of her chair, and aske
as she whisked by, "Something to drink?"

"Gwen," I yelled after her, "you know I wanted to talk with you about something.'

Although she was already in the kitchen, she answered, "Oh God, I knew there ha
to be something. I'd hate to venture what," she added nervously. "Whatever. Go ahea
and hit me with it."

Glasses were rattling. I could hear the sound of their tinkling, one against the othei
Then the refrigerator door was opening and closing. She was pouring something.

adobe settlement seemed to kiss the clouds and push right on through the giant slow-moving flotillas of the sky world. Directed to turn off the roadway, we drove onto dirt. It wasn't much more than a rutted path.

Several times Gwen had to ride the high side to avoid dragging and possibly taking out the oil pan. Every time she did, the car almost rolled. It forced us over onto each other.

Finally we were in the shadow of a mesa. Huge crumbling boulders littered the jagged earth. A walking path skirted an earthen mound and seemed to disappear into the mountain at its base.

Gwen and Bellimino waved a "Come on" as they sped away in a kind of friendly race with each other along the foot trail. It was impossible to catch up to them. Then they were just gone. The path abruptly ended. Beyond was a very steep ramp of rippled windswept rock.

Waves of stones, I thought, trying to navigate in a breathless struggle upward. Bellimino and Gwen were nowhere to be seen. Then, in unison, their voices reverberated from all directions at once and no place in particular. The sound echoed like a thundering musical chorus off the giant outcroppings of the mesa. It was hard to know just where their exact location was. Then—shock. A part of the mesa just seemed to open up like a gigantic funnel, and at the back of this giant mouth there was a kind of holy sanctuary—secure and hidden.

At that precise spot sat the ruins of a centuries-old adobe. Two or three walls still stood as reminders of what had been a home. Legend spoke of it as the motherland of the very spiritual "little people." There must have been some truth in the old stories. Only little people could have

stood upright in the doorway we had to crawl through. After going inside, we sat for the longest while. It was a place of meditation. Then, as the sun passed over the flattened plateau of the mountain's parched peak and dropped lower and lower in the sky, we realized it was time to go before dusk began growing up from the basin's floor. Bellimino had taken us to one of his people's veritable spiritual centers few outsiders had ever entered. All because of Gwen.

Now I was back. This time, however, the reason for visiting her was far different. Gwen always signed her letters "In God's Light." She had agreed to tell her whole story after she had learned of my journey to those who had encountered God.

Coming out of my recollections, I was not content to sit alone, so I sauntered through the dining room and into the kitchen. Watching her, I couldn't help but think of the first time I had seen her. She had looked so familiar. It was as if I knew her. I didn't, but strangely, it was as if I did. There had been something about her voice, the way she talked. The shape of her face. Her eyes. Expressions. Her blond hair. Then she reminded me that she had been with CNN and *Headline News.*

Funny, I reflected as I stood in the doorway and watched as she finished icing the refreshments, when someone's on television, everyone seems to think they know them personally. Even if they've never met. So I was no different. But that's changed now, I thought to myself. I really do know her.

She had gone beyond just drinks and had some snacks ready. I asked, "Want me to take this to the coffee table?"

"You can," she said, "but I've got one more thing to do. I'm coming. Go on without me." Turning, she pulled on the refrigerator door, reached in, picked up a plastic lemon, and pushed the door shut.

"If you're not finished," I said, "I'll wait."

"No, no, no," she protested. "This is for the ants."

Not the ants again, I thought. Then I laughed. She did, too.

"No, no, no," she repeated. "Not what you think."

"Oookaay," I droned, not knowing what she could possibly be up to.

"You've seen me do this. You know what this is for," she tried to remind me.

But I didn't. I quickly searched my mental reservoir, but nothing was there. My mind was a complete blank, and she sensed it.

"I feed the ants outside so the whole population won't have to come into my house looking for food," she stated flatly. "But some do anyway. And I refuse to use those pesticides. That stuff'll kill ants and who knows what else. You know it gets into our systems, too." But using concentrated lemon juice as a way of keeping her home free of what I considered to be pests? That was a first for me.

As I all but gawked, Gwen squeezed out a line of the extract on the windowsill. Then the window frame. And, finally, along the threshold of the door to the garage. "Lemon?" I asked.

"Yeah," she replied. "It's natural. I don't use the other stuff."

"Does it work?" I asked in amazement.

"It doesn't kill them," she said, beaming, proud not to be a killer. "I don't want to execute them," she laughed, adding, "Just make them know this is my home and not theirs."

I laughed as well. And she added, "They're part of the kingdom, too, but I don't want them in mine. Not in this part of it, anyway." And as she spread a line along the floor with the juice, I could see the critters fleeing. They couldn't get away fast enough.

"Lemon," I said. "Of all things. It works," I admitted, in disbelief. Gwen smiled as I carried the drinks away.

Within minutes Gwen joined me. We sipped our drinks without talking. The silence was nice, but the longer I sat there, the more I couldn't contain myself. Finally I blurted out, "Why, Gwen? Why did you walk away from your career when you were at the top? You had it all! What happened to make you do such a drastic thing?"

She didn't hesitate answering. "I got to the point where I just couldn't see tomorrow."

"And you just quit?" I asked.

"No, there's more," she said with a dread that arose with the memories. And she went on. "I was lying in bed with a thirty-eight-caliber gun on my chest. And I was trying to come up with one reason, just one, to see the next day. I couldn't do it. I couldn't find a reason. It was very dark, a spiraling abyss of 'Ooohh, I can't even think of a . . . I can't dream a dream that would make me want to be here tomorrow.'"

"Whatever brought you to that point?" I asked with concern.

Gwen did a "ha, ha, ha" kind of laugh that I had come to recognize. She did it whenever something was said that touched her. So I waited, hoping she wouldn't let my question die.

"There's not that big a deal to it." Gwen stopped, thought, and then went on. "It is a big deal to me. That's when the angel . . ." She paused.

"The angel?" I asked.

Gwen sighed, "Yes. I'll have to explain."

"Take your time, but not too much."

Slowly Gwen began telling her story. "I was working for CNN in Atlanta," she said. "It was about 1990, and I was anchoring *Headline News*. At the same time I was living with a man and the relationship had gone sour. He and I had known each other for twelve years, but it was clear it wasn't working. It was really very detrimental to my soul." She stopped, falling into a reflective mood.

"When you say detrimental," I asked, "what do you mean?"

"Oh," she picked back up, saying, "he had his old ways. He was an airline pilot. And he tried really hard to give up his ladies and the drinking, but he just couldn't do it." She paused, then added, "I wasn't going to live that way. He understood where I was, but he couldn't be what I needed."

"What were you looking for?" I pried.

Gwen quickly stated, "Somebody who was faithful and sober."

"I've heard of romances failing and taking people down like that," I said, knowing after thirty years of marriage how much hard work goes into a relationship. "But," I quickly went on, "you were still at *Headline News* and at the top in your field. Wasn't that going well?"

Gwen smiled. "Nobody knows this unless they've been there, but as an anchor you absorb all the pain of everything you have to tell people about. And you can't react to it at the time. But you carry it home with you at night. Whether it's the two hundred elephants that were slaughtered by poachers or the Somalian refugees who are starving or Rwandans who are being shot, you carry that home. It's very real. It's in you.

"The news business," she went on, "is a very brutal life. It's very competitive. It changed from when I started, when we actually had conversations about 'What can we do to help people? How can we help people to cope? What can we do to make the world better?' Then it evolved into, 'How do we get higher ratings?' It was too much all at the same time."

"So, there you were," I said. "Everything had just built up, and you were going to kill yourself!"

Her hands became animated. They were dancing across the coffee table. Then she clasped them together and rested her chin on them. Finally, she admitted, "It's very personal. It's very hard to talk about in one way, because it shows a terrible personal weakness. It wasn't some high drama, 'Aaaah, I'm going to kill myself.' It was just very cold. You know, 'What am I doing here? I'm a drain on the planet. I'm not contributing. I see nothing beyond.' I couldn't understand why I was even here. I just didn't see the point."

A sadness fell over her face. For a minute she sat quietly. Then she started talking again. "I don't know . . . one or two in the morning, and all of a sudden it's a pitch-black room, and at the end of the wall there's this like bright light that comes. It's so tiny but bright." She looked at me, her eyes spreading wide, but she didn't stop talking.

"This is on everything I hold holy," she promised. "That light starts to glimmer. It's almost like a firefly but ten times brighter and I'm . . . now I'm fascinated. I'm staring. Into my head speaks a voice. I can't tell you whether male or female, very androgynous. It says, 'Close your eyes, for if you look upon me you will be blind.' "

"Gwen," I said, "you saw a light and heard a voice! You had a vision?"

"I didn't have a vision. We're talking about an angel here! That was a true being. On everything I hold holy," she went on, firmly now. "I was like, 'Okay. I'll do it.' And I closed my eyes. But I could see through my lids, 'Cause it was so bright, this light coming and coming and coming. And it came all around me. It was an angel. 'Cause even through my eyelids, I could see the image. I don't know how else to explain . . . it was so bright it came through my eyelids. Wasn't male or female, but the wings I felt come 'round me and it said, 'No, no, no, don't do this. You are loved. The Mother has sent me to tell you, you are loved in the kingdom and don't do this. You'll be all right. We're with you.'

"And I was like, 'Oh my God.' I can't even imagine it happening to anybody and it happened to me. Now I grew up an Episcopalian and, God bless the Church, they didn't put anybody else down, but one thing they didn't do is talk about the Mother. To my great disgrace I had never given Her a second thought. But if you look around my home now, She's everywhere. There's a reason for that, because She sent that angel to me and I didn't even know Her and I never thought about Her. Never gave Her a second thought.

"Of course, that changed my life," she said, pausing.

I didn't know what to say. So we fell quiet for a time as I absorbed what she had told me. Then I began to wonder how she had handled quitting. I asked, "After the angel came, how did you end up in New Mexico?"

Picking her story back up, Gwen said, "A friend invited me to come to New Mexico to visit. I wasn't here two seconds and I knew it was home. I went back, packed my stuff, and started my journey out here. I was in a big old rental moving truck, everything in it, but I knew I had a new destiny and it was here in New Mexico. I didn't know why. And I got cowardly, as we all can do, and I thought, 'Mother, I know you told me my journey's prepared, but I just can't imagine I'm going to make it all the way across the country . . . in this big truck. Give me a sign!' And with that I looked down—I swear this is true—and the license plate on the car in front of my truck said, 'All's Well.' And I say, 'Okay! I'm sorry! I'm sorry I ever doubted.' And I had a great journey out. Within six hours of being here I had a home, a job, everything was prepared. I was totally blessed." And she paused.

Then, to make sure she made her point absolutely clear, she added, "That was an angel sent by the Mother."

"When you saw the angel—"

"I saw! It said, 'Close your eyes, for if you look upon me you will be blind.' And it's interesting, because when you're a child and you're having Bible stories read to you, you're told about the blinding light of the angel. That doesn't mean anything then. You don't really understand that.

"I'll tell you. It's a light not of this world. When I closed my eyes and as that angel engulfed me, I still felt blinded. It was so bright. Even through my eyelids, I thought I was going to be blinded."

"I'd have been scared out of my wits," I laughed. Then I asked, "Did you feel like running away in fear?

Gwen was quick to answer, "No! My gosh, no. I felt . . ." Her words trailed off. She was searching for a way to explain it to me. Then, she said, "I felt just . . . an ab-

solute 'thank you' verification of always knowing the Mother's there and 'thank you' for showing up."

"Would you say that the Mother must have thought you were really going to shoot yourself?"

"Exactly. I was not hysterical. I was very rational. It was the thought of 'Okay, enough space taken up on the planet. You're not really contributing so much.'"

"You had it thought out, cold and calculated."

Gwen paused to think. Then she added, "For me, it was like 'This is tough here. The other side is easy.' My thinking was 'This is one tough journey, and the other world's a cakewalk.' I was just tired. Really tired. And it was the Mother's way of saying, 'Not yet. I have other work for you.'"

"Have you regretted leaving *Headline News*?" I asked.

"No," she answered without a pause. "There hasn't been one second, not one, where I've regretted one thing. See, that's other people's priority. That's like saying, 'Don't you want to be a company CEO?' It's the same question. I wouldn't trade, oh my Lord."

I had touched a chord, and Gwen continued, "If you're a CEO, that doesn't put you in any special place. Some of the most profound people I've met have been street people, the disenfranchised. Jesus was a street guy. And I always think about that when I pass someone walking down the road. I always send out a blessing, because I'm sure there's somebody there I'd want to know."

Now Gwen had touched me. Her words carried me back to Atlanta, not to CNN and Gwen's world as she had lived it there. I was thinking about my experience with the homeless. And she was right. The street people did have something to say. They had certainly given me something without their having to make pretenses. They gave of themselves. The church people had, too, but it was of a far different nature than those at the mission.

After telling Gwen of my experiences in Atlanta, I turned back to her story. It still drew me in, and I was interested in hearing more.

"Wasn't everyone saying, 'Don't do this! You've made it to the top'?"

"Everybody," she said, laughing hard. "They were going, 'Oh, she's lost her mind.' But that was okay. In the end I know it's my journey, and if you don't take it, it'll haunt you."

"Gwen . . ." I seemed to be yelling in the stillness that had surrounded us, yet my voice was just above a whisper. "Have angels come to you before or after?"

But she didn't seem to hear me. She was rising to make her way back to the kitchen, as it was time for dinner. So I let the question drop, thinking we would pick up the conversation at the table as we ate. Instead, our talking was more chitchat and, in time, Gwen drifted back to CNN.

"I was with CNN first," she said. "I started working there around 1984. About 1987 my mom got really sick and I left CNN to go care for her. I stayed through her passing. That was two or three months. And I lived in her room, sleeping on a futon by her bed. It was such an experience that I just couldn't go back into that business environment. So I went to Italy for a couple of years. I just needed the time for myself."

"After you came back to the States, did you go back to CNN?" I wondered.

"Not directly," she answered. "I did come back to Atlanta, but I worked at a local station. It was just starting up and they wanted me to anchor. I was there about a year, then CNN rehired me. This time, however, it was as anchor on *Headline News*."

After dinner we returned to her living room and relaxed. Instead of continuing our conversation, we sat quietly and listened to music. Finally, Gwen was ready to call it a night. She showed me to the guest room. She had already laid out my towels, which were neatly stacked at the corner of the bed. She told me she had prepared the coffeemaker, and all I'd have to do in the morning, if I got up before her, would be to flip the switch to on. Then she excused herself and climbed the stairs to her room.

The next morning I did indeed get up before her. And when she came down, I was sitting on the sofa sipping my coffee. Before she joined me, she fed her cat, Merlin, and started watering her plants. In time, she poured herself some coffee and, again, plopped down on the floor by the coffee table. Because of the number of plants around us, I thought of asking her about them and did.

"You know herbs and do herbal medicine for people. Was that to be part of your work?"

Gwen nodded but was quick to add, "I've come to believe that 'medicine' is such a broad term. It's the simple act of loving that is the greatest medicine. And that might be some of the best medicine that you can ever give. Sure I do herbal medicines, but sometimes the truest medicine is simply truly loving and caring. And that can be expressed through a hug. Love really is the greatest medicine. We don't want to recognize its simplicity, because that makes it too simple."

"When did you know you had the ability to know what someone needed?" I asked.

Rising from her restful tranquillity, she didn't hesitate, "I don't really remember." Then she stated frankly, "But it scared me. So I asked for it to go away . . ." She made a sweeping motion with her hand as if to be brushing something away.

I blurted out, "Why?"

Gwen replied, "'Cause I didn't know what was happening."

"When was that?" I asked.

She tried to remember. "Maybe fifteen, twenty years ago. I got a little afraid of its power."

"When this happened to you, what was it that gave you the sense of its power?" I probed.

Gwen rolled her eyes, thinking back. Then she said, "A friend of mine fell out of a tree. She was a grandmother, and she was having a tea party with her grandson in a tree house. She fell on her back on a root. It was a very bad injury.

"When I went to see her, I didn't know she'd had the fall. And she started telling me about it. She was sitting across the room, and I looked at her. The only way I can describe what I saw is it was like a neon X-ray. I saw her skeletal outline in neon.

"There was another time. A friend of mine was a hairdresser. One day I was having my hair done by him. He knew of my proclivities." Gwen laughed, adding, "He said, 'I have a friend whose hair I cut. He's very ill. Will you work with him?' and that's all he told me.

"I said, 'Sure.' He took me to visit him. When I went to put my hands on his head, I saw three neon triangles in his head. And it turned out those were where tumors were. But I wasn't ready to handle it."

"And . . ." I stopped, going no further. My word hung heavily in the air.

Gwen paused, said, "It was Chief Two Trees who taught me to handle it. Then I was blessed. Deepak Chopra! He's become such a big guy now. I got to study with him when he was not a big deal. He's the most centered person I've ever met."

"What is the process when you do medicine?" I asked.

"First of all, it's not me. It only comes through me. But it's like a recipe book is being opened to me and saying, 'This is what the problem is, and this is what you do. Later, even I sometimes go, 'Huh!' That's why I have a lot of reference books to go check that information I get. But I start to lose it if I'm interrupted. So there can't be any questions until I'm finished."

Stopping to sip her drink, Gwen fell into contemplation. After a few minutes, she went on. "Healing power comes through us and comes in its time," she said, growing very serious. "I believe this from the bottom of my soul"—she took a deep breath and quickly continued—"that every human walking this planet is like an antenna. And the information only comes through us. It's truly given to you, but you've got to be sincere. Ego will trash it out. Big time. That's why Western medicine is having so many problems. Money and ego. When you bring garbage, like ego, into it, the results are changed. Trashed. You can't do good medicine with those elements. Doctors today don't even touch people, which is the first thing you need to do. You have to put your hands on them."

"Is it a business?" I asked.

"Ooooh no!" she almost yelled. "Can't be. It's love. Medicine is sacred. Absolutely sacred."

"Is there a charge?" I came back.

"Never, never!" she insisted. "Something is given to the healer just as a way of completing the circle. And it's up to the one who wants to be healed to decide what it's worth. If it's a dime or twenty dollars or fifty, I don't want to know. One of my first great teachers would put a basket out and say, 'Whatever you believe this was worth.'

"Problem is, many don't give anything. If that's the case, then surprise! They don't get anything out of it. There's got to be an exchange.

"It always amazes me the people who just trip through life. They just don't realize . . . have no clue! You can't cheat the universe. It's really true. Oh, you might think you can. You might even think you can skidaddle here or skidaddle there, but I've never seen it work. It'll catch up with you. Like people who are greedy. They take something and they think they've made off with it or they tell a lie. It never serves you. Never!"

"But now you're talking about something different than doing medicine," I said.

"Now you're into life. Oh," I corrected myself, "medicine is part of life, of course, but you're going into the deeper realm of 'What's it all about.' Well, do people ever really learn?"

Smiling, Gwen got up from the floor, sat down in the chair beside me, and nodded. "Sometime on the journey they will. Something'll happen. They'll get it. What's more, I do believe we have a forever journey. But we're here to get it right. This is a classroom."

Slouching deeper into her chair, she held her cup close to her mouth and went on talking. "When I look back on my youth, I admit I did some crazy things. I thought I could tell this little white lie and serve myself. I thought I was serving me. When I look back now, I have to laugh. None of it served me. Ever! It comes back, always. And truth stands forever. So that is the final cosmic joke. And all these beautiful teachers that have been sent are saying, 'Don't sit in the middle of the road. You're going to get run over and it will hurt. Don't do it.' And we're all like, 'Aaah, man, I wanted to sit in the middle of the road. Daggonit, I wanted to sit in the middle of the road.' These teachers came to tell us how to be happy and peaceful and joyful. They didn't come to deprive us of all the wonderful things around us.

"We've got it all backwards. We're taking away from ourselves. And they were just trying to help at great expense to themselves."

Gwen was not in a mood to slow down. But she was ready to move again. Up from the chair she rose, dropped to the floor, and walked on her knees to the far side of the coffee table. Fumbling for a coaster, which she found, she put her drink down on it. She took more time to munch on a snack she had placed there earlier. Then she continued, "I cannot believe the choices brought to us every day from the kingdom," and she stopped with a grin. With a cherubic expression sweeping across her face, she said, "Everybody teases me about always saying 'the kingdom,' but I call the creative power the kingdom. All the time."

With that explanation over, she flatly stated, "We have choices. Major! Even more interesting is the fact that the choices get easier and easier. I believe, too, we are tested. It's one thing to say, 'Here I am,' but be careful what you ask for. You'd better be ready. It's going to come for you."

Contemplating the process she had described, I blurted out, "That leaves you open—no control—doesn't it?"

"For me," she said, going on, "it's the easiest and most beautiful way to live there is. I wouldn't change it. I wouldn't. On the other hand, there can be some melancholy along the way. Like, here was Jesus, and He's walking around and trying to share with everybody and do His best, and He's got these few friends gathered around. They're His

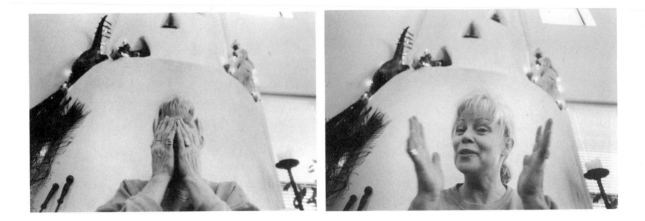

pals. They believe in what He's doing. They listen to Him. And He allows Himself to open up His vulnerable, human side. Then, one He loves very much gives Him a kiss that he knows will put Him through the worst physical pain a human can endure. For forty pieces of silver! And I'm positive He wouldn't change one second of His time here on earth, but the melancholy that must've overcome Him at that moment in time . . . the disappointment. The sadness. From someone you love."

"But Judas was betraying Jesus!" I injected.

"I believe Judas was just thinking of a different kingdom," Gwen cautioned. "He wanted to go to war and set up a kingdom on a physical plane. Then he recognized he had goofed. That's what I mean about realizing things sooner or later.

"Yet, there are a kazillion Judases out there. Not mean-spirited humans, but just those with misunderstanding and who do terrible things in that misunderstanding. I've met, in my lifetime, only one or two what I would call truly dark or left-sided people. Ninety-nine percent are good humans. They just have not quite figured out the choices, like self." She pointed to herself to be sure she had made it absolutely clear. She included herself in how hard it was to see the choices.

Gwen looked down. I could almost see her mental wheels turning. Finally, she raised her head and added, "It's sad, though. You see somebody that you care about self-destructing, and you are just sad as hell for them. But we're all part of God, there's no doubt about it. Still, it's hard to understand. Everything is for a lesson. We just never seem to learn. I think we've lost the wisdom."

Gwen was leading up to something. I didn't have a hint as to what it might be, but there was one thing I wanted to know first. She had mentioned choices and God. I was eager to know what she meant when she signed her letters with "In God's Light." And I asked her.

"Light." She frowned, thinking. "Oh, oh, *that!*" she cried, surprising me with the reaction. But she didn't go on. She jumped up. "Mer Mer!"

"Murmur?" I asked.

Gwen was already to the stairs and bounding up them. "Merlin," she corrected. "Merlin's not back yet." Racing across the balcony, she reached the door to the second-floor patio over the garage. Pushing it open wide, she leaned out.

"Mer Mer!" she called, almost frantic. She waited. "Mer Mer!" she repeated, raising her voice. Then, coming back inside and leaning over the banister to look down at me, she said, "With the city widening that road . . ." She pointed toward the backyard. On the other side of the fence bumper-to-bumper traffic constantly roared by. She was concerned, and her words were pouring out. Barreling back to the door that was still ajar, she all but yelled, "Coyotes go for the cats," and she was calling Merlin again.

Shouting back at her, I said, "In the city?"

"Mer Mer," she pleaded sweetly but sternly, without answering my question. Then, not forgetting me, she momentarily leaned back over the railing to say, "It's still the desert. We live on the desert, but so many people are moving here, there are new dangers for our pets. And she went back to the door. "Come, come. Come now. You don't want to be run over," she said in warning to her wandering furry companion.

Gwen was nervous and impatient, her concern mounting. She paced and called again. Time was passing and the window of safety seemed to be narrowing.

Then, out of nowhere, Merlin slipped through the opening, rubbed against her leg and casually sashayed down the steps. Without a sound, not even a meow, Merlin pranced into the dining room to sniff his bowl for any replenished food that might have been added. Gwen followed, relieved.

Without even catching her breath, she remembered my question and began answering it. "I believe God is light," she said. "I think that's why people used to worship the sun. I think light is the key to it all. I can see the truthfulness of light.

"A friend of mine used to say light was intelligence, that intelligence was contained in light. We use these expressions all the time, 'Stand in the light,' 'He sees the light.'

We use it over and over. Then we counter to that in the next breath. We use dark, dark, dark. I think we all instinctively know intelligence and spirituality have something to do with light.

"Einstein said that by just looking at a piece of matter we change it. It's a very difficult concept, because if you turn that around people say, 'The observer and the observer's prejudices create whatever.'

"No, no, no! What Einstein did was he took light. He saw that whoever was observing it and their thought about it changed the quality of it. So then, that leads you to believe we do, in fact, create our universe. We create!"

"Isn't that putting us up there alongside of God?" I asked.

"I see the universe as God's huge body and we're part of it. Like in any body, every molecule, as it evolves, changes. And as each one of us individually evolves, then we change the body of God. And the universe is God's body. We're a speck, a sneeze, or whatever, but a molecule in my left baby toe does affect my whole body.

"One of my brothers is always saying, 'You always think you're going to change the world.'

"'No, no, no,' I go. 'You don't understand. I'm just trying to change me, because that's all I can do.'

"The way I see it is that if I can become a good cell or molecule in God's body, He's happy, I'm happy. In doing that I'm affecting all those cells, meaning others, around me.

"Just ask anybody how they felt when someone did something really good for them! I really believe that if you give people the opportunity to do good, they will leap at it. People will only do negative things out of pain and hurt and what they perceive as lack of opportunity. So if you give people that doorway to do good, they'll run through it. People want to, because they know the feeling. It's beautiful. Ask people if they feel better when they smile as opposed to frowning. You don't even have to intellectualize it. Ask yourself! When were you the happiest? When you gave to somebody, or when you took from them?

"Our generation got carried away. We forgot! We forgot how to be real people. Oh, did we forget!"

"Things are a mess, or seem to be," I agreed. Then I mumbled on, adding, "Like what you said about being in television."

Gwen frowned and said, "If you think broadcasting is pitiful, try to be a politician in Washington. The rules are set. The game is bought and sold and there is no turning back. What is amazing to me is that anybody can step in that arena and do anything good. I think it's overwhelming. I think they're meaner than broadcast people. I think they will cut your heart out, and I think anybody who can do kindness in that arena should be called great. Broadcasting is vicious, but in politics they will kill you if you try to do good. Think about it . . . the CIA and murder. Ask John Kennedy and Martin Luther King!"

"What can anyone do," I asked, rhetorically.

"The answer for the problems of the world is love, love, love. God is love. You can have the knowledge but still not be able to apply it. Every single human walking this planet has the potential for love and reaching that higher state of awareness. I'll say to you that I am here because I'm not a fast learner. The universe has a system and it's a system of learning. All the great teachers came to say, 'Here it is, guys. You can do it.' We've lost our way. We're off and crazy in this material, technological world. In this society, it is difficult to grow spiritually because of the way we're raised, because of the material focus. We have created a nightmare for our spirit. We're just not getting it. It is sad that we have evolved. so far away from that which we should be and could know somewhere deep inside of us. This society is just not conducive to developing spiritually."

When she paused, I chuckled, "Who's got the power to change it?"

Gwen shot me a humorous glance and said, "Who but us? We created a system that is fairly overwhelming to try to circumvent. That doesn't mean we shouldn't try, or that we're not trying. Just look at us now, though. Look everywhere. Look around the world. What could be more barbaric than how we humans behave? I can't imagine doing anything worse than what we do to each other. We rape our children, kill women, discard old people.

"There was a young woman from Rwanda who came under my care for a while. Happy Matusi. Happy was one of two people in her entire village to survive an attack in 1994. The only reason she survived is the attackers dug a huge pit and they threw everybody in it and the bodies of her mother, her father, her brothers, and her sisters absorbed the majority of the bullets and grenades. She still had grenade fragments throughout her body and her arms and legs, and she had two bullets removed from her body. She was only one of two people to survive in that entire village," Gwen repeated. "And she was a beautiful, beautiful spirit who came to Albuquerque to be healed."

"I can't deal with suffering," I injected. "It's beyond me why we do what we do to each other."

Gwen whispered, "If anybody can tell me what's more barbaric than humans in this universe, what behavior they could possibly fathom . . ." She wiped away tears that had welled up in her eyes. Then she continued, "We've been cannibals. We kill animals for fun. We dump poison into the very thing that feeds us. I'd like to know what's more barbaric! Maybe there is something, but I can't, for the life of me, imagine what it could be. What could you come up with that's worse than this? I mean, genocide, molesting and beating our children, treating our old folks like throwaway garbage, treating women like we do all over the world, where, when they displease us, we kill them . . . thirteen million in the Spanish Inquisition alone. Look at India today. Please, please! I can't imagine a planet or a society that . . . what more could they concoct? Nothing! And still the great teachers have come, time after time, to point us to a better way. You'd think we'd start listening!

"We all want an easy fix. I look back in my life and I have to say the reason the Lord told me not to judge anybody is because I know if I recognize it, I did it. If not in this life, another life. If I recognize it, I did it, therefore I cannot judge it."

"We're all guilty," I admitted.

"I'm right in there, too," she conceded. "Looking back over my life, I have to admit that I've lied, I've cheated, I've stolen. What else can you do? On some level or another I've done it all. I just can't sit in judgment of anybody, because I know I've done it. Judgment is not my job.

"But it's hard. I get . . . if I see somebody being cruel to an animal or child, I get a little crazy. I just can't contain myself, because I feel like animals and children have been placed in our care. We are their guardians. They don't have the options to say, 'I don't like this.' In the case of an animal, 'Please don't hook up all those electrodes to me.' Or a child, 'Please don't beat me. Please don't molest me.' They're stuck with it." Gwen became overcome with emotion, and she didn't try to hide it. She let it show.

"Don't you think there's going to be a payday?" I asked.

Gwen was quick to answer. "You better believe it! When you do something harmful to someone else, then in that very second you have done it unto yourself. If we could only understand that, then everything would be fine. Because then you would never hurt another human. You would never think another bad thought. You would never do another hurtful thing, because you would understand the interconnectedness and know the hurt done to yourself.

"We're so goofed in this society. We're so programmed in so many wrong ways." With that, Gwen began clearing the coffee cups off the table, and set about preparing lunch. We'd spent the entire morning talking. It had passed like a flash of light. And now it was mealtime, again.

Trying to volunteer, I was swished out of the way. Although the kitchen was small, I wanted to help. But she was adamant, and there was no changing her mind. So I followed her instructions when she said, "Go. Go. Go listen to music. Smoke. Nap. This I'll do. But tomorrow morning," she added, laughing, "you can buy me breakfast."

It was to be breakfast at a Mexican restaurant. Gwen had already planned where we were going. The eatery was not a fancy place, not one of those high-dollar places, but it

was a daily gathering place for those in the know—the locals. Gwen was one of them, and everyone in the place knew her.

There were hellos and hugs for Gwen as we made our way toward a table. Immediately upon seeing her, a waitress ran from the back of the restaurant. Gwen introduced her to me as Martha. Grabbing Gwen's arm, Martha ushered us to one of the tables to which she was assigned. Once reaching the table, Martha pulled out Gwen's chair and said, "Sit."

As soon as Gwen was comfortable, Martha started talking. It wasn't enough for her to show her enthusiasm at seeing Gwen, she had to tell her. Back and forth they talked. Gwen asked her about her health, family, and work. At that, the kindly waitress told Gwen about her troubled financial condition. Martha thought aloud how some had so much and she had so little.

"You love people and you're kind," Gwen said, trying to console her.

Martha whispered back, "I don't have nothing." And tears came to her eyes. Quickly she wiped at them to keep them from running down her face.

Gwen was quick to say, "You are one of God's angels."

"I don't even have a VCR," Martha said.

Gwen told her friend, "The more stuff people get, the more burdened they are." And she used herself as an example. "One time I gave away everything I had but two suitcases. I've never been lighter in my life. Never felt better! And I keep giving away and it keeps coming back. I can't get rid of it—"

"I see all these people who have everything they want," Martha interrupted.

"I don't think they have the love you have," Gwen comforted. "Everybody loves you. Everybody carries you in their heart and in their prayers. What's more valuable than that?" she asked.

Martha seemed touched. "I'm always praying for everybody before myself," she said. "I pray every little while and at night or when I'm driving. I pray all the time."

"You are blessed." Gwen squeezed her friend's hand. Martha returned the show of affection by leaning over to place the side of her face on the top of Gwen's head. Then she stood tall and whirled around to run and pick up a waiting order that was getting cold.

After Martha left, Gwen proclaimed, "That woman is one of the sweetest people I know. She'd do anything for anybody. She's raised a half-dozen kids, and some who were not even hers." Gwen shook her head, then added, "It's hard on her, the way she has to work, and she makes so little. Then, to see others seemingly having so much more, she just doesn't understand. But what she doesn't see is that she has so much love. She's got so much more than any of those who brag about what material possessions they have. Theirs is just boasting. What she has is real." Gwen settled into sipping her coffee.

Occasionally Martha would pass by, each time promising that the food would be out soon. Then she would move on to other tables. It was a full house, and Martha was too busy to stop to talk.

Gwen watched her almost dance from table to table. Then she whispered, "They don't pay well at a lot of restaurants. The wait people have to live on tips. Sometimes they do okay, but sometimes money is slow coming. It's not really right, because these people have to pay bills like everybody else. It's not really just."

As I was about to speak up, it was as if Gwen knew what I was going to say. So she chimed back in. "I can't take injustice," Gwen stated. "I used to be a real rabble-rouser about it, like during the civil rights days and such. I was very vocal and very aggressive about it. The work I do now is centered on trying to do what I can in correcting injustices, but the manner in which I do it is very different. Back when, those were the Sixties and everybody was crazed and for good reason . . . you know, consciousness. It needed to happen, though. That revolution needed to happen in this country."

Gwen's drifting into the subject of civil rights had aroused some of my old passions, and I spoke up. "Prejudice comes from oppression," I said. "I've found that those who have been put down know more about their oppressors than the oppressors know about themselves."

"In my personal experience, and I've had a lot," Gwen said, "the African-Americans are the most spiritually evolved, loving, giving, kind, forgiving humans on this planet.

They are so quick to gather you in and forgive you. Who else in this country has suffered the way they have suffered and who else is so willing to reach out and be loving? I'll tell you, if you believe in reincarnation, I think that's one of the last evolutionary steps. Be a black woman in Mississippi, man, and you own it. You own the kingdom!

"I can name twenty black people in my life off the top of my head that I call blessed. They have every right to just hate Anglos. I'm humbled in front of that kind . . . It could be Curly Island or it could be Viola, could be Zachariah, could be all those beautiful people who saved me.

"Curly Island," Gwen repeated her name. "She's a beautiful woman. She's one of God's own. She lives in a shack in Mississippi, outside of Greenwood, to this day. And all her life she served this one family. But when I talked with her, she touched my soul because she has so much beauty and love in her. She raised nine children, five or six of her own.

"She lived on this plantation owned by the family of a man I was dating. And when I met Curly, I fell in love with her and we created our own little revolution. It was Thanksgiving and she had eight thousand dishes to do, and I went out and started helping her in the kitchen. That upset all the white folks and I was told that I was 'ruining the help.'

"But Curly said I was the only white person who had ever touched her with love. It was very sad. So Curly became real special to me. Unfortunately, she doesn't read or write, so I'll send cards and gifts, but I don't ever get a reply. And she has no phone. In fact, she just got indoor plumbing and electricity a couple years ago. Sometimes her daughter will write. Curly's pretty old now and she can't go anywhere. She's just there.

"There's an Hispanic lady here who said, 'You know, you're the first white woman I could ever talk to from my heart.'

"I started thinking of how many times that has been said to me. I realized that maybe that's what I am, an ambassador . . . that not all Anglos, not all of us, are creeps. Some of us have old souls . . . Don't hate us too badly, although I know that a lot of what we've done is hateable."

Gwen paused, leaving me to think more on the subject was forthcoming. There wasn't. Not only had she said all she was going to, she had finished her meal and was ready to go. Earlier she had said she wanted me to meet some of her friends. Martha had been one. Now Gwen was eager to get to the next stop. I couldn't wait to find out who I'd meet next.

Martha caught up with Gwen at the door, And they embraced again. Both held on to the other for a long time. Then, we were out and in the car.

"Where are we off to next?" I asked.

Taking her time to negotiate a few turns before answering, Gwen finally said, "Paula Dimit. She's my angel artist. She carves angels and you'll love her," she explained. And we were out of downtown Albuquerque and on our way to Bernalillo, a small town north of the city.

"How did you get to know Paula?" I asked.

Gwen replied, "She used to live in the house where I do now. That's how we met. I got here from Atlanta with all my stuff on the truck, but Paula didn't have to move out for another week. I had a problem. I could stay in a hotel, but the truck had to be returned. So she was kind enough to move all of her tools and such out of the garage so I could un-load and get the truck back to the rental company.

"After she moved out and I moved in, she called one day to say, 'I have a little house-warming gift for you.' She came over and gave me one of her carvings. It was a beautiful Mother. She did that without ever knowing my connection to the Mother. We hadn't so much as spoken about it. It's been by my bed to this day.

"She's always carved angels. Big ones. After she went through some very rough times, she realized a lot of folks had been through them, too. So carving the angels was something she could do to help them through their troubles. Because of that, I think she developed even a deeper sense of spirit and belief that she had a gift. And she could use that gift to help others in a small way. Of course that has a ripple affect. It just keeps on giving. People have come back to her and said, 'You know the angel you gave me? Well, I met somebody who really needed it more. So I gave it to them.' And now her angels are everywhere. We believe they're out there protecting those who have one."

Gwen smiled. "That's one reason I wanted you to meet her," she said. "The other is that she's been through so much. She has a connection with the Mother, as well. That's what really brought us together. And since first meeting, we've been a shoulder for each other. I think she'd be willing to talk to you about it, if you're interested. If you want to know about God, Paula can help fill you in."

"Yes," I said. "I've learned that you can find out a lot when you're least expecting it."

It was almost shameful the way Gwen and Paula took on over each other. Had I not known Gwen, I would've been shocked. Instead I understood completely. There was only one way to describe the two of them. If I crossed my middle finger over the index and squeezed as hard as I could, that's the way they were with their feelings toward each other. Close. Tight. And because I was with Gwen, Paula gave me a breathtaking bear hug in hearty welcome. Then she laughingly exhorted me to follow her outside to the front of the former gas station that had been converted into her gallery. Now in her fifties,

she was in business for herself. For the first time in her life, she was a full-time artist and wanted to show me some of her work.

The front of her gallery looked like a zoo. There were carved animals all lined up in a row, drying in the sun. Because of her flamboyant sense of humor they were all chained. First impressions, from a distance, drew sadness for the creatures and anger toward the one who would do such a thing. But with a closer look, one could only laugh. They weren't real. It was Paula's art. They were wooden. But they were so realistic, it took two glances and a stare to know it.

Paula saw my reaction and she laughed. Gwen and I laughed, too. And passersby stopped to get in on the commotion. They nodded their heads and chuckled, too.

Bending down and unchaining one, Paula said, "I chain 'em so they don't go out in the street and get run over." Then, she cradled a wooden rabbit and started talking to it. "Duddn't that right, Notch?" And she explained, "He's a fightin' rabbit. He got his ear damaged and he's saying, 'All right, bring on somebody else.'"

"I always say they're 'don't mess with me' rabbits." She reached for another carving. "But, then . . . See! Look at little sweet . . . this little Buddha bunny. This is a new one. She's just so innocent and helpless. Look at that."

Moving back inside, Gwen turned to Paula and asked if she'd be willing to talk to me about her angels. At first Paula was hesitant and I suggested that it wasn't necessary. But I told her I was interested in the stories of people who had seen God or angels.

Paul responded, "God has been with me. I guess telling you about it would be okay since you're with Gwen."

Immediately Gwen pushed us toward another room and said, "Go in there to talk. It's quieter and I'll take care of the customers. I'll sell every one of them something or they're not getting out of here," She laughed, closing the door behind us.

Paula chuckled, then grew serious. She said, "I don't think anyone would be interested in hearing what's happened to me. But, if you insist, I'll tell you. It's not so exciting. It's just what I've lived through."

After offering me a seat, she started, "I went through all these years of doing things. Teaching school. Raising my daughter. And over time I came to realize that things exist on four levels. We exist on the physical, the mental, the emotional, and the spiritual. Some people say three. I think there are four. But we spend so much time on the physical level. That's where we think we're supposed to be.

"So I was going through my life and being able to pay bills and so on. But I had a great change. All of a sudden I didn't have any way to pay those bills. I came to this understanding through adversity." Paula stopped talking. For a moment it was awkward. Then she yielded, "I'm a recovering alcoholic. But—" Paula's words stopped.

"Paula," I said, "I don't want to pry."

But she went on. "When you get to that place, it comes, you're stripped to nothing. I hit bottom. I had to do something. But I always say I had more slips than a pig on ice in recovering from alcohol.

"There was a marked day that really changed things for me. I started out on borrowed money. And this one day, the owner of this building said to me, 'Paula! Wait a minute. We only get one day at a time. Don't worry about the next.'

"So I started sitting here talking to God. I said, 'Okay. Keep my heart pure. My thoughts pure. My words pure. Help me to go out and about and do the best I can with trying to make other people feel good.' Then things started taking care of themselves. It's an ongoing process.

"When I started this business, it was so scary. I was starting it in the hole. I'd sit here and start asking . . . I'd ask God to, 'Take me home. I don't want to do this anymore. Take me home.' And I'd say, 'I'm ready to go home.'"

"You wanted to die?" I whispered. "What happened to make you want to live?"

"I realized, 'No! If I'm supposed to be there, I'd be there.'

"So I know there's still some living to be done on this earth. Then I'd say, and I know there's a guardian angel with me, I'd say, 'Just wrap me in your angel wings. Give me some peace and comfort.'"

"And you started carving angels?"

"I've always carved angels. And for years I've given angels to people. If someone was sick or in the hospital, I would just take an angel down and set it on their table. Later I learned that those same angels would be given to others by the ones I'd given them to. They get passed on. I think that's great.

"God loves us. He's passing that love on to us. We're supposed to pass it on, too. You know it wasn't until just this last year that I realized that God really and truly loved me." Paula stopped and opened the door to check out what was going on with the gallery. Gwen was standing in the middle of the next room admiring one of Paula's carvings and telling someone how wonderful Paula's artwork was. Paula took a deep breath and said to me, "Gwen! What a blessing. What a friend."

Then she picked up where she had left off. "If a person told me that they felt better being angry and hateful and vicious and mean and passing that on so that gets passed on and on and that really made them feel the best, I wouldn't believe them. Our journey is supposed to be a joy and it takes fifty-six-year-olds, like me, to learn that lesson. And maybe my giving little angels help."

"Why do you give them to people?" I asked.

"You benefit from giving. The spiritual journey is supposed to be a joy. And sometimes it takes real adversity to wake you up to that journey. It's not just for the folks you're going to help. It's for you.

"Life's supposed to be a joy. I began to understand this hitting bottom with my alcohol, stopping drinking, but there was still a long path before I got to this point. When you learn to love other people, that's the greatest thing. Love. It's not because we love God. It's because He loves us. What a wondrous thing life is. Just realize what a gift. The greatest gift of all is to realize that life is supposed to be a joy . . ." Paula grew quiet.

I sat with her in the silence, but we both could hear Gwen talking away in the next room. Then I asked Paula, "Do you think it does any good to give angels to other people?"

"I don't know," she said. "I hope it does. I've heard it does. That's what people have told me. But the giving is for me. It helps me, I know that. You grow on this path, and one of the things I've learned is that when you feel you should do something for someone, you should do it. Doing it really matters for your journey. Some only play the game. I've decided I'm not going to play the game. It's going to be real or not at all.

"I am grateful and so thankful to God that I can do this thing with the wood carvings. What a wonderful gift God has given me that I have something I can give to people that makes them smile. It's my joy. It's my joy that I get to give and I feel that joy in my heart from giving."

"I've heard it's better to give than to receive," I interjected. "It does feel pretty good, I know that."

Paula was quick to respond. "The thing about giving is that it comes back. Maybe it doesn't strike you like some big revelation, but it will come back. And it's in those little things that count so much. It's like the jeans."

"You're talking about pants? Clothes?" I asked. "What's that story?"

"I needed some jeans," Paula said, adding, "and I knew I didn't have the cash to go out and buy them. Lo and behold, this is completely bizarre 'cause it's not even worth mentioning, but this lady came in and I hadn't seen her for quite a while. Some time ago I'd given her a bunch of these big, baggy jeans for her daughter because I had lost some weight. This all happened this month and she said, just out of the blue, 'Paula, would you like to have those jeans back? My daughter can't wear them.'

"That was two or three years ago that I did that. So, here the next day, in a bag sitting in my gallery were all these comfortable clothes." Paula laughed.

From her tone, I sensed she saw this as a gift of God. I guessed that I would have, too, if I needed clothes and didn't have the money to go out and buy any. Looking at Paula, I said, "Yes, I'd say that was one of those little miracles." Then I added, "Have you had any other things like that happen?"

"Well," she mused, "there was another odd little thing that happened. I don't know if you'd call them miracles, but they're just happenings. I looked down one day. Here were these little angels. Like sequins. But they're shaped like little angels. And someone had sprinkled little angels right here and over there. I had no idea who had done that.

"For months, two or three months, every time I tried to clean this sawdust, which gathers every day, I cleaned around those angels. And I'd move them and I'd clean. Couldn't just take my little broom and dust everything off 'cause I had to clean around those angels.

"Well, lo and behold, this person comes in and looks down and there were the angels. She said, 'I sprinkled those angels there when I was here two or three months ago.'

"And here she came back from Michigan, came into the gallery, and the angels were still here. She came in yesterday. And she's coming back Saturday. She said, 'Do you need more angels?' And we both laughed."

"I'm all ears, if you want to go on," I said.

"There is more. This kind of thing goes on all the time. You give and it comes back. Like my sister recently sent me an angel as a gift. She was thinking about me and did that. Now these are just physical things, but I believe so much in the angels. It's all about giving.

"I'll tell you the story of my Blessed Mother. She's the only carving of mine that I won't sell. Oh! She's a rough-looking Mother. But light a candle and turn off the lights and she becomes beautiful." Paula motioned for me to do it. She wanted me to see the change.

When Paula pointed out the carving, I had to confess. She was a . . . I couldn't put words together to describe her. "Rough" was Paula's word for her, and she was right. It was a rough-looking Mother.

"If you notice," Paula said, "she has great big hands. Her hands are very large. And they seem to get larger in the candlelight."

She was right again. The Virgin's hands were extremely large and grandly out of proportion. Then Paula laughed, "I carved her years ago. When I first started in wood," she explained. Her work had improved, yet there was something about this Blessed Mother.

Paula went on, "I was working on her and her hand broke off. Oh, I repaired it like you can wood and I finished her. I had her all done and wrapped very carefully. I was taking her to a gallery to sell. Before I could get there, her other hand broke off.

"At that time, believe this or not, my hands had arthritis. It was so bad that I would have to use two hands to lift a coffee cup.

"Someone told me, 'She's meant to protect your hands. Maybe you shouldn't sell her.' So I brought her home. I repaired her other hand and I kept her. And I don't have arthritis in my hands now. Later I told someone that story and I said, 'I wish she had done my knees.'

The man said, 'Well, you didn't break her knees!'

"And that story is true. When I made her, I didn't even realize I was making her hands so-o-o large. So now, when I'm sitting here talking to God and praying, I always know she's there. I looked the other night . . ." Paula just shook her head and said, "And . . . and . . . she really is not a beautiful . . . she's not just another pretty face. But when that candle's on her, she just looks beautiful and peaceful and wonderful."

Paula went over and picked her up. Gently caressing her, she whispered, "It's all about giving. And you never know where the gifts are coming from. That's the beauty of it. It can even be from my beautiful Blessed Mother."

"Paula," I asked, "do you really believe the Mother had a connection to that piece of wood?"

"I couldn't pick up a cup. I know that. Now I can. But I can't prove to you it was the Mother."

Paula and I talked on for a while. Every once in a while Gwen would check on us, eventually indicating she needed to go. Our visit with Paula was over. As we were preparing to leave, Gwen and Paula hugged again. Theirs was one of those "no matter what" friendships. It was ongoing and forever enduring. I opened the screen door for Gwen, but Paula lagged behind. When I nodded that my holding it open was for her, too, she eased by me. As she did, she pressed a tiny wooden angel into my palm and followed Gwen. The talk between them was still just as intense as it had been when we first arrived. For them, it was never a good-bye. It was a "we'll pick up where we left off" kind of farewell.

Once we were back in the car, Gwen turned to me and said, "I wanted you to meet Paula because there are many people who have the connection to the Mother. Paula's one of them. And I didn't want you to think I was the only one. There are a lot of people who are seeing Her. She's out there working. Almost every week you'll read in the newspapers about someone else who has seen the Mother."

All the way back to Gwen's home we sat without talking. Once we were settled, I brought up the subject of the Blessed Mother again. "Gwen," I started, "what is it about the Mother?"

Gwen sat for a minute, then responded, "People forget that She was human, a great spirit, or whatever you want to call it. God chose Her for a reason. But She was a human. So She really has an attachment to humans because She knows our condition. That's why, of all the spirits, She is the one who continually works double time. If you'll notice, whenever there are sightings or visions, it's always the Mother. Have you noticed that?

"It's because She was human. Completely. And God chose Her because of Her beauty and compassion and loving nature. Because of Her empathy for us, She's always trying to help out. She understands. In my life, anyway."

Gwen waved and I looked around. It wasn't until that very moment that I realized just how many statues, carvings, and paintings of the Virgin Mary she had on shelves, tables, and walls.

"She's all over my house," Gwen confessed. "Every image that you see of the Mother in my house, pretty much, is Guadeloupe. Now I have a couple of exceptions that have been gifts that were given to me because everybody who knows me knows that I love the Mother. So they'll bring me images of the Mother that aren't always Guadeloupe. But

She is over my bed. She hangs on the wall . . . a beautiful Guadeloupe that was made by a Mexican artist out of tin. And it's painted."

"Reason?" I said.

Gwen looked at me and hesitated before going on. That left me wondering why, and I asked about the reluctance.

"The Mother appeared to me twice," she said. "I told you about that time in Atlanta. That was when She sent the angel. Well, She came once again after I got to New Mexico. She came personally. But if I talk about it, people think I'm saying, 'Oh. I'm really special. The Mother chose to recognize me,' and I don't want that. I'm so scared that people will think I'm being braggy or setting myself apart. And then they would look at me and go, 'Well, what makes her so special? Smokes cigarettes. Drinks. Curses.'

"What I really want is to let people know that She's there. She is there!

"I'm a regular guy. That's me. And this didn't make me some great human. In fact, quite the opposite. It made me recognize how humble one must be."

"I'm listening," I said. "And I know this is the reason you're here in Albuquerque. Please do tell," I gently coaxed, leaving it up to her to decide if she wanted to continue.

Gwen raised herself up on her knees to lean over the coffee table. Then, lighting a cigarette, she continued, "There's a woman in Madrid. She lives in a bus. Tina. When I met Tina, she just needed love. Her comment to me was, 'Somebody told me I needed perfume today. I wish somebody'd offer me a bath.'

"I said, 'Come down to my house.' One thing led to another. She was a frequent visitor in my home, and it was my great pleasure to share it with her. So one time, out of the clear blue, this is the lady that has not two dimes to rub together, she called me. She said, 'I have a surprise for you.'

"And I said, 'Really! What is it?'

"She said, 'It's a surprise. You just have to come up. Pick me up and I'm going to surprise you.'

"I said, 'Cool.' So I picked her up and she said, 'Ah, we're going to Santa Fe. Ten Thousand Waves.'

"Well, that's like this very chichi Japanese-run spa and healing center. And I'd never been there. She had paid for it and made reservations for us to take the hot baths and whatever. What you have to do is go into this little hut and undress. Then you go out onto a redwood deck and there's this huge hot tub and it's boiling hot and it's freezing cold outside. So you jump in, get down low. Then all of a sudden you're okay, but you're outside and in front of you everywhere are the Santa Fe Sangre de Cristo Mountains and, of course, New Mexico's clear, clear sky.

"So this is her treat to me. It was beautiful and we're there and we're sitting and just being quiet and I looked up. Out of a glowing thing, I assume a star, came this growing and growing and growing. I'm like, 'Oh my God.' And I'm staring and I'm staring. That's why I'm so attached to Guadeloupe. 'Cause out there in that sky I see . . . about the size of a big . . . not an ostrich egg, not a chicken egg, but some egg in between . . . I see Our Lady of Guadeloupe. Brilliant! I cannot—there are no words to describe the l-i-g-h-t. There is no light in this kingdom like it. Reds! Yellows! Greens! Just as She's always depicted. You know, She's very colorful. The colors are shining from Her!

"I wanted Her to say something. I have to tell you, wretched old me, I wanted Her to say something. I really did. Just anything, I didn't care. But She didn't. She just was there.

"It was humbling, totally humbling, 'cause I'm just a wretched human." She stopped talking and said nothing for some time. We both just smoked.

Finally, referring to the effect the experience had on her, Gwen added, "Every morning I pray to Her, 'Today, let me do your work. Please, today.'"

Now I had an understanding as to why Gwen cared so much, even for the ants. Call it whatever, but to Gwen what had happened to her opened her eyes and heart to the universe around her. She even stopped for dead animals smashed in the road. She had told me on the way back from the visit with Paula, "I bury them. I pull over and get my rubber gloves and my fold-up army shovel out of the trunk of my car. They deserve some dignity. Even in death."

Gwen sat quietly when I got up and went into the kitchen. I was only going for a glass of water, but usually when I headed in that direction, she was ready to beat me there, asking as she raced, "What do you need? I'll get it." That's just the way she was. Always the proper host. But not this time.

Turning on the faucet, I saw them. Taking a step back, I glanced into the living room. Gwen was still where I had left her. I shut off the water and considered if I should call to her. I decided against it. I wouldn't even mention it since it would spur her into action. So I simply walked out of the room and flipped off the light as I did. She would discover them soon enough. And when she did, out would come the lemon juice concentrate. She wouldn't kill them. Just squirt around them.

As for now, the countertop would be a secret playground. And it would be peace and freedom, maybe even a little fun, for the ants.

8. *FERNANDO MERCADO*

SAN ACACIA, NEW MEXICO

The visit with Gwen came to an end. I was ready to move on. It wasn't that I was eager to leave, rather I was looking forward to be rolling again. So, as she helped me carry my bags out to my truck, Gwen quizzed me as to which way I was heading.

"West," I told her, adding, "just as far as I can go. Guess I'll stop at the Pacific Ocean." Then I told her I'd probably turn north, maybe even end up in Seattle. At that point I figured I'd swing east and go home. It wasn't that I knew anyone who had seen God out that way, but it was my hunch there would be those who had stories to tell.

After opening the truck door, Gwen rushed up to give me a friendly "be safe" hug. Then, I slid under the steering wheel, slammed the door shut, and eased out into the street. Glancing back, I saw that Gwen was still standing in the drive, waiting for one last wave good-bye. I rolled my window down and yelled to her, "Adventure!"

"Experiences!" she shouted back. Then she blew me a kiss.

Interstate 40 was as unwelcoming in Albuquerque has it had ever been on previous trips to or through the city. As I angled down the on ramp an old dread surfaced—fighting traffic congestion. On top of that, the speeding cars and trucks were always a major concern for me. As I slammed the accelerator to the floor, slipping between a minivan and a freight hauler, I cursed and prayed for patience at the same time. All I was hoping for was to get through the mess safely and reach the wide-open spaces of the desert in one piece. Fortunately, by staying with the traffic's flow, I managed to go the distance without an incident.

As the number of cars and trucks dwindled and with speed no longer a necessity, I throttled back and relaxed. For a change of pace, it was good just to listen to the mesmerizing sound of my tires roaring along over the pavement. And the sights of the desert were incredible. Because it was impossible to take everything in with one visual scanning, I quickly studied one view after another.

Miles and miles rolled by, and in time, Albuquerque was no longer a part of the landscape. The city had fallen far behind me, becoming only a dot on the map that occupied the seat next to me. After tiring of constantly trying to see everything around me, I began to think of all those I had met on this trip who had encountered the divine. One by one they came to mind. And as they did, it was as if the scene was playing out before me for the first time.

I was in the church dressed as a homeless man. Someone was whispering, "But God, look at his dirty socks." And the preacher was pointing at me, telling the whole congregation that anyone could rise up out of the gutter and follow Jesus. By then, everybody knew he was talking about me.

Then there was George and Little Willis at the mission. George was worried about my not having enough to eat, so after tapping the side of my leg, he was offering to buy me a hamburger. Little Willis was throwing a coat to George as he hurried to deliver a friend a few fried chicken necks.

There was Sarah making arrangements for Pretty Girl so her bird would always have a home. Tate was staring down the barrel of a gun that would not fire and believing God had intervened to spare his life. Floyd was talking to God at the bottom of the river. Germaine was being protected by angels at the door of the old post office. William Jesus was holding his buddy's headless body after a bombardment in Vietnam and hearing an unfamiliar voice comforting him. And Gwen was being kept from killing herself by an angel sent by the Virgin Mary.

The miles rolled on. And, as they did, I remembered each and every person I'd met and marveled at the stories they had told. Amazingly, I thought, not one of them had complained about anything. Some had been homeless. Others had lived their lives with very little in the way of material things. A few had risen to the top of their professions and had freely given up their careers. One had lived a lifetime of physical ills. Another had so much compassion for others that she had sacrificed her own health in order to serve those around her. The Vietnam veteran, although the conflict had long been over, faced the horrors of war daily. Yet, none harbored any ill will toward anyone. No one was filled with anger for any reason. Their lives had been touched by something they saw as being far beyond themselves, and they had been transformed. No matter how hard life had been or whatever conditions they had endured, what happened to them transcended everything else in their lives.

Then, as I neared Interstate 40 after leaving Gwen's, the idea "Head for home" appeared like a billboard out of nowhere. Admittedly, it could have been that I was more than a little homesick and didn't need too much of a push to make the decision I did. Nevertheless, as I turned eastbound, I inwardly thanked Fernando Mercado. Mercado's story was different from all the others. He had not seen just one revelation; he said he saw God every day. And now as I passed through Amarillo, I flashed back to him. It was something he had said that kept coming to mind. And because of that I was now traveling east instead of west. I was not going to California or even Seattle. I was going home! His words had been simple. Two little words! They were "Pay attention."

As I drove in the direction of Virginia, I thought of him. Our meeting could have just as easily never happened. When I called Gwen before leaving home to ask if I could come for a visit, she had said, "Stop in San Acacia. Meet Fernando. He's a great artist, and you've got to hear what he has to say." Then before our conversation had ended, she added, "Please see Fernando. Just drop in on him at his gallery. It's in an old school. He's always there. He lives in the bell tower. It'll be okay. Just tell him you and I are friends."

But I wasn't going to do it. Friend of Gwen's or not, I wasn't going to knock on the door of a great artist without an appointment. My mind had been made up before I ever left Richmond. I still wasn't going to do it when I crossed into New Mexico after dropping William Jesus off in El Paso. My thinking had been the same when I pulled out of Las Cruces after spending the night there. Yet, after passing Truth or Consequences, I changed my mind. It could have been just seeing the name of that New Mexico town that caused me to alter my plan of going directly to Gwen's first. No matter what it was that made me reconsider, it was clear what I was going to do. So when I reached the San Acacia turn-off, I slipped off the interstate. I was going to chance walking in on the artist cold.

It had not been difficult to find the old school. Because it had recently been remodeled and transformed into an art gallery, it stood out from the few old adobe houses that remained in the withered community. The village of San Acacia seemed to have always been a sleepy little hamlet, and my first impression was that it was still asleep. The

Catholic church had been abandoned long ago. A house here and there had fallen into ruin. But the school had been impossible to miss. And someone seemed to be there, since an old 1970 Oldsmobile was parked out front.

After knocking on the thick wooden doors of the gallery, I waited. No response. I knocked again. Nothing. Then, walking over to the tall windows, I peeked in but saw no movement. Going back to the door, I banged once again. Still there was no movement.

In desperation I tried turning the handle of the door. It moved freely. As I pressed against it, the door began to open. Hesitantly I inched part of my body inside, just to see if anyone was around. I heard nothing, so I called out, waiting and listening. This time there was a rustling sound, but it seemed to be coming from above me. When I glanced up, I saw a foot dangling from a passageway leading from the loft. Surprised, I didn't know whether to stand where I was, retreat, or proceed into the foyer of the old structure. Standing dumbstruck, I remained in place, hoping the person above me would be friendly.

As he descended a primitive ladder bolted flat against the thick adobe wall, I jumped to explain, "I knocked," and swallowed hard. Taking a breath, I went on as fast as I could, adding, "I didn't hear you and took a chance on sticking my head in."

There was a response, but I couldn't tell if it was a "welcome" or not. The man's voice was muffled since his head was still in the tight confines of the attic. Feeling awkward, I blurted out, "Gwen told me to stop by," without knowing whether I was talking to Fernando or not. But I went on without stopping. "She told me to just introduce myself. No need to call."

The man took his time descending the old handmade ladder. As he carefully but slowly made his way down, more of his body came into view, the figure growing longer and longer. Not knowing who I was talking to, I grew more uncomfortable with each rung he negotiated.

Finally the man was standing in front of me. He was smiling, and for the first time I relaxed. I sensed I was not considered to be an intruder. Then, with a hand outstretched in greeting, the man took mine in his and introduced himself. He was Fernando. Immediately he led me through the foyer and into the main part of the gallery. I could easily see that it had once been a large classroom. Now, instead of chalkboards, desks, and rowdy kids, various artists' work filled the room. Since I had never much cared for school, I appreciated the transformation.

Because of my interest in art, I asked Fernando if I could see some of his work. At that, he gave me a tour of his studio. His paintings were exquisite. It was as if light were emanating from them instead of reflecting off of them. Even if direct light had been shining on them, it would have made no difference. They had a quality about them that cap-

tivated me and even seemed to embrace me. As I stood there, it was difficult for me to imagine how he could put on canvas what he did. Because I was so moved by his work, I asked, "How is it that you do this?"

Fernando was a little surprised by my question, but he quickly recovered and stated, "All my paintings are about music and light and movement. The subject matter really isn't that important. It's just an excuse to work with the light and music."

"Light and music," I repeated, adding, "Do you hear or see?"

"All the senses are put into play. It's not just visual, it's also audible and all the other senses—taste, smell, and touch, too."

"What do you mean?" I asked.

Fernando laughed, stating, "I don't try to analyze it too much. It isn't about intellect. It's something else. I've never found a word for it yet, but to me it's a sense of being."

After returning to the gallery, I told Fernando of my journey to find those who had seen God. Immediately he responded, "Who's She?" And we both laughed.

"You may be right," I chuckled again. Then I asked, "Have you seen God?"

"Every time I wake up," Fernando stated matter-of-factly.

Caught off guard, I sat for a minute without saying anything. Finally I asked, "Was there a moment when God came to you?"

"It didn't work that way for me. It was a process of growing, of seeing things differently," he said.

"When you say, 'Seeing things differently,' what do you mean?" I wondered aloud.

Fernando took his time to answer. Then, he explained, "I was born and raised a Catholic. With my life, things that happened along the way gradually made me question some things, like organized religion. And slowly, it happened—through reading, thinking, seeing, observing, and experiencing. And I realized that religion and God are two different things. Religion, like politics, is a business and has nothing to do with God."

"Do you think you were able to see more clearly because of your art?" I asked.

"It's very hard to talk about this," Fernando said softly, "but that may have had something to do with it. What we're talking about isn't a cut-and-dried type of thing." He paused, then asked me a question. "When you ask me these things, what are you seeing? Are you thinking of me as a Christian?"

"No, absolutely not," I quickly answered. To clarify, I added, "I'm just wondering if you've seen God. That's not asking if you're Christian."

Fernando seemed satisfied with that response. "The reason I ask is that I just went to visit my daughters over Thanksgiving. One of them is a born-again Christian like my former wife. And I had to go through a whole routine of trying to defend myself and my beliefs. I don't know whether I should have or not, but it ended up that way. It's just that sometimes Christians have a narrow point of view."

At that moment I understood what Fernando had been up against. I had been raised in a strict Baptist household myself.

Now, as I headed for home and remembered Fernando's story, my mind carried me even further back. As I crossed the Oklahoma state line, I couldn't fight away the memories. My parents had lived for the church. It had been the central focus of their lives. Because of their religious beliefs and the influence they had over me, I enrolled in a fundamentalist religious college in Chattanooga, Tennessee. Much to my surprise, it had been more rigid in doctrinal interpretation than even my hometown church had been. After graduation, I promised myself I'd never set foot on the campus again.

Shaking my mind away from that time in my life, I gazed trancelike at the road in front of me. Then I was thinking again, but this time it was not about Fernando. It was that I had an uncontrollable urge for coffee. With exits off the interstate few and far between, it was miles before I came upon one with a service station that was also a convenience store. There was no second thought about it. I flipped on my turn signal and took the ramp off the highway. After getting my drink, I was soon back on the interstate and again remembering Fernando.

I guess my thoughts of religion were still with me, because I was hearing Fernando talk about his religious upbringing. He had said, "I was brought up a very strict Catholic. I was taught God was an old man with white hair. Later I came to realize that God doesn't hang out a shingle. God's everywhere. We're all gods. Jesus said, 'You are God.'" Fernando's voice dropped, then he stopped to take a swallow of the coffee he had prepared earlier.

Finally he was ready to go on. "It isn't easy to describe to someone else what you feel and what you know. Everyone has his or her own experience and relationship with God. It's an individual relationship.

"I guess it's growing up," he said. "You're taught as a child by your parents or by your community all these things, then you start questioning and you start seeing things differently. It's just a slow change."

Fernando had piqued my interest because they could have been the very words I would have used had I been the one talking. Because I wanted to know what had helped influence his transition, I asked, "How did that change come about?"

It was obvious from his expression that he didn't really like talking about himself this much, but he went on to answer my question anyway. "I grew up in El Paso. I couldn't get away from there fast enough. That's why I joined the Navy. I wanted to go to

Japan, but when we got to Hawaii, they took me off the ship because I played basketball too well. So I spent my enlistment there, doing lay-ups for the Navy.

"When I was discharged in San Francisco, I took a bus straight to Seattle. I wanted to get as far away from Texas as possible. In Seattle, I worked for Boeing, but I knew I wanted to be an artist. And actually I was a graphic artist with Boeing, in the aerospace division. While I was there, I met an artist who did fine art. Boy, he was a real artist, I thought. Anyway, he taught art in his spare time. He was supposed to give me lessons, but it was more philosophy than lessons in drawing and technique.

"About a year or so later, I moved back to San Francisco and got a job as a commercial artist. It was the early Sixties and I was involved in the things that were going on in the city at the time. Hippies and such. I was part of the movement, but I skipped all the drugs.

"One day I put together a photo album of my paintings and took it to one of the galleries. So I opened it up and I asked the gallery owner, 'Can I show you my paintings?'

"At first he said, 'No!' But he glanced at the album as he was turning away from me. Then he turned back around and said, 'Wait a minute.' Later he drove me to my home and bought everything I had in the studio. I was hooked and gave up commercial art. And I've been painting ever since."

After hearing of the many things that had happened to him, such as the breakup of his marriage, his giving up his commercial art career in San Francisco, his loading up everything he owned in his 1970 Oldsmobile and heading for New Mexico, I asked how he came to where he was in his relationship with God.

"I had an agent when I was working with a gallery in San Francisco," Fernando explained, "and we talked and talked. At that time I was very much in love with Jesus. Not in the church sense. Anyway, we talked about that.

"One day my agent invited me to her home. On her piano was a picture of an Indian master. He was a guru." Fernando paused, finally adding, "I hate the word 'guru.' It always has a connotation of artificiality.

"Anyway," he continued, "she suggested I meet him. And sometime later I did. What he had to say agreed with me. It didn't negate any religion. His teachings simply said, 'What all the saints said is the same thing—go inside and see for yourself.' He also pointed out that after the personalities were gone, organized religion took over.'"

Fernando and I refilled our coffee cups. "It sounds as if this was a profound time for you. Were there other things going on in your life as well?" I pried.

He thought for a moment before answering. Finally, he added, "I had been divorced by then. My wife had taken the kids and moved back to Tennessee, where she was from."

There was Tennessee again. But I didn't allow myself to start recalling what my life had been like when I lived in Chattanooga. Instead, I turned to Fernando and asked, "What about your move to New Mexico?"

He settled back in his chair, glancing up at the ceiling and then over at me. Finally, he answered, saying, "My niece, who lives here in New Mexico, is like a little sister to me. I'm sixty-one and she's only a few years younger. She and I have always been close, and she knew how things were for me. So she called one day and asked, 'Why don't you come visit me?'"

"So I did. While I was here she brought me to San Acacia because she knew about the old school and she knew the family who owned it. After some talk, the owners and I worked out a deal where I'd fix it up in exchange for living here and being able to use part of it for a studio. And that was that. I sold everything. Put whatever would fit in my car and that's what I brought. I came and moved in. So now I've been here for four years."

"But this is sort of like a monastery," I said, "and you're here all alone. Don't you get lonely?"

"What is there to be lonely about? God's here," he said, adding, "God is with you every second. That's why I say, 'Pay attention. Somebody's with you all the time.' You can't stop being with God."

"How do you know?" I asked.

With that, Fernando leaned close to me and said, "You asked me earlier if I had seen God. Yes! Every day I look outside the window and there's God. Everywhere."

"A lot of people would argue with you because of the way things in the world have gotten," I said. "Look around. It's crazy."

Fernando raised his hand and made a sweeping motion as he responded. "We're scattered. We're not paying attention. All the things in front of us keep us from being what we're supposed to be. We're so fragmented. And we all keep seeing these things when we think of ourselves. We let things get in the way of the message from God. He's trying to tell us something."

"What is that?" I quickly asked. "What is the message?"

"Love and respect," he said, adding, "and pay attention!"

"And what do you pay attention to?"

Fernando smiled. "Don't ask questions. Just pay attention."

"To what?" I pressed.

Fernando stayed patient with me, adding, "You meditate. You close your eyes and you meditate. Stop thinking about the world. And if you're truly seeking your own special relationship with what you're trying to call the Almighty or the divine, then it'll find you. But you have to go inside and see for yourself. Don't take anybody's word for it."

Now, as I made my way across the country, Fernando's words kept coming back to me. When I had asked him what respect was, he told me that respect was not about judging.

"What is love?" I had asked.

"Love is light," he had responded, but did not elaborate. Then he pointed out that it was not for him to tell anybody anything.

There had been at least one thing Fernando had said that I knew was the truth. It was that everybody had to develop his or her own relationship with the divine. The way to do that was to pay attention. With that I agreed.

Still, I wondered what to pay attention to. Had I paid attention when I turned east instead of continuing west after I left Gwen's? Here I was about to go into Arkansas wondering if I had made the right decision back there in Albuquerque. Fernando would say that I wasn't respecting myself if I was now judging what I had done two days earlier.

"Stop it!" I told myself. "Just pay attention."

The road seemed never to end. And on I went. Occasionally I tried to take my mind off all I had experienced by turning on the radio. Switching from station to station, I just couldn't find anything that was worth listening to. Finally I turned it off and went back to my recollections. In my mind I heard Fernando's words, then mine, and every once in a while I'd internally argue about this or that. This went on for hours at a time.

Just as I was nearing Nashville, my thoughts changed altogether. I was actually thinking about the college I had attended in Chattanooga. Immediately I fought the memories away. That had been a long time ago, and I had no desire to dwell on those

days at college. But Chattanooga! That was a different story altogether. It was where I had met my wife. She and I had started our family there with the birth of our daughter. It was where I had begun my career in journalism. As I recalled living there, a warm feeling came over me, and I smiled to myself.

"Pay attention!"

The words came at me out of nowhere. They seemed audible, but I knew they were only a thought. And I wondered why they would ring out as they did. For a while I tried to pay attention, but I didn't know what I was paying attention to. So I gazed off into the distance as I paced my speed to that of the traffic around me. I'd at least pay attention to that. I certainly didn't want a speeding ticket.

Then, up ahead, I saw the road sign signaling the I-40 and I-24 interchange. Then I saw CHATTANOOGA spelled out in big letters. "This is where I'd get on to I-24, if I was going there," I told myself. Immediately my mind began to wander. It would be fun to visit the old town again, I thought. Someday, I went on, I'm going back to see my old friends at the newspaper where I started out in photography. And I'd drop in on Bob Sherrill, a photographer with whom I had worked. Then I laughed, "Yes, someday."

"Pay attention!"

There it was again. The thought was back.

Then, just as I was about to pass the exit, I swerved to take it. I didn't know why, but I did. It was the last thing in the world I would have ever considered doing. I was on my way home. But not any longer. I was making a detour. I was on my way to Chattanooga.

9. BOB SHERRILL

CHATTANOOGA, TENNESSEE

"Madonna!"

That was it. The muscular young fireman had said enough. The name of the street was all that was needed for direction. But he hesitated from divulging more. A look of skepticism quickly replaced his genial smile. His eyes suggested a rising suspicion. Neither of us said anything, each waiting for the other to speak first. With his foot propping open the steel door connecting the lobby to the firehouse, he seemed to grow impatient. We looked at each other. I said nothing, while he was hedging in an obvious attempt at trying to protect an old friend of the department and an icon of the community from any unwanted intrusion. He was waiting for an explanation as to why I was interested in the venerable elder of East Ridge.

Embarrassed by my lack of insight, I tried to fill the chasm my silence had created. Before finishing my first sentence, he was eager to interrupt me with directions to

Bob Sherrill's house. My body relaxed with an audible sigh of relief. It was good news to learn that Bob was still going strong after all the years since we worked together as photographers for the *Chattanooga Times*. And, of all things, he still lived on Madonna Avenue.

Taking pictures for the East Ridge Fire Department had always been an integral part of Bob Sherrill's life. Although he worked a forty-hour week for the newspaper, he had made time in his schedule to help the department any way he could. With that knowledge in the back of my mind, I knew that would be the one place I could go to find out how Bob was and get directions to his place. After overcoming the initial awkwardness my request had generated, the fireman stated somberly, "He can't take pictures anymore. Doesn't get out too much. Can't drive. If somebody picks him up, he'll come by once in a while. Why, he's in his eighties. Still lives in the same place. Alone. Well, he's got his cats. Don't know how many. Don't think he does, either. His sight isn't what it used to be."

In maneuvering the maze of streets of the small town, memories came rushing back. It was to this very village next to Chattanooga that I brought my new bride to live after our wedding in Indiana. We rented a three-room house from another fellow photographer and set up housekeeping. It was also here during that same time that I met, and came to appreciate, Bob Sherrill. He was fifty-five years old then, in the year 1967.

Turning onto Madonna was like going back in time. Everything seemed as it was in the Sixties. The houses were in the same perpetual state of repair and disrepair. Peeling paint flaked from one; the home next door stood neatly trimmed. Some lawns were well manicured; others cried out for the attention of reluctant residents. A car, long past its prime, rested in a graveled driveway. Next door, a brand-new one sparkled fresh from the dealership. Thirty years may be a lifetime somewhere else in America, but here it was only yesterday.

One. Two. Three. Four. Then there was Bob's house on the left. His home blended in nicely with the others on the block. It was, however, a little more tired than his neighbors'. A Seventies Chevrolet station wagon was right where it had been parked years earlier. The tires had gone flat, not from wear but from lack of use. Although it was protected by a simple sagging aluminum carport with decorative wrought-iron columns, the car was covered with dust and dirt that had built up over time. The used-to-be-white paint had turned brackish with mold and mildew, causing it to become as rough as sandpaper. Bob had always taken great pride in his car and had pampered it with as much care as he had his vintage wooden Chris-Craft boat. The cruiser had been sold long ago. The car should have been, too, yet the relic of better times sat there like a monument to longevity. I imagined it a shrine as I walked past it on my way to the front door.

I knocked. As I waited, several frightened cats darted from under a rusting chair and a half-beaten-down cardboard box on the small porch. Scrambling about for a new hiding place they couldn't find quickly enough, they leaped with all their might out into the yard. Crisscrossing back and forth in panic, they screamed like refugees from the pound's incinerator and then disappeared from sight. The cats were not alone in their fear. I was a little frightened too. They had made sure of that, and all the hairs on my body standing straight up proved it. Regaining some composure, I leaned forward to see if I could detect any sound from within the house. But there was nothing, not even a board creaking.

Three more knocks. And, "Bob! You home?" Then the wait. Glancing about, first at the panes of the door, then to the darkened lace curtains on the other side, out to the tall grass in the front yard, up and down the street beyond, and finally at the old station wagon, I turned back to the door. When I did, I jumped at the sight. There had been no sound, but there was a little white-haired man, slightly bent with age, peeping through the glass.

"Bob!" I said out of a shocked reflex. "It's me," and I called out my name twice.

Now there was a crack as the door opened a few inches. He peered out, his vision having faded, trying to figure out who it was. I gave my name again, and his face immediately lit up. He remembered now. The door swung open wide, and he was at my side with one step. It was indeed Bob Sherrill, wearing his trademark double-knit sweater, plain shirt, and heavy, baggy cotton slacks. He looked no different than he had three decades earlier. The only thing missing was his trusted black-and-chrome camera. If it had been draped over his shoulders, I was sure he would have been whispering curses just under his breath and gently pushing me out of the way in a huff to get to his assignment. He never could stand to be late, even if he had been shafted with the worst possible kind of shooting job.

"I can't believe it!" he said, absolute shock written all over his face. After shaking hands up and down, over and over again, he said, "Can you believe, I'm eighty-seven!"

"You're eighty-seven," I said, truly amazed, although I knew he had to be close to that age. Then I added, "You don't look a bit different than the last time I saw you."

"I don't feel any different much. Got a bad knee that's hard to get around. I lost my eyesight. I can't see anymore."

His next words came suddenly, catching me off guard. They sort of hurt my feelings

a little, since it was I who was visiting him. But I let it pass with only a second thought about it.

"Whatever happened to Ken Touchton?" he asked, bringing up the name of a fellow photographer with whom we both had worked. Ken had been my closest friend through all the intervening years. "Do you hear from him anymore?"

I gave him an update. Hearing about Ken pleased him. When they had worked together, they had developed a close relationship, and Bob, the older, experienced photographer, had become a mentor to Ken, the young college student, the newcomer in need of a lot of encouragement in the unforgiving world of news gathering. Bob beamed upon learning of Ken's accomplishments. He didn't say it, but his smile gave him away. He was proud he had played a role in Ken's life.

Bob was now ready to move on with his questioning. "How did you happen to be in Chattanooga?" he asked.

After explaining I had been traveling around the country working on a project about God and was now on my way home, I told him I wanted to see him if I saw no one else in Chattanooga. He seemed very pleased. Then, turning the conversation back to him, I asked, "What are you up to?"

With a hint of sadness he said, "I'm not doing anything now," letting his words drop into a silence. Finally, after a long pause, he added, "Of course, I've been retired for quite a while."

Not thinking, he started retelling stories. Some I already knew. It had slipped his mind that I was there when some events had taken place. But I listened respectfully. I remembered as he talked. "I went to the *Times*. I left the *Free Press* after twenty-nine years and I worked at the *Times* the last eleven years before retiring. You worked at the *Times*, too," he stated without waiting for a response.

"Well, let's see! Charlie Pennington's passed away. Mrs. Homberg's retired. John Popham retired and he went to law school and got a law degree. George Baker died about three months ago. I went to his funeral. Mrs. Spence passed away and also Roy McDonald. He's no longer living. Charlie Quenton, E. T. Bales passed away."

After going through his mental list of those who had died, he said, his voice lowered, "Eleanor, my wife, you know. She passed away and also my daughter who lived in Huntsville passed away. I have two granddaughters who live in Alabama, and that's the only kinfolk I have. I don't have anybody here."

Eleanor was gone. No more Bob and Eleanor. It was hard to imagine one without the other. They went together like peanut butter and jelly. Bob was the quiet one, reserved, even shy. He avoided the limelight. He stood back, alert and listening but saying little. Yet with his unbelievably dry wit, he was quite funny. One had to pay attention to what he said, then think about it. And all of a sudden, his comments would hit and there would be no holding back the laughter that would erupt.

Eleanor was Bob's opposite. She was a charmer, but she always spoke her mind and said it like it was. She was spontaneous, outgoing, lively. Any room or gathering she entered, she was immediately the center of attention. And she liked it that way. Wanted it that way. Worked at it being that way. Wherever she went, she left a trail of laughter that was contagious. And she had a zest for life unequal to anyone's. Her attire and even her makeup flaunted it. She lived the whirlwind. Actually she was the whirlwind.

They were an extraordinary couple, like George Burns and Gracie Allen, but Bob didn't stop to dwell on that or on Eleanor's passing. Showing no self-pity over being alone, without his wife, his daughter, or any other close family member, he said, much to my surprise, "You know the building we worked in? They tore it down," and he shut his eyes so tight, his thick bushy white eyebrows almost touched his checks. Then, opening his eyes so wide his brows lifted his look into an expression of stark alarm, he shouted as best he could with the controlled cool manner for which he was known, "They tore the whole thing down!"

Standing side by side in silence, both with our hands in our pockets and staring out toward the street, we must have given drive-bys grist for conversation. Here we were, two men looking out into nowhere and not speaking to each other. Finally, out of concern, I asked what he did about his meals if he had trouble seeing.

"Oh, sometimes somebody'll come over and take me to the grocery store. I get things I can heat up. I do pretty good. I get out some . . . when I can get someone to take me. It's not so bad. I make out.

"I've had to stop watching TV. Can't see it. So I listen to the radio all the time."

There were no regrets in his voice. He showed no outward remorse. He begged no sympathy. Although he stood no higher than my shoulders, I saw him as a towering giant.

"Something I want to show you," he said. Slipping through the partially open door, he quickly disappeared into the darkness of his living room. All the blinds, shades, and curtains had been pulled closed. He had no need of light. So it was impossible to make out what he was doing. Within minutes he was back. In his hands he held a shipping box about the size of one that would be used to mail a coffee-table book.

He said, "That's the plaque. Slip it out of the plastic. They . . ." His voice fell, his sentence never completed. "You can read it, if you want to," he said. So I did.

The plaque, a resolution from the City of East Ridge, read, "Resolution. Honoring

Bob Sherrill for his outstanding dedication and service to Hamilton County, Tennessee, and its citizens. Whereas Bob Sherrill was born on November 9, 1910, and whereas Bob Sherrill has made the City of East Ridge, Hamilton County, and the State of Tennessee a better place in which to live because of his outstanding dedication and service to his community."

As I read it, I could see with a glance now and then that a big smile had spread across his face. It was a tribute well deserved and I said so. Then I added, "That's beautiful, Bob."

"Yeah. That's full of bull, all right. It's nice, but they waited too long. They waited until I was so old that I couldn't use it. It won't do me much good, but it's nice, I guess. If I was younger, I could kind of promote myself and maybe it would have helped my career. Now I can't even see to read what it says. That's a funny thing! After you get old and harmless to everybody, they give you this plaque and do nice things for you. I could have used that when I was . . . twenty-five or thirty years ago. But now . . . it's funny how those things work out. It's nice, though. I like all that flattery on there."

I couldn't tell if his dry wit was coming out or whether, although uncharacteristic of him, it was sarcasm. Nevertheless, we both chuckled.

When I handed Bob his plaque, he took it and stroked the edges of the frame several times. He could say what he wanted to about it, but his care with it clearly revealed it was one of his prized possessions. Together we worked it back into its plastic sleeve and then back into the elongated box. As we played with it, trying to find its exact fit, I said, "Well, Bob, I'm working on this project. I'm looking for people who feel like they have had an encounter with God." I stopped, my mind on the plaque, which wouldn't go back into its groove. Then it hit me. Suddenly, my thoughts raced about, remembering some of the tales he used to tell about his newspaper days during World War II. Bob may have had an experience like that for which I was searching.

With the plaque now secure, I repeated, "I'm looking for people who feel like they've had an encounter with God. Have you ever had something like that happen to you?"

Shaking his head, he said, "I haven't thought about it right offhand."

His words were so matter-of-fact, I sensed his dry wit was coming out. Trying not to let him know that I thought what he said was humorous, I added, "So you haven't seen God?"

Bob's hand went to his head, and with a quick stroke he pushed his fingers through what hair he had left. He was grabbing for what to say. Then he started, "Well, I . . . I have—no, I haven't seen—" He went quiet. Just as suddenly as he did that, he blurted out, "I can't see anything. I'm blind!"

His immediate laughter shocked me. I hadn't been expecting the outburst. And he continued to laugh, so I joined it. He was funny and the way he so bluntly said, "I'm blind," was funny, too. I found it refreshing that he could joke and laugh. Even about that.

"So," I said, "if God showed up, you wouldn't know it?"

"Well, He might have. I don't know. Can't see! I'm blind," Bob proclaimed. Then he thought for a minute before going on to add, "He . . . He works in mysterious ways . . . from what they tell me."

I was about ready to launch into another question, but he stopped me. "About God . . . you ought to go over and see Lee Roberson." Bob chuckled.

He had made a wry joke, and I caught it. Bob and I both knew that some speak of the charismatic Roberson—the former pastor of a local church and founder of a Baptist college—and God in the same breath. That was only part of what Bob's humor was about. He was needling me. It was his way of letting me know he'd never forget I had graduated from the ultra-fundamentalist college that Roberson, a white-haired Moses-like figure, had started in the 1940s. What's more, Bob surmised I had no plans of making that visit while in the area. So he pushed all the more.

"You ought to go over to Tennessee Temple and look the place over. Have lunch with Dr. Roberson." After a short pause, he added without remorse, "I think it's about to fall apart. It's nothing to what it used to be. They hardly have any students anymore. I don't think it's as big as it was."

His thoughts then turned to recollection. "I haven't been around that school in a while. I went there on an assignment when I was still working for the paper. It was the school's thirtieth anniversary and they had a big crowd for that. And do you know Dr. Roberson remembered me. He remembered all the newspaper people by name. He was good at that. So he introduced me by name to the audience. Kind of embarrassed me. Then he told the audience . . . it was the honest truth . . . I went out there and took a picture of him when he announced in 1946 that he was going to form that college. I think he started out with about five students and it grew from there. And do you know the last time I saw him he was still wearing the same kind of double-breasted blue suit. I wonder if it could be the same one after all those years." Bob chuckled.

I laughed, too, and asked, "Did he have the same red leather Bible? With gold-edged pages?"

But Bob didn't let on that he had heard me. He was thinking about the past. Catching his breath, he added, "I did some movie work for 'em back in those days." Then he abruptly stopped for a minute. In the pause I could swear I heard him gritting his teeth. In a slightly agitated tone, he picked back up where he'd left off. "I never did get my money and I had a hard time even getting the money for the film. I finally gave up. I said,

'If y'all just give me the money for the cost of the film then . . .' and of course they used the movie and sent it around to different places and tried to encourage students to come to school there. And I said, 'If you'll just give me the money for my expenses, I'll forget everything else.' I got my money, it was just for what I paid for the film, but that still took some time."

He pressed his lips tight. With his face being so round anyway, his expression exaggerated it's shape even more so. Then he started again. "If they saw a chance to get something for nothing, that's what they do! Tennessee Temple had a way of using people."

Now wound up, he was not ready to stop, "They had some students working down at the newspaper office at night. If there was anything on the desk . . . like a desk set or a picture in a frame, it would disappear. They stole everything that was down there, and that's why they finally ran them off. That's the honest truth. I'm not saying that all the students are crooks, but they sure had some down there that would take anything that wasn't nailed down."

"I don't guess we have to worry about any of that anymore," I said, putting my arm around his shoulder. "Neither one of us," I added with a hearty laugh. "We're gone from the paper. And I'm out of the school." He nodded in agreement.

Just as I was about to say my good-byes, he stiffened. At first I thought it was a reaction to my heartfelt affection. After all, my arm was still resting across his back. But that wasn't it. He had lapsed into a memory.

"Your writing project!" he said. "I never told anybody."

Not able to imagine what he was going to say next, but eager to hear, I waited anxiously. The wait was short.

"I happened to think about something," he said. "It happened about fifty years ago. It was up on Daisy Mountain, above Soddy Daisy. That's out Highway 27, north of Chattanooga."

I knew where Daisy Mountain was. One of the very first assignments I was given, just a day after starting to work for the *Free Press,* was on Daisy Mountain. No one else would take it, but I didn't know that. Nor did I know why.

The assignment had been a simple one. Take pictures of a bridal shower. Simple enough. No great creative skills were required for that. Just bunch the people side by side in front of the gifts and "mow" them down, as we called that kind of lineup in the newspaper business. Navigating the treacherous mountain roads and finding the place was the first real challenge. But the most painful lesson and the more difficult feat was to learn how to deal with the principal of the residence where the shower was being held. One encounter would have been enough, but three times was to be the charm.

Upon my arrival, I was taken by the chain-link fence that surrounded the house. I let my initial surprise fade as I pushed open the sturdy gate and briskly walked, with great youthful confidence, toward the front door. After all, I was a newsman. Although only nineteen, I thought myself "somebody." A professional. Hotshot news photographer.

All too soon my self-confidence evaporated. Instead of being met by appreciative subjects, I was facing two attack dogs. In a flash, the two high-strung Doberman pinschers, boiling in rage, were charging me.

"Now, now," came a calm voice I only slightly heard from what seemed a very distant place. It was the lady of the house. At the commotion she had come to the door and was now standing on the stoop.

The dogs froze. Their growls continued, however. Trying to breathe, I caught a gulp of air and then started panting like the dogs I was facing. I knew they were not through with me yet. Their black eyes told me that as they stared me down.

Still, I couldn't move. I may as well have been made of stone. I was a statue. Nothing about me worked. My legs wouldn't move. My feet felt as if they were blocked in cement. To make matters worse, the kindly lady said, "Come on in. They won't hurt you. They're just all bark, no bite."

With my spine now turned to jelly and my fear surfacing in huge goose bumps that had raised every hair on my body, I tried to take a step. When I did, the dogs bowed their backs even more and bent their legs like runners readying for the gun at the start of a race. I stopped quickly.

"They won't bother you, honey," said the woman, who I was now beginning to really dislike. "Just ignore them."

Keeping my eye on the one closest to me, I started to walk. That was a mistake, because the other one jumped for my leg. Quickly, as fast as I possibly could, I turned my gaze on it. It stopped short, but the other one tore at me. I yelled as I flashed my eyes on it. It fell back. But then the other one was back.

"Just pay them no attention," the woman said sweetly. "They won't hurt you. Come on in."

I couldn't talk to her. My head was turning back and forth so fast. Eye on one, then on the other. One would stop and the other would make like it was going to attack. But I did reach the steps without getting bitten and without any help from the woman. Once through the door, I thought I was going to fall into a dead heap. I was exhausted. Sweat poured from my forehead and from my armpits. My shirt was soaked. If that was not enough to endure, every lady in the room roared in laughter. One who was bolder than the others spoke up and said, "Oh, sweetie pie, they know you're afraid of them. That's why they do that. Just don't be so scared no more."

After a cool drink of mountain well water, I calmed myself enough to line everyone up and take a picture. Then another. One more still, for good measure.

Upon leaving I demanded in the kindest way possible for someone to pin the dogs so I could leave. With that done, I raced down the mountain and asked God to spare me any trip back up. Ever!

That was not to be. My flash had not been synchronized with the shutter. I had exposed only half of the frame. Even the "one for good measure" was ruined and I was ordered to reschedule the picture. Having done that, making sure it was understood that the dogs had to be locked away, I drove to the mountain again the next week. All the ladies had reconverged to fake the shower. I lined the women up and retook the shot. It was over.

But it wasn't. Something happened that to this day I cannot explain. There was nothing, absolutely nothing, on the film. The chief photographer was furious. And no, he would not allow anyone else to go back. I had to do it. And I did. A week to the day from the second visit I was lining the same women up. False gifts had been wrapped and the trimmings of a shower rehung. With no confidence left, but ever so thankful there were no dogs to deal with, I attempted to get any image on film that I could. I wanted my humiliation to be over. Finally, it was. I had succeeded, and three weeks after my first visit, the picture ran in the paper. I swore I would never go back up that mountain, even if I had to quit the paper to avoid it. I never did return. For work or, God forbid, pleasure.

"Oh, Daisy Mountain," I whispered to Bob.

"Yeah. I had an assignment up that way one time about fifty years ago. I was on my way back and I heard a call on the police radio—always had one in my car in those days—saying they had a shooting up on Daisy Mountain. Well, they'd been having some family feuds up there and some of the people had been shot at and some had tried to burn their houses down, different things. Had quite a bit of trouble.

"So I thought, well, I'd never been on the mountain before, and I was right there at the road that goes up the mountain on my way back to the office. So I thought, 'I'll drive up there and see what's going on.'

"It was in September, I guess, and was already dark. Never been up there before. Just as I got up to the top of the mountain, I happened to look across and I saw a body lying facedown in this yard . . . little old shack of a house with the light shining out the window, and so I stopped and just looked over there a few minutes. There wasn't a thing moving.

"So I went on up the road and turned around, and I sat there in the car a few minutes 'cause I was going to wait for the county police to arrive and then I—I'd, you know, go over there with them. Well . . . everything was quiet and I didn't hear a sound. So I just sat there a few minutes. I thought, 'Well, I'm going to walk over there.'

"I had a four-by-five Speed Graphic camera back in those days. I got the Graphic in my hand and flashed a bulb, using flashbulbs then, I took a picture of that, uh, body lying there on the ground. It was a bloody mess. He looked as if he'd been shot with a shotgun, then hit in the back of the head with an ax. He was good and dead. That was the person they'd had the call on. As soon as that flashbulb went off, three men came out the door. One had a bloody ax in his hand, other'n had a shotgun and the older man with him. Apparently they'd been drinking moonshine, and they just got real mad, you know, wanted to know who I was, what I was doing there, and all that stuff.

"I was trying to explain it. Well, they got to arguing between themselves. They wanted to finish me off right there on the spot! And that's when the Lord was with me." Bob's voice quivered as he relived every detail.

With almost a shout, he stated, "I'll tell you the honest truth. I know how . . . how it feels, you know, going on your way to the electric chair.

"I was standing . . ." He paused, then went on. "The Lord was there! And these men were all grouped around. The older man thought it'd be better to take me to the nearby woods and dispose of me." Bob visibly trembled. His words fell out of his mouth, one after the other, in sentences that were now running together from his excitement. "And if they had done that, why then nobody would, ah, they wouldn't find me right away and associate me with that crime they just committed. And, anyway, they's arguing about it and so I didn't know what to do 'cause I knew if I ran, they'd shoot at me because that's what happened to . . . this dead fella. Fella's name was Boots Parker.

"So I was standing there and 'bout that time . . . Coulter's had a funeral home . . . Bob Coulter was in one of their ambulances all by himself. He had a radio in there and had heard the same call I did and he came up the mountain and saw that I was in trouble and he went right over there and started talking to these fellas. He told them that I was all right, that he'd known me a long time and I'd do whatever I said I'd do . . . trying to help me out. He saved my life.

"He arrived there in just a matter of minutes, I'd say seconds. Anyway while he was talking with those men, the county police car came up and they had two men in it.

They jumped out and one grabbed the shotgun, and the other'n took the ax away from these fellas.

"While the police were talking to 'em, I just backed off in the darkness, got in my car, coasted down the hill, and didn't even turn my lights on . . . till I got out of sight. Way down the hill I turned my lights on and started the engine.

"I came back to the office. I never told a soul I'd been there. And all these years I'd never mentioned that to anybody. But I did, eventually, develop the film and made a print of that picture. But I didn't tell anybody 'cause those fellas had families and they'd 'ave come after me. Hunted me down. And that's when the Lord was with me. That's about as close as I think He ever came to me."

With alarm still plaguing him after all the years, he sighed, "That scared the daylights out of me. It really did. I didn't think I was coming back. That's the honest truth 'cause the way these fellas were, you know, and they just killed this fella lying there on the ground. And I knew they wouldn't hesitate to kill somebody again 'cause they'd been . . . apparently drinking and were in a bad mood. They were real mad.

"I guess that is as close as I've ever had anything happen. I used to respond to all the fire alarms and I've been in buildings on fire. I remember starting into a kitchen when the ceiling fell in just before I stepped in there. I've been in some close places, but nothing like that place where I felt like I was going to be murdered.

"If that guy had not been listening to his radio or if he'd been somewhere other than the bottom of the mountain when he heard the call, any other place and he'd not gotten there in time, that's how close it was.

"Bob Coulter said they had buried some of those people that lived on the mountain and that there was no questioning about it, they would've gotten me 'cause they wouldn't hesitate to kill somebody. He said, 'Those people are mean up there.'"

Bob then proclaimed, "That was pretty close. Everybody's going to die someday, but I just wasn't expecting that it might be that night. I had divine help!"

The mountain! We both knew it all too well. And it was the one place neither of us could be made to return to. Yet for all the years, it was locked in our memories. It always would be. Although for both of us there had been a little heavenly help, his had been a lot more dramatic. I had merely escaped pain. He had been spared his life.

As I was leaving, Bob called out, "Tell Touchton to come by and see me if he's in the area." Then, laughing, he teased, "That thing about God," he repeated, "better go by Temple. Have lunch with Dr. Roberson."

"Think he'd pay?" I yelled back and waved, forgetting he couldn't see me.

After getting into the truck, I sat for a minute to make sure he got back inside okay.

Slowly he pulled open the storm door and disappeared behind it as it closed. After starting the engine and dropping the gear into drive, I muttered to myself, "No way! Never going back to Temple." Four years of classes and mandatory church attendance five or six days a week had been enough. Besides, there was not one sermon out of the thousand or so I'd been forced to sit through that I could even remember. But Bob's story! It would be with me forever.

10. PETER FREED

CHATTANOOGA, TENNESSEE

It was high noon and I was hungry. But I wasn't about to take Bob Sherrill's advice. There was no way I was going to drive through the campus of Tennessee Temple. Instead, I drove straight for the old eating joint that some of my classmates and I frequented during our undergraduate days at the Baptist college. And to my surprise, the place had not changed much over the years. Just as it was then, the little restaurant was jam-packed at this time of day. And the lunch crowd was impatient. Very impatient. Waitresses hustled as fast as they could move, filling orders, taking new ones, and struggling to refill empty worn porcelain coffee cups and giant plastic iced tea glasses. They were way behind and sweating it. The blue-collars were hungry and demanding. They wanted service. For them "now" was too slow. And they were loud.

Indeed, the noise was so great that everything in the place seemed to vibrate, even the masonry walls and the imitation oil paintings hanging on them. But that changed when he walked through the front door. By the time he had pushed his way through the line of customers blocking the entrance as they waited to pay, the roaring chatter slowly died to whispers with every step he took. As he pressed deeper into the eatery in search of an available table or empty stool at the counter, he left a trail of eyes following his every move. Mechanics, truck drivers, parts men, and delivery women gazed at him suspiciously. With his tailored suit, coordinated tie, stiffly starched pure white dress shirt, and shoes polished to a mirror shine, he more than stood out in the crowd.

It wasn't that he just didn't fit in, he was different. Everyone not only sensed it, all knew it. It went far beyond his impeccable dress. There was something unexplainable about him. Like all the others around me, I joined into the neck-craning and stared, too. I just couldn't help it. I had been taught better, but that didn't stop me.

As parties rose to leave, new ones rushed to take their places even before the dirty dishes could be cleared from the greasy tables and the crumb-riddled chairs could be wiped clean. Finally, in desperation, he propped against a paint-faded pole to wait for a seat. He glanced about the smoke-filled dining room, hoping to determine the next group's planned departure before any other would-be takers caught the movement. His eyes, ever so alert, rolled slowly over the bustle. Then he saw me.

I looked away as fast as I could, praying he had not noticed my lack of manners in watching him. But it was not me he was interested in, nor did he seem to care that I was engrossed in his actions. He saw that I was at a table for four and that there was just one of me. Three chairs remained unfilled. His eager expression asked the question without his uttering a word. Although embarrassed at having been so easily caught, I nodded a yes, and he went limp with relief. Dazed at my own behavior, I avoided making any further eye contact with him, but I heard him sigh. Then, his voice rising above the now somewhat muted commotion, he said, "Thanks." After a few more seconds, making a real effort to strike up a conversation, he added, "It's just impossible in here today. They'll fight you over a table. Thought I'd never get a seat."

He and I laughed, and I finally looked up. I could clearly see that he was holding no resentment over my earlier blatant curiosity. Relieved, but still feeling a touch of guilt, I eased out of my shell and said, "I got in just in time. Before the storm. Guess I was lucky. Even got to order"—I shrugged—"after a while." I paused for a breath, then added, "But the food's not here yet."

"You're in. That's what counts at this joint," he laughed. "By the way, name's Peter." He stopped, waiting to see if we were going to exchange names.

"Steve," I returned, getting my name out just as the waitress arrived with my long-anticipated coffee. Beginning to pour, she quit at half a cup and slammed the pot down hard on the table. I looked up and her mouth was wide open. She seemed about to say something, but whatever it was just wouldn't clear her throat. Maybe she's choking, I thought and quickly glanced at Peter then back up at her.

"You choking?" I shouted, trying to be loud enough for her to understand me but not too loud for others around us to hear. I didn't want to create a small panic.

She shook her head no. Then, with her eyes targeted on Peter, she blurted out, "You a movie star or something?"

Somewhat shaken, Peter responded, "Or something. That'd be more like it." He smiled sheepishly. Nearby customers, most of whom had never taken their gaze off him, leaned closer to hear more of his explanation. But he said nothing else.

The waitress wouldn't leave it alone, however. Determined to get what she wanted, she demanded, "You're a movie star, ain't you? I've seen you on TV. That's it, ain't it?"

Bowing to her pressure, Peter said, "Long time ago. Probably 'bout the time you were born."

"I knew it," she nearly screamed. "I knew it! You *are* a movie star." Then, unexpectedly, she whirled around toward the lunch counter and yelled so everyone in the entire place could hear her, "Scott! Scott! He *is* a movie star! I told you. I was right."

Peter raised his hand in protest, hoping to calm her, but the waitress was having none of it. She was in her element. To her, Peter may have been a movie star, but she was center stage and getting all the attention the hamburger heaven could muster.

Not content to let the moment die, she swung back around and, with hands on her hips, bent over to talk right into Peter's ear. "I knew it. I told Scott back there. He's the cook. Calls himself the chef. Anyways, he and I had it out. I told him you were a movie star. He said you were something else. 'No,' I said, 'a movie star.' And I know some things. It's like this. Ain't no man alive brave enough to come in here with makeup on less he's a movie star."

I looked at him and realized that she was right, as she continued on.

"And that's what I told Scott. What does he know, anyway? He's just a cook." She caught her breath but kept talking. "And he ain't a good one, at that. His food tastes funny. Don't eat it myself. Scared of it. And he takes too long to fix the sorry stuff. I just serve it and get chewed out for it being so late and cold when the customers finally get it. Hurts my tips, what tips I get, but what am I going to do? I just work here."

Both her hands were now pressed white on the table. She was crouching, but making no effort to leave or, even, to finish filling my cup. Sensing that something must be done, Peter pulled a menu from its holder and with an inviting gesture said, "Want to join us?"

She beamed and in mock argument whispered, "I can't. Want to get me fired! But if you got any spare parts . . . I'd quit and take them. I can act, you know." She inched closer to Peter, her face nearly against his, and with an overly flirtatious smile grinned to exaggeration.

The three of us laughed, without too much obvious insincerity coming from Peter's chuckle. He remained ever the gentleman. Then, with an understanding tone in his voice, he said, "I bet you can. You'd be terrific. But, you see, I'm no movie star and I hear it's hard to break in. That's a hard world." Ever so slyly he scooted his chair at an angle over toward her and smiled warmly, saying, "Right now, if you don't mind too much, it'd be great if I could just go ahead and order."

Muttering to herself, but loud enough for both of us to hear, she said, "Don't tell me you ain't no movie star. I got eyes." Then, with an edge of sourness to her words, she yielded, "Hey, what's the difference. Let me serve ya. What d'ya want?"

So taken aback by her apparent pain at what she had seen as a rebuke, Peter changed his expression. Trying to make amends, he tapped the menu a couple of times and made like he was going to order. He didn't. Instead, he told her, "You really have me pegged wrong. I'm not a movie star. I was in television a long time ago. I do training films now. All I do is stand up in front of a camera and talk into it. It's no big deal. But I'm no star. Hollywood doesn't know me from beans, and that's all there is to it. Forgive me if you've mistaken me for something I'm not."

"Okay," she said, her expression softening, "so you're not a movie star. Let me get your order so you won't starve to death."

On leaving, her prance said it all. She was satisfied she had not only waited on a movie star, she had talked to one as well. And it had made her day, probably several of them.

Peering at me, he didn't wait for questions I might have for him. "I knew I shouldn't have come in here like this. But, you see, I had no choice. I was hungry and I didn't have time to get out of character, if you will. I just didn't think. I'm so used to makeup. Doing stand-ups. You know . . ." He hesitated, then corrected himself. "Maybe you don't know," he apologized, "but doing video you've got to have make-up or the camera . . . video is a hard taskmaster. You play by its rules . . . For television, you wear makeup. Remember what not wearing it did to Richard Nixon? He lost the election. Kennedy was media up. Or his advisors were and he listened to them. He won. I'm not saying television was the only thing going for him, but it was pivotal."

"I've heard about the makeup thing," I said. "And I know just a little about television. Flirted with it a while back. But I learned too much too fast. There's a difference in being on television and being in television. Being in television is vicious. Those in it will eat you alive, if you let them."

Interrupting me, Peter jumped in. "News directors. General managers. And you got to watch out for your peers. They'll do you in, too. But the consultants are the worst. They waltz in with a lot of talk and nothing to lose. They stir the stew, then turn it over to the administrators . . . the cannibals. I have former coworkers who've had their lives just about destroyed. Good people. Wonderful human beings. And the only thing they can do is just get out of it altogether.

"And sometimes consultants won't stop with the talent. They've been known to take down a station with their cockamamy advice."

Then, with a shake of the head, he added with a deep sadness, "Look where television is today. It had so much potential for good. That's one of the reasons I got into it in the beginning. It could do such wonderful things. Maybe I stayed longer than I should have. May have had more than a little ego tied up in there somewhere. But look at what it's become! I know I got out for the right reason. I realized I couldn't change it for the better, to do something worthwhile, and I couldn't continue working with those getting into it. Money and the desire for fame attracts some very interesting people. And for companies, it got to be that it was only the bottom line that counted. They pushed out the old-timers. The ones with heart. The consultants probably had something to do with that, too. Wanted pretty faces. Empty heads. No soul. I just couldn't take it any longer, so I walked. And here I am."

"You know what I found back there?" the waitress said, as she rushed up to bring our conversation to an instant halt. Not waiting for an answer, or even an acknowledgment of her presence, she cried out, "Food! I told Scott I had a movie star out here and he had to get out the order but fast. And he did. Got both meals at the same time. How do you like that, Mr. Movie Star?"

Without waiting for a response, she lowered his meal down in front of Peter with exquisite finesse. Mine she slid in front of me without even a glance in my direction. It was Peter she wanted to impress and did everything in her power to do so.

"What's more," she joked, "there's something odd here. You guys both ordered the same thing. Ain't that something! But it's cool," and she flitted away as quickly as she had arrived.

During the coarse of the meal, Peter was constantly getting refills on his tea, whether he needed them or not. Once in a while I had my coffee refreshed, always without even a word from our star-struck waitress and wannabe actress.

After she had delivered our food, Peter and I studied our dishes. Our orders were identical. Reacting first, I mused, "Hamburger man, too, I see."

He and I laughed. Then I asked, "How's it that you picked this place out of all you could've gone to?"

Peter didn't hesitate in answering. "Habit! When I was in college here, this is about the only place I ate—outside of the school's cafeteria. Now when I come back to Chattanooga, I like to stop in. It was the only place then, and it's the only place now, for a good hamburger. And it brings back some good memories."

What he didn't know was that he could have been speaking for me. That was why I had ordered the hamburger platter, just as he had. As we both smothered our burgers with catsup and mustard, I remembered those days so long ago.

Lost in thought, I barely heard him asking, "Do you come here often?"

Going for a bite with great anticipation, I took my time to answer. Stopping just short of chomping down, I said, "Only every time I get back to Chattanooga. That's not very often, though," and I bit down. It was so good. I didn't want to have to say another word. I just wanted to eat . . . and think about eating my long overdue burger. The taste seemed not to have changed any over the years, except I thought maybe it had been better back then.

Memories have a way of getting proportionately better as the years go by. At least some do, anyway. Then there are the others that get worse, I reasoned to myself without bringing Peter into my one-sided conversation.

Swallowing hard, Peter couldn't wait to wash his food down before he was talking again. "You don't live here?" he asked.

"No," I answered. "Worked at the newspaper once. Actually both of them. First one then the other."

"Oh." He seemed satisfied and took another bite.

We ate on quietly for a time. Then he asked, "What are you doing here now?"

"Actually just passing through. Saw an old friend from my newspaper days. On my way home to Virginia. Been across the country working on a project," I said between gulps, leaving it at that.

We ate on, but I could tell he was pondering how to ask more without seeming to be nosy. Finally he broke through his hesitation. He couldn't help himself. "You a writer?" he asked.

"Writer, photographer. Take your pick."

"If I can ask, what's your project?"

"God," I said, sipping the last of my cold coffee.

"That's a subject," he coughed, nearly strangling himself with a mouthful of tea that tried to go down the wrong way.

"You okay?" I jumped half out of my seat. "Do this if you're choking," I barked, wrapping both my hands around my neck so tightly I lost a breath and snorted when I finally regained it.

Furiously Peter shook his head from side to side and held up his hand to say, "Hold it."

Part of me said, "Go on and slap him. Slap him on the back," but I stayed put, poised on the edge of my seat. With my hands still around my neck, I watched his face carefully for any indication he might not be breathing. When he leaned back and smiled, I couldn't help it. I started laughing uncontrollably. I couldn't quit. He didn't quite seem to know what to make of my reaction, but he snickered lightly.

"What—what—what's so damn funny?" he managed to ask, brushing tears from the ordeal from his cheeks.

Laughing and trying to talk, I sputtered, "Th-this is the f-first time I've ever seen a, a man's makeup run!" I burst into heehaws.

Immediately his hands flew up to cover his face. And he laughed hard. With his palms over his mouth, his words came out muffled but plain enough to understand, "I guess it's time to get this stuff off. I'll look like Peter the Clown. Be back in a minute," and he lit out for the rest room as inconspicuously and in as straight a line as he could.

"Want more coffee?" a voice said from behind me.

Saying, "Yes," and turning to raise my cup to our waitress, I saw that she was holding only a pitcher of tea. No coffeepot.

"Where's our movie star?" she asked. "He gone? Thought he might want a filler-upper, too."

"He'll be back. Gone to the little boys' room," I explained as I watched her top off his glass.

Paying me absolutely no attention, she started for the kitchen. Over her shoulder she shouted that she'd be back with the coffee. "Got some brewing. Take a minute."

"Bring our checks," I called after her, not knowing if she had heard me or not. Fortunately she had, because in no time she was back. Two checks fell to the table. And then the surprise. I was getting fresh, hot coffee. And more. She was talking to beat the band.

"Say, listen. You a friend of the star? He'll hear you out." Sliding a torn slip of paper beside my plate, she continued, "Name and telephone number. Give it to him when he's in a good mood. Better then. I can do a mean script."

I looked up at her, my expression showing my astonishment. She stepped to one side, one eye twitching nervously, and reacted fiercely, "Oh, no! Nothing like that."

"Like what?" I asked, then realized in a flash that she thought I was thinking she was trying to come on to him. I wasn't. I knew what she really wanted, but that didn't stop her from explaining herself.

"It's just that I could do a mean script, if I had a chance. That's all I need. Maybe, if he needs somebody like me, he could call. You got the name and number. I really could act."

In a little while, Peter returned from the rest room smiling. His step was livelier. No more tears. No more runny makeup. But he looked a little older.

"Now about God," he whispered while taking his seat.

"About God," I echoed. "What?"

"What!"

"What," I chuckled. "You want to know about my project?"

"Yes. Yes, I do," he said excitedly.

"I'm searching for people who say they've experienced the divine. That's all."

"Anybody in particular?" he questioned.

"No. Anybody. Everybody."

"Well—" he started, but I interrupted him.

"You sound like a reporter. I'm supposed to be the interviewer. Got this thing all turned around," I joked.

Turning all seriousness, he said, "Sorry. But you got my attention. Can't help it." Then he fell silent, his elbow rising to rest on the tabletop. His hand dropped under his chin and his head eased down on his clenched fist. He was studying me or thinking deeply about something. He blinked and held his eyes closed longer than would usually be normal.

"Got a question," I said, and he opened his closed lids to look at and into me. There was something there, something on his mind. I could see it, and I knew I had to ask. But he spoke before I could.

"I was afraid of this," he murmured, "but go ahead. What you got?"

"Want to tell me about your experience?"

"Had lots of experiences. Lived a long time. Which one?"

Folding my arms over my chest, chin down, I pushed up in my chair and said, "The one with God!"

"Treading on dangerous ground now," he said, his voice dropping an octave in tone.

"Oh, yeah!" I teased. "Tell me 'bout it."

Taking his time to ponder if he was going to say more, he slapped his hand over his mouth. His thumb pressed deep enough into his face to find a natural support under his cheekbone, and his other fingers curled downward to encircle his chin. He was in no hurry, leaving me to wonder if our conversation would go any further.

Finally he spoke. "People don't cater to anybody tampering with their God." He stopped and then started again. "I should say their idea of God. They want you to play it by the book, whichever one that may be. Different places, different book. You can do anything, but don't mess with their God. In some places they'll kill you over their God. Could happen here in America, but . . . but more than likely they'd try to hurt your reputation, keep you from getting a job, stop your loan from going through. The more fundamentalist, the more the chances."

Raising my hand as if I were in school, I waved it for him to stop speaking. He paused and I said, "You saying you've had an experience?"

Before I could go on, he countered, "Who hasn't? But that's beside the point. The only real question is 'Who'll talk about it?' "

"You?" I asked.

"What makes you think I've something to talk about?"

"Who hasn't?" I said, turning his own words back on him.

He grinned. "Crafty, crafty, crafty." Then he asked, "What about you?"

"Remember, I'm the interviewer," I chuckled.

"Getting mighty deep in here. Isn't there someplace you got to go?"

"Here. Here for now. As long as it takes," I said firmly, meaning it.

"How much time you got?" He eyed me.

"Long as it takes. Want to get started?"

"Okay," he yielded. "But let's get our checks and get out of here. Got something to show you. Let's go for a ride."

"Bill's paid," I said. He tried protesting, but I stopped him, adding, "Done that! While you were in the bathroom. Figured the laugh awhile ago was on you. The meal's on me. Least I could do."

"Got me! But the next one's on me. Meal, that is," he quickly corrected so as to have no misunderstanding as to what he meant. Then he interjected, "I'll drive. You can leave your car here. Nobody'll bother it. They'll never check the parking lot. Don't care."

Peter all but attacked the streets of Chattanooga. At every turn he was pointing out what was old and what was new in the city. He was at once talking about the new library, new since he had attended college here, and the aquarium, the old building recently renovated to house the *Times*, where the old *Times* building had stood, the developing riverfront, and all the vacant downtown buildings. His eyes grew animated with each detail. When we passed the old Tivoli Theatre, I sensed how dazzled he was over its architecture. As he talked about the theater's gilded interior, his hands were everywhere but on the steering wheel. His actions made me more than a little nervous and I prayed he would stay in his lane.

Soon we were headed east out Ninth. Then Bailey Avenue. Memories rushed back.

I felt as if I were that kid again just arriving in the city and starting my first year of college. The sensation of being far from home and away from my parents for the first time returned as if all the intervening years were a dream.

"Bailey Avenue, then Union and Orchard Knob," I said to myself but unconsciously loud enough for Peter to hear.

"Know it well," he added, taking the words right out of my mouth.

"You got to watch finishing my sentences," I demanded.

"Say," he said, changing the subject, "you move here to work at the paper?"

"No," I answered, "to go to college. Second year of college started working at the paper."

"To go to college?" he said, surprised. "What college? University of Chattanooga? I mean, before they changed it to the University of Tennessee at Chattanooga?"

Not waiting for me to answer his question, Peter proclaimed, "Here we are. This is it!"

"This is what?" I exclaimed, so surprised that my words squeaked out.

Peter looked over at me after parking in front of the school's admissions office. "This is it," he said and repeated, "This! Is! It! What I wanted to show you."

"This is Tennessee Temple College! Excuse me," I corrected myself, "Tennessee Temple University."

"Yep. The one and only."

"Hey." I held up my hand. Lifting myself nearly off the seat, I glared at him. "Wait. Wait just a minute," I commanded. "You went here? To Temple! This I can't believe. You went to school here? Here?" Collecting my thoughts, I backtracked, "I've got to say something, then. Back there at the restaurant . . ."

Peter was attentive.

"When you came in . . . I'm sorry, but I stared at you. It wasn't right. I'm sorry, but there was something about you that was different."

He listened, his lips trying to complete his half smile but didn't.

"Well, when I found out you were wearing makeup, I thought that was the thing about you that was different. You know, at first, I couldn't put my finger on what it was. Now I know. It's because you went here."

Immediately he held out his hand to shake. His entire body was laughing. Then he said, "Got me pegged. Temple grad," and he eased to rest against the door.

Absolutely confused, I slapped my knee and laughed. "Something I missed back there when we were talking about God? About religious fundamentalists? And you brought me here? You know we're right now in the center of all that? But you know that. You graduated from this place."

Peter turned all seriousness. To make his point, he leaned over toward me and whispered, "Met God here."

"Oh," I coughed, "you're preaching their message. They'll love you here."

Not even acknowledging my last statement, Peter reached over and put his hand on my shoulder and added, "Or I should say, God found me. Right here."

Straightening back up and surveying the scene, he gazed out through the windshield. Slowly he turned to look at the buildings that made up the sidewalk campus, as it had been referred to when I was living in Chattanooga. There were no campus greens and no tree-lined walkways. Here there were only buildings constructed right up to the concrete sidewalks, and on the other side of them was the curb and the street beyond that. There had not even been an attempt at matching the structures architecturally. Even if the place was considered a campus, it was still ugly. But Peter didn't seem to be considering that. He was seeing something else. It showed in his eyes. They twinkled.

Leaning back over toward me and bending far too low for comfort, he dropped almost to the seat. Then, with his body contorted in a position I marveled that he could perform on his own, he turned his head upward and strained to look up and out my window. Pointing his long finger, he said, "Look. Up there. That window."

Following his gaze and the direction of his finger, I twisted around to look. "What about it?" I asked.

"That's where my room was. That was my room! That floor of the Temple Building. Men's dorm, top two floors. And"—he choked, his voice breaking—"God . . . God was there. Came to touch me right in my room. Never been the same since."

"Like I said, they'll love you here. Aahh, I mean," I corrected myself, my caution rising to a question, "they love you here?"

Peter flew up from his curled position. Unable at first to talk, he worked his shoulders to and fro and bowed his back to reset kinked vertebrae. Finally, in very stern tones, he uttered, "You think . . . they . . . I . . . this place . . ."

Peter's calm exterior cracked a little. He was so upset, he couldn't get his thoughts together enough to say what he wanted. And that made him angrier.

"Hey," I jostled him, "I didn't mean to get you so riled." Then, trying to turn a possibly bad situation into a joke, I laughed, "You're out of joint. Set your bones and straighten those tired old muscles."

Finally, he relented, and we both chuckled like brothers making up after a trivial spat. With a few twists of his torso in semicircular motions to loosen strained muscles, he relaxed even more but sternly stated, "I asked if you had some time. You said you did. And we're here. But I'm telling you, there's some things you got to know before you come to any rash conclusions about this place loving me. Got that?"

Whoa, I thought, I've made him mad as a hornet. And I don't even know him. We just met. At a restaurant. Back up, boy.

"Okay, Peter," I soothed, "I think I've jumped off the deep end here. I hear you and believe you. You met God here. That's all I know. Now, please, just tell me what you want me to know. We'll leave it at that. Okay?"

"You really want to know? You're absolutely serious? You sure?" he quizzed.

There was a lightness now to his demeanor, but the edge was still there. His face began losing its pinkish redness and slowly returned to its normal skin tone. The tension around his eyes faded. A big grin spread across his face. He thumbed the steering wheel. He was thinking, and I kept quiet. If either of us was going to talk, I figured he'd have to be the one to speak first.

After a few minutes of our trying to get ourselves back together, I couldn't resist and answered the questions he had posed, "Yes! Absolutely. What else can I say? Want me to plead, 'cause I am interested. Wouldn't be here right now if I wasn't. What d'ya say? Or you can take me back to my car. Up to you."

"Okay," he said, his voice dropping, "but it's not so simple to explain. It's a long story. Lots of things happened. God didn't just show up. God wasn't just here and I bumped into him. Lot of things . . ." And his voice trailed off.

After a breath or two, his voice returned louder and stronger. "I came here. Back in the Sixties. Young. Just out of high school. I loved God. Thought I did, anyway. Loved God. The only God I knew, the one I had been taught in church. Got saved in junior high, and got baptized. Walked the aisle a couple times to give myself over to serve him. Going to be a missionary or preacher or something. But I was going to serve him. That's how I found out about this place." He paused to look down Orchard Knob and glance over at the chapel on the corner. A couple of students, Bibles in hand, passed by our car and eyed us, but they kept walking.

Racing his fingers through his well-trimmed hair, he went on. "The preacher back home cornered me after church one Sunday. Said there was just the place for me. It was a place where I could go and get my education and be trained in the service of God. He said, and I remember, 'It's a school that's God centered. Everybody there loves God. Serves God.'

"Then he wrapped his robust arms around me and pulled me into his immense belly. He breathed into my ear, 'God's there, son. It's just the place for a God-fearin' young man like you to go. You'll make a great preacher one day. But . . . you got to get the training first. You'll go to Temple. I'll take you myself.'

"And he did," Peter went on. "My parents were ecstatic. They were going to have a preacher in the family. In their minds, I was going to be somebody. Going to make the

family a name. And make them somebody in the process. That was understandable. Well"—he took a breath—"it's understandable now. They were just working people. Regular churchgoers. Went to church every time the doors were opened. Tithers. Sunday-school teachers. The choir. Did all the right things. Good people. But their son was going to do more. I was going to serve God . . . going to give myself over completely to his Will.

"Maybe you don't understand." Peter eyed me patronizingly. "But from where my parents had come from, my going to a Christian school and studying to be a Christian worker was *something*," and he emphasized the last word. Then he continued, "To them all their love and hard work raising me was going to pay off. I wasn't going to be a hoodlum. No! I was going to serve God and make them proud. So my preacher brought me to Temple and I was enrolled."

Laughing, he paused. For a moment he closed his eyes and said nothing. Then, with his big eyes flashing, he said, "I was proud, too proud. And I was cocky. I thought I was about the biggest thing going. It didn't take me long to get the wind knocked out of my sails, and I was shocked.

"See, I thought everyone here loved God. That this was a place of freedom, but what I soon discovered was that this was a place of rules. Strict rules. There was no thinking for oneself, for following God as one saw fit. It was the most regimented place I had ever been in my life. And everything I did, what any one of us students did, someone was watching and eager to report. Down to the most minute, most insignificant things. And there were demerits for the least of infractions. Very quickly I came to realize that the God I thought I knew was nowhere to be found. And I was left wondering what happened to that caring God who loved me. I didn't just feel forsaken, I was lost. It was a strange place where everyone talked about God but lived only by rules and gladly passed judgment.

"Let me tell you," he proclaimed, "there was no choice. You had to go to the approved church for every service. Sunday school. Sunday morning worship. Sunday evening. Wednesday evening prayer service. Chapel Monday, Wednesday, and Friday. Student body service on Thursdays. And you were given a number and had to check in. First thing during chapel on Monday morning you had to fill out a form and declare, on the threat of punishment, that you attended all the services. And they checked out your statements. If you fudged, never mind. There was always someone peeping. You didn't see them, but they were there, lurking. Besides, they had room checkers who walked the halls of the dorms. You would be caught, bet your life on it.

"Then there were dorm meetings. Why I don't know. We never discussed matters relating to living conditions. I tried to bring up the cockroaches. They were everywhere and they were big. Some about two inches long. Just crawling the walls in the night. Sometimes one would fall on you in the middle of the night. Talk about a bad dream! Although I'd jump up, turn on the light, and try to find the sucker, sometimes killing it, the rest of the night I would get no sleep. Felt it crawling all over my body. All night. All the next day.

"But they didn't want to discuss that. The meeting was for Bible reading and praying. That was all. All!"

Interrupting him, I asked, "What about the cockroaches? Ever get anything done?"

Peter yelled and laughed at the same time. "Get anything done? Are you kidding. Never got the place sprayed. But I'll tell you what I did do. I collected some and put them in a small box. I marched right over to the president's office in the back of the chapel building. It was late one evening. Very few people were about. I had arranged with a friend who had a work scholarship to unlock the back entrance and let me in. I was scared to death someone would catch me. But that didn't stop me. I bent down, opened the box and angled it so the opening would be toward the president's door. There was a crack at the bottom of his door. It took awhile, and I was sweating it, but finally they all took off into his office. Believe me, the next day that office got sprayed."

"And the dorms?" I asked.

"Nope. Couldn't even pray them away," he laughed. "To use what they call Bible language here, I learned to live with adversity."

Our conversation briefly died. He was lost in reverie. After a while, he said, "Talk about adversity! Let me tell you something. Going here was like listening to one long sermon. No matter who was brought in as one of those great distinguished speakers, all of them preachers, the messages were always the same. Three points and a poem. And then the altar calls. They lasted longer than the sermons. Each speaker begged, pleaded, and prodded. The success of the delivery was always measured by how many came forward to turn one's life over to Christ. But don't you see? We had all done that. That's why we were here."

Peter's voice was now rising. He wasn't angry, he was hurt. Then he continued, "It wasn't long before I didn't know if I was coming or going. I was confused. In a mess. Walked the aisle many times and actually got rebaptized three times. Three times! I was convinced that I wasn't saved, then told I was after getting baptized, and then convinced by more preachers that I wasn't. It was maddening. Believe me, my mental state rapidly fell apart. Today, they call it depression. Know about that.

"But once in a while there was a kind of salvation. At the beginning of each new school year, there was registration. Everyone had to sign up for classes. It was horrible. We had to go to each professor and wait forever in line to get approval to take the classes. There was this one professor who stood out. When I finally was next in line at his table, he jovially asked, 'Got any problems?'

"Sure it was a joke, but I said no.

"'Yes, you do,' he said. And I argued that I didn't. He repeated, 'Oh, yes you do. Not knowing you do means you got some.'

"Back and forth we went. Finally, he told me I had better take his class so we could get to the bottom of them. I wasn't sure if I wanted to, but I took his class anyway. And I learned during the semester that there was at least one person at that school who knew God."

Interested, I asked, "Who was it?"

"Dr. Frank Lee. He's the most important man who ever came into my life. He's what a human being should be. He restored my faith that there was a good God. And if ever I thought about teaching, I'd want to be just like him. Don't meet many teachers like him, but when you do, you never forget them."

Peter pulled on his ear, then rubbed the underside of his nose with an extended index finger. In time he continued. "Dr. Lee was tough," he laughed, remembering. "He came to class prepared and he demanded that of his students. He cut no slack. And in grading, you got what you deserved. But he was fair. And consistent. He pushed every one of us to do more than we thought we could. And we did! Besides all that, he demanded, no, forced us to read books and position papers. He challenged us to study viewpoints other than those we had been taught. Viewpoints that may conflict with the college's philosophical stance. Many times he would say, 'How can you know what you believe until you learn what you don't believe? That means reading what other great thinkers think and believe.'

"What he said over and over again stunned me. Gnawed at me. Turned me upside down. It got my attention. He shouted, 'It's a fool who believes something without knowing why. And you have to think to know. Don't ever take someone else's word for anything, because they may be as big a fool as you. Learn to think!'"

Peter stopped to rub his right eye with the knuckle of that same index finger. To lighten him up, I joked, "Going misty on us?"

He chuckled deep in his throat and added, "That man started me on a journey that goes on to this day. He led me to believe that I, too, could be a great thinker. Maybe one of the greatest—that's what he inspired in me, anyway. Now! I'm far, far short of a great thinker, not even close to being one, but he made me question. That opened the door for me to start thinking for myself. His point was in one other thing he taught: 'Even if you question what those around you believe, then you can always know that you came to your belief on your own and you're not just going with someone else's thinking. Don't ever ride blind in the mind, intellectually drive your own course!'"

Peter was excited. It showed in his actions. He couldn't be still. His hands moved. He rolled his head and cracked his neck. His breathing became very audible. And abruptly he said, "Dr. Lee could not accept mediocrity. He decried it. And he roared against the anti-intellectualism all around him here. It was especially fierce when the 1968 school annual came out. I would never have noticed it, but he saw it. That's why I remember the statement so well. For weeks he quoted the passage. It said, talking about the faculty and their relationship with the students, 'What a person thinks, the way he feels, and the path he walks are the responsibility of his educational supervisors.'

"He blasted that as heresy. He told us that his main responsibility was to get us to think for ourselves. And we could take care of the rest. That we'd know how to get information and know how to process it. He said, 'That's what education is. That's all it's about. Thinking!'

"One day after a chapel service as we were all coming out of the auditorium, I ended up going out the door at the same time as Dr. Lee. We were all smashed together, after all there were a lot of students going here in those days. Now I think it's like a ghost town around here. Not even a third of the students. Anyway, Dr. Lee was in a foul mood. We had just sat through a sermon by a preacher from up in Middle Tennessee. He came here a lot. Well, Dr. Lee was really griping. He looked at me, and there was fire in his eyes. I didn't see that often. What he said, though, was serious business and I knew if one of the stool pigeons heard, we'd all be gone. Dr. Lee snapped, 'Not since King David, until today, have so many people been slain with the jawbone of one ass.'"

Peter stuck his head out the open car window, took a breath of fresh air, and turned to me, saying, "Frank Lee was a hell of a teacher. What I wouldn't give to be back in his class just one more time."

Bowing in toward the steering wheel, he added, "And he was a brave man. He bucked the system by trying to get us to think for ourselves."

Finishing on his praise of Dr. Lee, Peter jerked open his door and bounded out. Popping his head back through the open window and raising that finger again, he said, "Got to do something. Going to check something out. Be right back." Instantly he was around the car, taking two or three steps across the walk and opening the double doors of the admissions office.

Speeding into the building, he nearly tripped over a young woman down on her

hands and knees sponge-washing the glass. Halting momentarily, he nodded an apology and disappeared beyond my sight. Several breaths later, he was out the door and bouncing back into the car.

Panting, he said, "Got one!"

"One what?" I asked in wonder.

"A school catalog. What else? Want to see something?" he snorted.

Slowly he flipped through the pages. As I looked on, I could catch glimpses of what was on a page here or there. I caught "51st Edition Volume," and he was on to the next page. In passing I saw a picture of the founding president, Dr. Lee Roberson. Then came the table of contents. And it was gone. A few more pages. Then he stopped.

"Here it is," Peter boasted. "Confession of Faith! Down here. Look. It's here!"

"What is?" I asked.

"Right here. And I quote, 'Every student who expects to graduate from Tennessee Temple University will be required to sign a statement indicating agreement with the Confession of Faith.'

"That's new since I was here, but down here on the next page. 'Objectives.' Read down," he demanded. Here! Number Five. 'The student will develop skills for independent thinking and analytical reasoning.'

"See anything interesting in that," he asked rhetorically. "Right there. That's what got Dr. Lee dismissed. What they say, anyway. After I graduated, he was forced out. Heard that some students went home for the summer. Parents thought they were different and questioned them. Their ideas, rumor had it, were radical. Their preachers called the school and demanded the teacher responsible be held accountable. Guess who that was?

"Even back when I was here, we joked, but it was the truth, that this was the only place that taught you to think for yourself and then kicked you out if you did. Now they've made that policy official. Dr. Lee failed to establish his point with the administration, but he succeeded in the lives of some of us."

"So you were changed that fast," I said and carefully studied his reaction. Peter frowned and pursed his lips, crinkling that section between his nose and mouth.

"No," he said, his tone matter-of-fact. And, "No," again. "Just started it. There was something that happened a short time later that forced me to consider who I was, where I was heading. Pinned me to the ground."

"Wrestling match?" I laughed.

"Could call it something like that, but no. It called me to question if there was really a God."

The way Peter responded took away any thoughts I may have had of continuing to joke. It piqued my interest. From somewhere inside of me I sensed he had experienced a profoundly moving emotional event. I asked, "Something you can talk about?"

"Oh. It's at the crux of who I am today," he started. "And yes. I think I can share it. Most of the student body had to deal with it. So there are a lot of us out there who've had to live with it all our lives. It may not have registered with some, but it did with me. It called into question my belief system. Thank goodness Dr. Lee had gotten me started on how to deal with issues."

Peter stopped and fell silent. For a long time he just sat and turned the steering wheel back and forth. Any onlooker, and there was some who passed, would have thought he was playing driver. It was almost comical. There he was—a middle aged man acting like a kid with the wheel as his toy.

Slowly he started talking, his voice low, "There were these two guys. Roommates. Lived right up there. Near the end of the hall. Far end."

"One day the dean says he caught them in bed with each other. All kinds of stories came out of that. But anyway, they were called on the carpet. Told they'd have to get up in front of the whole student body, tell all of us what they had done, and, if they wanted to stay in school, apologize and ask forgiveness of us. Can you imagine!

"At the time, I thought, 'What do we have to do with it? Ask God, not us!'

"One of the boys said he wouldn't do it. He was told to pack his things and get off of campus in hours. It was done fast so he wouldn't have a chance to tell anyone. He was actually told that. And he left. But not before talking to some of us.

"The other one wanted to stay. So he was ordered on Thursday, student body chapel, to get up in front of all the students. His day finally came. One of the school officials stood up and told us a little of what had happened, then he introduced the guy.

"You can be sure that the auditorium was quiet. No one was moving. I don't think even one person coughed. There was dead silence.

"When he started to talk, he couldn't. As far back as I was, I could tell he was crying. And I really felt so sorry for him. He was being humiliated and it made me furious. I wanted to jump up and yell out how wrong it was to make him go through that. But I was young and I went along. Regretted it then. Regret it now."

Pausing, Peter wiped his eyes. "A lot of wrongs go on because no one speaks up. It's happening to others, maybe in different ways, even today. Anyway, I'm getting off the story and starting to preach.

"That kid told us what had happened and that he was sorry. He said he had prayed to God to forgive him. We were all simply dumbfounded. Most of us, I think, didn't care about what he had done. We were upset at his having to go though that trauma of having to stand up on that platform, from that pulpit, and tell us all those details.

"At the point when he just couldn't get another word out, somebody got up and said, 'Our brother has told us his story. He says he's prayed to God to forgive him of his sins.'

"Then, he said, 'If you forgive him, stand up. He cannot stay in school here unless you, his fellow students, forgive him, because he betrayed you, too. He has stained this campus and only your forgiveness can cleanse that stain. Do you forgive him? Stand up now. Show him.'

"Well, you should have been there. Probably over fifteen hundred, almost two thousand students got up, and you couldn't even hear the rustling. It was so quiet.

"At first I thought everyone had stood. Then, like everyone else, I started looking around to see if everyone was standing. I learned. It was a real surprise, too. Not everyone was.

"Down at the front. That's where all the preacher boys sat. First two or three rows. For every service. Not a one of them stood. Not a single one.

of training Christians.' Sounds like opinion to me, what about to you?" he asked, but didn't wait for an answer.

"Got to see this." He pointed down the page. "'Since moral virtues are essential to scriptural obedience and successful Christian living, pornography, fornication, adultery, and homosexuality are not tolerated.' Can you see anything out of place here?"

The inconsistency was clear. Before I could speak, Peter was talking again. "When will people ever understand that homosexuality is a state of being? Part of the soul's code. It's how somebody is, not what they do. It's not an act. Anyway, when did an act stop anyone? There was talk thirty years ago about male teachers being involved with female students and they never had to stand up in front of the student body and ask forgiveness. That was pushed under the carpet.

"See what this does to me? Now I've started preaching. I'll get back to why I told you all this." Peter scratched his chin and sniffed. Coughed. Then he said, "That brought me to God. Dr. Lee had pleaded with me to ask God if my attitudes on a variety of subjects were glorifying to Him. I told him that I prayed about them. But I didn't. And almost every time we talked outside of class, he questioned me about talking to God. I told him the same thing each time. But I didn't pray about such things. He knew it. Finally, with the chapel thing, I couldn't hold off praying any longer.

"One afternoon, after my last class, I was so tormented about my relationship with God, wondering if there was a God and, if there was, where He was, I went to my room. No one else was around. All my roommates were gone somewhere. Most, if not all, of the other boys on the floor were gone, too. It seemed I had the whole dorm to myself. So I closed myself in my room and fell to my knees beside my bed. I didn't want to do it and appear like I was falling into line with the school's way of doing things. But I did get down and start to pray.

"'Dear Jesus,' I started and I don't know another thing I said. I can't tell you to this day. Something happened and I wasn't even there anymore. I can swear that there was a flash of light like I've never seen before and I've been in some pretty hellish lightning storms. There's just no way to describe that light. It was in me, on me, around me. It seemed to explode inside of me, like it was coming out my pores. And in that instant, I felt . . . I can't describe it . . . except to say it was like love, but I've never come close to getting that sensation with any love I've had, and I've had a few."

Peter's breathing grew faster. He was talking nonstop. It was hard to distinguish where one sentence stopped and another started, yet they were not run-ons. He just didn't worry about periods. Occasionally he would pause to suck in air and then proceed.

"I was somewhere else. It was beautiful, but I couldn't see it. I felt it. There were

"To this day, I think they made a pact, planned sitting there and not standi
they didn't budge.

"Well, because the majority of us stood to say we had forgiven him, the sc
lowed him to stay. But, you know, he didn't last long. He couldn't survive in t
ronment. Everyone knew what he had done, and no one would have anything t
him. And he couldn't take that ostracism. Before the end of the semester, he s
have disappeared. One day he was there, the next he was gone. I don't think r
noticed that much. Before long, the episode was as if it had never happened.

"There was a rumor that circulated for a day or two that one of those gu
ten drafted because he had lost his student deferment. Then word got arou
had been shipped to Vietnam and had been killed over there."

Peter's words had stopped, and I looked over at him. I thought I was
sympathy or pain or something other than what I did. There was rage c
thought it best to wait on him to continue. Finally he did.

"There's one part of the story I haven't talked about. Kept it to myself
you just don't bring up and throw around," he said, now willing to s
preacher boys, only ones who stayed seated! Let me tell you something," h
"there was at least one of those preacher boys who should've stood up. If
the whole place stood, he should have. But he didn't! By not standing, h
self. They all did. Let's face it. Everyone should've stood. No, that s
never've happened. But it did. And all of those preacher types should'
out for the way they acted. But I can't change that. And at least one of t
ticular, should have supported that kid. And he didn't. He disgraced hi

At that Peter pounded the console between us. His voice cracked a
one of those preacher boys. Knew him well. And he knew me. I knev
couldn't hide that from some of us. Yes"—and he looked at me, checl
"we go to Christian schools. And go on to teach, to preach, to lead th
still go to church. I'm a deacon, but I can tell you I go to a church t
honors life, and respects each person's soul's code. We're all God's c

"Well, I know for a fact that that preacher boy went on to marry
in the South. But, I'm telling you, he failed that kid that day in ch
Then, sorrowfully, he added, "We all did. And it's been hard for
for it."

Peter started flipping through the catalog again, seemingly to
story he had told. Then as a surprise to me, he said, "Look at tl
duct.' Page seventeen. Get this." He started reading, "'While instit
inspired in the letter of the Word, standards must always conforrr

hills and valleys and flowers and birds and animals and people and . . . and . . . and I knew I was in the presence of God. No, I couldn't see His face, but it was there. Right in front of me, around me, in me. Everywhere! And I knew. I knew . . . knew everything. I knew who I was and that I was part of God and God was part of me and part of everybody else and . . . and everything was one. Even the teachers at Temple and all the scoundrels and robbers and preachers and . . . everybody. All things one!

"At that very moment I was no longer a racist and no longer better than anyone else. I no longer hated anyone, because I knew I was part of love. I knew what my life was to be about, and I wasn't going to be a preacher or missionary.

"Then, and I don't know how long I was in this thing, I was back. Right there beside my bed. But I was not the same. Yet all I could remember was that something had happened. It was like I knew things, but I didn't know all the things I knew. So much had gone from my mind. I guess I couldn't hold it all. And it's taken me the rest of my life for some of the things to come back. When they do, I know I knew them. And it was from that time in my room on my knees.

"Now I've learned things over the years, but the truths, the major ones, I knew I knew them when they cropped up."

Peter was tongue-tied. He knew what he was trying to say, but he was having a hard time expressing himself. Finally he said, "I know what I'm talking about, but I don't know how to explain it to anyone else. I just know that I was changed and others noticed it, but the particulars were hard to come to grips with. It took time. But this I know. Some people thought I had lost my mind. Others thought I had turned radical. And I had. Being consistent was an ordeal for me. My pendulum swung far out and then back. It's taken all these years for me to become fairly steady, to find the harmony in life that I know is there. Maybe it's just age that does it to you. Whatever! I know peace and am learning more to accept what that means everyday.

"One thing I'm certain of. God showed me the way and has given me a long enough life to find it. It's been there from the beginning, but some of us have to be hit in the head to wake up. I had to go to Temple for God to get through to me. So I'm thankful for the experience. If I hadn't come here, I don't know where I'd be today. It was here that I . . . no . . . God found me. I figure I was where I was supposed to be or I wouldn't have been here."

"You're a better man than me," I mused. "I'm a little more stubborn."

"What do you mean?" he said, playing with the car keys on the steering column. "Going serious on us?" Then he chuckled, "Confession time? I think there's probably a pope in the temple around here somewhere," and he laughed deeply at his own joke.

"That's the problem," I said. "Just can't let go of some things. Know I should 'cause they don't mean much of anything any longer. Still they hang on. I let them. A character flaw, maybe."

Wincing, Peter turned toward me and said, "What in the hell—oh, around here it's 'what in heaven's name'—are you talking about? Character flaw? You are troubled, aren't you?"

"Yep. Been going on a long time. See, I didn't really want to come around."

"Mean Chattanooga? Bad memories, huh?"

"No. Here! My photographer friend, Bob Sherrill . . . I told you I just saw him. Well, Bob wanted to know if I was coming through here. Temple. I said no but, look, here I am. With you. At Tennessee Temple, for God's sake. In front of the Temple Building! And you brought up those two guys. And that one having to get up and do that! In front of us students!" I realized I was actually shouting.

"Stop! Stop right there. Wait a damn minute. What do you mean 'us students'?" Peter's eyes were wide and showing suspicion and disbelief at what he thought I might be saying. "Go on. Say some more," he coaxed.

"You heard me," I confessed. "I was in chapel that day. Way in the back. And I just stood there like a dumb ass. Let it happen . . . without so much as a whimper. And those self-righteous preacher boys." I choked up.

"Hey," Peter blared, "think you're missing something here. This ain't about that horrible scene. Ain't about preacher boys. Hear me? If I could get over that, so can you. But this right now is between you and me. You left something out, way back at the beginning. Like when you let me start spilling my guts and go on doing so. About this place! Like we were strangers."

"Hold on." I struggled to contain the damage. "We *are* strangers."

"No. No! And, no. You went here. I went here. We aren't exactly strangers. May not actually be friends. Maybe could've been. But certainly not strangers. We lived in the same house, so to speak. Dealt with fundamentalism and extremism. And survived, a little tougher for the emotional and spiritual wear and tear. But you're missing the point. You didn't tell me. That ain't exactly right," he said, his voice pained just about to the point of being belligerent.

"That wouldn't have been good journalism if I had told you. Would it?" I said, trying to create a rational defense.

Peter nearly jumped out of his seat and said, "Journalism! Hell, journalism's not journalism. No such thing as true objectivity. It's an entertainment, just like this place. Here, some theater, too. Mostly tragedies. But you aren't getting off the hook that easily. Why didn't you tell me? I feel very foolish. Think about it."

"I was wrong," I said, "Wrong. Understand—you shocked me by bringing me here.

Then I thought I'd just let you talk to see why. Then I realized you really had something to say, that it wasn't a plan to save my soul. It was your story of how you found salvation. Even here. Then I knew I'd have to come clean, but I wanted to hear everything you had to say without our getting into this like we're doing right now. If you had known that I went here, you might have been just as skeptical of me as I was initially of you. That's the only explanation I have."

Turning to me, he smiled. Relief, at least what I took for relief, reflected through his eyes. I was taken at how much kindness there was in them. "Good point. Good enough. And you're right. And we are adults. Newspeople." He laughed at his little joke and I understood completely. "Age has a way of maturing you, doesn't it?"

"Sometimes," I said, hedging. "Not always. Some get there and some don't. I hope to get around to it before I drop off the planet."

"Can't do that yet," he said. "We just got to really know each other. But the maturing thing, we're all working on that."

Then we laughed and he started the car. He said, "I guess we should get out of here. There'll be rumors if we don't. Hey, they may even try to kick us out, if you know what I mean!"

"Wait a minute," I protested as he put the car in gear and inched it back to squeeze out from between the cars parked too close on either side. With his attention stranded somewhere between what he was doing and the revelation I had thrown at him, I said, "Since we're here . . ." and I hesitated.

He kept rolling, angling the car, changing gears, and moving the other way. Then I spoke, a little too loudly, "Up there. There. That was my room."

Absentminded, as if he had just come out of a deep sleep and was trying to get his bearings, he braked hard before I could finish what I was saying. He nearly slammed us through the front windshield. Good thing we weren't going any faster. We would have been picking glass out of our teeth. "No!" he shouted, and we were now bouncing up and over the curb. He seemed dazed. Then, regaining control, he backed up and eased off the sidewalk. "You got to be kidding!" he blared, his words exploding out.

"Nope! Room was right there on the third floor," I said.

Shocked, he questioned, "Temple Building?"

"Yep. None other."

"No-o-o. No way! We were neighbors?"

"Can't say, but must've been," I said.

"What did you say your name was again?" he asked, shaking his head. Then he let it flop back against the headrest. "This is just about the damnedest thing that I think has ever happened."

Before he could say more, three Bible bearers turned the corner several car lengths from us and walked in our direction. Two of them had passed going the opposite direction earlier. Now they were coming back.

Peter laughed, "Hey, they've brought somebody with them. I think they're checking us out or something."

"Something, I think." I grinned. "Want to leave now?"

"Hell no. Let them be suspicious. Would be nothing new, anyway."

The strollers walked by, looking straight ahead. As they passed, they shifted their eyes onto us without turning their heads. Just as they passed, Peter admitted, "I remember. Couldn't forget your name. A lot of people thought you'd be running this place one day. Then the devil got you. Rumors, you know. Said you went crazy. Became a radical. Fell from grace."

"No," I corrected, "had some experiences. I'd say I saw the light, but that wouldn't sound right. Not after what you just told me you went through. But, it's amazing to me how similar our experiences have been. Maybe amazing's not the word I should use. It's unbelievable. Our stories are just about the same. And all the time I thought I was the only one seeing things the way I did. Sure there are differences, but . . . What I learned in short order about Temple and the way things were done here came as a shock. I really thought I was heading into a utopia. Paradise! Then I found out how things were, you know, the way the place was run. I had looked forward to being a part of something so wonderful."

"I said that already," Peter injected.

"Well, I was so excited, too. When it hit me what I was in for, it was too late. I couldn't go home, I would've had to live in disgrace. So I stayed and did the best I could under the conditions. It's taken a lot of time to get over, yet sometimes I don't think I've completely worked through all of it. As a matter of fact, there's something that happened that's stayed. It's really childish on my part. Pretty trivial. The bigger issues, like philosophies and doctrines and dogma, that stuff I dealt with." I stopped speaking, wondering if I should even bring it up. The child in me said to go ahead. "What the hell," I said, weakening. "Want to hear it?"

"It's show-and-tell time. This is good," Peter said. "Think we're going to know each other pretty damn well before this is over. Anyway, go ahead. I'm all ears. This is bound to get very interesting. If it doesn't, I'll tell you and we'll get out of here."

"It's just that my family never had much in the way of material things," I said. "My father never made more than seventy-five to a hundred dollars a week in his job. It was pretty hard to take care of my mother and us two boys on that kind of salary. My parents did the best they could, and I know they would've liked to have done better, but that's just the way it was. Some families had more than we did, and we knew the difference, but we never felt deprived. Sure my brother and I wanted more, but we were glad to get what we did.

"When I announced that I was going to go to college, a Christian college, and study for the ministry, my parents were thrilled. By going to college, I would be the first on either side of my family to be college 'edjimacated,' as my daddy put it. I could see the pride in his face when I told him. His whole body seemed to grow larger than his already huge six-foot-three-inch, two-hundred-ten-pound frame. His golden skin, handed down from his partial Cherokee ancestry, seemed to glow. My going to college was, for him, his accomplishment. He had always inwardly harbored the desire to be a preacher.

"But I'm getting away from the story," I backtracked. "Both my parents came from large families, very large. My mother was one of ten children, my dad one of sixteen. Mother and Dad's parents had been from large families, as well. Out of over seventy first cousins and all the uncles and aunts and grandparents and great-aunts and great-uncles and second and third cousins, I was going to college. But more than that, I was going to study Bible and go into Christian service.

"In making my decision I didn't think about all the family stuff and my parents' pride. I was going to college! Besides, it was not just any college. I was going to a school where Jesus was number one and it was going to be a place where everyone would be going for the same reasons."

Peter waved and I stopped. "Sounds like my story," he whispered. "Got to get your own," he joked.

Nodding over at him, I laughed and went on. "Mom and Dad didn't have the money to send me. That didn't bother me. I was bound and determined to go anyway. I knew I could make it. Then I discovered that Temple had a work scholarship program. You know the system. A student got his tuition, room, and board in exchange for working thirty-seven hours a week for the school."

"Like that young woman right there," Peter pointed with that index finger of his. "I almost tripped over her when I went in a while ago. Down on her hands and knees. God, this place worked them like slaves. Looks like they still do."

"Tell me! I know," I snapped. "I applied, got accepted, and was on work scholarship my first year. Didn't know what I was facing, didn't matter at first. Just knowing I was going to college was enough.

"Chasing rabbits," I laughed. "Back to my parents. Night after night I could hear my parents whispering after they had gone to bed. That's when they dealt with serious matters so my brother and I couldn't hear. Anyway, they decided to do something special for me. With some budget juggling, my mother announced that she was taking me to town to look around for a sport jacket to take to school.

"'You'll need something nice to wear to class and church,' she told me. 'We'll get something that'll go with different-colored pants. That way you'll have different outfits, to mix and match.'

"In high school I had only a couple pair of pants and shirts and one pair of shoes. Now, my mother had taste. She may not've had many dresses, but what she had were nice. She was the same way with my brother and me. Like my shoes. I had only one pair, but that pair was what was in style at the time. They were name brand. All the 'in' kids wore them. It didn't matter if it was all I had, they were the best.

"Don't know how your family was financially, but the way Mom worked it out to get finer things was calculated. I'd say she was a little sneaky. If my brother or I needed another pair of pants or a shirt, she'd lay them away. Every week she'd fudge on her grocery allowance by just a little and pay a dollar or two on them until she'd finally pay them off, and by then we were really in need of those clothes. In other words, they'd come at just the right time. She'd do the same for herself. Dad would just go get what he needed, and that was seldom. Come to think about it, I can't remember his ever going in a store and buying anything for himself. I know he must've, he had clothes to wear, but I can't recall how he did it.

"Sometimes Dad would accuse her of tricking him when she'd slip into a new dress for church. He'd bellow good-naturedly, 'Now where did that come from? Did you go buy a new dress? When did you get that? I don't remember it!'

"'Aaaahh,' she'd say sheepishly, 'this ain't no new dress. I've had it for years. It's just an old thing I've not worn for a while.'

"Dad would know what she was pulling, and so would my brother and me. But we all let her get away with her little schemes.

"The day finally came when we made the trip to town. You can imagine how excited I was. I knew where we'd be going. In our little town there was only one place where respectable people shopped and probably the only place where the clothes were halfway in style. That was A. V. Wray and Six Sons. A. V. Wray's! The year before that's where my mother laid away my London Fog windbreaker. Now I was going shopping for a new sport coat.

"As I walked into the store, I was immediately seized with an overriding fear. Lay away! And I immediately wondered, 'How long will it be before I'll get it and be able to wear it?' My mother must've noticed that my walk had slowed and that I didn't seem to have the same enthusiasm.

"Motioning me over, only as my mother could do, to the coatrack, she whispered, 'I'm opening up a little account on account I ain't' got no money.' Then she laughed at her own sense of humor. She'd made a joke out of it and the heavy air lifted. I was relieved and perked back up.

"Something about my mother's sense of style and taste must have rubbed off on me, because it didn't take long to pick out the coat. It attracted my attention immediately. There it was, a dark tweed with blacks and browns mixed with little knobbies of interwoven threads of reds and greens. It was perfect. I could see myself in it rushing from class to class, my necktie that I'd surely be wearing flying over my shoulder as I hustled to beat the bell. I knew I'd be impressive in it. Oh, did I say that it was the most expensive one in the sport-coat section? Thirty-seven dollars. Thirty-seven dollars! My joy turned to sadness as my mother disappeared downstairs to the accounts department. That coat was costing my parents about a half week of my father's paycheck.

"When I realized the magnitude of the expense, I nearly leaped down the old wooden stairs in an attempt to stop her. It was too late, the papers had been signed. The coat was on account. Not really wanting to give it up, I still tried to get her to come back upstairs and select another, cheaper one. 'Nothing doing,' she said, 'that's your coat now.'

"It was settled and inwardly I was pleased. Hopping. Hardly able to contain myself until I could wear it in public. I would've, too, had it not been August and the hottest one in years to boot.

"On the Sunday before I was to leave to come here, I just couldn't stop myself. I had to wear that coat to church just to try it out. With it still being August and still hot as blue blazes, I began to roast in it before I could even get to the car to head for church. But I endured the discomfort to give everyone the chance just to see me in that coat.

"That was just about the proudest day of my life. Not only was I going away to college, I was going to study to be a preacher. Growing up, our minister had called that the highest calling on God's great earth. Besides that, I was wearing my new coat and getting a few smiles from the girls I'd like to have dated. 'Yes,' I thought as I strutted out after the benediction, 'this coat will serve me well in college.'

"Once here, I wore my coat with pride and more than a slight arrogance. However, there was one thing I hadn't thought about. Men wore suits to class every day. Suits in every class, every day! I began to feel a little self-conscious in my 'one coat for all seasons and all occasions.'

"Then one day the worst imaginable thing happened. I just can't forget it." I looked out the window. Through the doors of the Temple Building, I could see dark figures moving about in the admissions office. After watching the silhouettes for a time, I returned to my story. "It was totally unexpected. One of the kids living in my dorm, one who seemed to have come from a family with money and, therefore, had more clothes, came bouncing down the stairs from the dorm floors above. As I was just about to take a drink at the watercooler next to the staircase, he yelled loud enough for anyone around to hear, 'Hey, you must really like that coat.'

"I looked up, startled at the sound of his voice, and was at first flattered he'd noticed my coat. I looked down to admire it myself and started to thank him for his compliment. Before I could say anything, he laughed and said, 'Do you ever have time to dry-clean it? You wear it all the time. Or do you like it too much to let it out of your sight to do that?'

"From then on I was the most miserable student here. It seemed that as I walked into any room, even the main auditorium of the church we were required to attend, with four thousand members in Sunday attendance, all eyes would turn toward me. I had no doubts they were wondering about that coat."

Opening the car door, Peter brought my story to a halt. He was getting out, but he poked his head back in through the window and said, "Keep talking. I'm listening. Just got to stretch."

"Don't want to bore you," I said sincerely.

"Not boring me. It's some story. Go on," he requested. And I did.

"It wasn't long before I hated that coat. It became a noose around my neck. I didn't want to wear it, but I had no choice. It wasn't proper to go in shirtsleeves, and besides, I had to have something to cover my skinny arms. At nearly six feet tall I barely weighed one hundred twenty-five pounds, and I needed something to cover my thinness and give me a small sense of body instead of being just arms and legs. My profile, I thought, resembled the side view of a zipper.

"But that coat! It had been my pride. Not only did I wear it, but I flaunted it. Then when the kid made fun of it . . . It was like he was talking about me, not the coat. Well, something inside of me went, 'Be that way, go on and worry about what you think everyone thinks or do something about it.' And I decided to take some action.

"Every week my parents would send me a few dollars for laundry, and once a week I got a letter from my grandmother with two dollars tucked in the envelope. She'd saved it just for me from her baby-sitting money. After reading the letters, and with my roommates safely out of the room, I'd quickly pull my cheap trunk from under my bed, unlock it, and dig to the bottom. Finding the tiny box that once housed a tape reel used by a radio station, I'd slip in the folded dollar bills with others I'd stashed away the week before, and then I would secret the box back to the bottom of the trunk.

"In order to make my plan work, I took portraits of graduated missionary couples. I was already taking pictures for the school. That allowed me to raise a few more dollars here and there. Also, I talked one roommate into throwing my clothes in with his laundry one week and my other roommate the next. It worked.

"This went on week after week until one Friday I had what I thought to be enough. Bumming a ride out Bailey Avenue, through the Missionary Ridge tunnel and into Brainerd, I got out to the mall. There was a men's store there, as well as a J.C. Penney. One place or another, I was going to get a new coat. Besides, spring was coming. My one coat had served me well, but winter was about over. And I needed not only a lighter one but a change.

"The specialty men's store had several I liked. They had caught my eye immediately, but I was not going to be in any hurry. Slowly, ever so slowly, I walked the aisles. Down one, then the other, trying one jacket then another. The clerks watched me eagerly, but finally their patience wore thin and they left me alone. Then I spoke up and their enthusiasm picked up again. 'I'm going to look around at another store.' Their faces dropped, and I added, going out the door, 'But I may be back.'

"Penney's had nothing that interested me. Their jackets, I found, were for much older men. Very conservative. I wanted to be more in style and, of all things, loud. To be seen! But to be seen the way I chose. I returned to the men's store and immediately grabbed the coat that had been the first I modeled. It was bright, couldn't miss it. There was a base of white with stripes of reds, blues, greens, and yellows. A madras! My coat of many colors!

"'Let them look!' I thought to myself as I paid from the money I'd scrimped. 'This is what I want to wear because I want to wear it and it makes me feel good!' I chuckled, very, very pleased with myself.

"After catching a bus west on Brainerd Avenue, again through the tunnel and down McCauley, I got off at Orchard Knob. Barely able to contain myself, I all but ran, coat in a box under my arm, the three or four blocks back onto campus. In my pocket I even had a few bucks left for a well-deserved milkshake I had deprived myself of for weeks because of saving for my new coat. The milkshake was sweeter than ever.

When I finally finished my protracted story, there was silence. Neither he nor I said anything. I waited. Still silence. We said nothing. Time passed. In a move to break the gulf between us, I spoke, "Hey, I didn't mean to get so carried away. Sorry to have bored you through all my ramblings."

"Ah, not boring. Actually grabs me."

"Then why so glum?"

"Aaaahh," and his voice died.

Prying, I said, "What's going on, here?"

Peter pulled open the door, slid back in, and let the weight of the door swing itself closed. He sat with his arms hugging the wheel. But he said nothing.

"So?" I proclaimed.

He could hardly speak but he tried. "One day I knew we'd have to meet again. Remembered you only when you said your name. Sure you've changed a lot, so much that I'd have never recognized you. But the name, could never forget the name."

"Well, we were at Temple at the same time. Nothing unusual about that."

"It's more than the name."

Coyly trying to get out of him what seemed to be eating him, I pressed, "Maybe it's because of the rebel I became. Gave everybody a hard time, especially the administration."

"Yeah, that was something. Kind of impressive, I'd say. Was even back then. Gave some drama to the theater. But that's not it."

Now my full attention was focused on getting to the bottom of what had so gripped him when just minutes earlier he had been so animated, as animated as a former TV anchor could be. "Just go on and get it out. We're friends now, wouldn't you say?"

In a rush his words came spilling out. "I-I-I'm the one." He stopped. Water filled his eyes and a quick redness followed.

"The one?"

"That coat. And the way you wore it with such . . . such . . . such pride. Me and my tongue. It always wagged before I could stop it . . . back then."

"What're you talking about? My coat? You remember me . . . and my coat?"

"Hell, yes. And I knew I'd have to face up. All these years, I remember. I regretted it the minute—the minute I said it and I knew that if I ever could, I'd ask you to forgive me. But I kept putting it off. Then we were graduated and you went your way and I went mine. I never could bring myself to talk to you face-to-face. Then it was too late. Years passed. Now it's been almost thirty. Thirty years! And we meet again. What goes 'round comes around. Something inside of me just knew that this would happen."

We sat silently. Neither moved nor spoke. I was in shock. I'd remembered the event, but I'd forgotten who had made the remark. True, I had taken it personally, but I had only vaguely remembered the image of the kid who had ripped out my heart that day. Thinking about the man next to me and the way he had been three decades ago, he was definitely the type who could have gone into television. I know the type now, or at least what type they become because of the nature of the industry. At the time, however, I could not have been that insightful. Youth is blind.

With a deep breath I stammered, "I—I never held it against you personally, just . . . just . . . it was the fact that I thought the place and everyone in it was Christian. The higher standard calling thing." Trying to console him as best I could, I added, "I didn't even remember your name. So it has nothing to do with you."

Valiantly raising his head and slowly taking his gaze from the deteriorating neighborhood, he whispered, "Forgive me! Forgive me, if you can."

So touched by his struggle to hold back his tears, I couldn't keep water from welling up in my own eyes. No! Not me, too, I thought, searching for a way to let him off the hook and finding only, "It's over, long time over."

He pushed my remark aside, "The look on your face that day . . . the look . . . when you realized . . . ooohh! I didn't know what I was doing. But I've lived with it all these years. Stayed like an instant video replay . . . over and over.

"With all I've learned since then, though, I'd never intentionally hurt anyone ever again. It comes back. If we had only known at nineteen and twenty . . . really known that's the way this thing called life works."

Thrusting his hand forward, as if an old friend greeting another after a long time of being apart, mine rushed to meet his. The clasp was more than a handshake. Immediately our fingers encircled the other's thumb, as I had learned from my Indian friends and he did naturally. Our left hands followed to enclose around the other's right.

We must have looked like two rather strange guys, especially at a place where even students who were married got demerits for showing any kind of affection. Yet we were men unabashedly displaying a deep caring for each other. There we sat doing a double handshake, faces flushed, eyes filled with water and engrossed in an emotion of a long-distant past that was somehow playing in the now.

I tried to say, "It's over!" but my lips uttered no sounds. Then, there in front of our former domitory residence, I reached over and put my hand on his shoulder as one more sign that everything was okay.

That was all he needed. In a rush he leaned over and wrapped his arms around my neck as best he could in the confines of the car. Immediately I returned the hug without any reservation. For a time we held the embrace. Finally, in a quivering voice, he said out loud what I had only attempted to say earlier. "It's over!"

ABOUT THE AUTHOR

Steve Wall began his career in journalism as a news photographer for the *Shelby Daily Star* in Shelby, North Carolina. He was a senior in high school. During his sophomore year in college in Chattanooga, Tennessee, he joined the news staff of the *Chattanooga News Free Press*, continuing his undergraduate studies and working full-time for the newspaper. Two years later, he took a staff position on the *Chattanooga Times*.

After several years with the *Times*, Mr. Wall walked away from a promising future in the newspaper world to plunge into the less secure realm of freelance magazine writing and photography. Within a year, he traveled on assignments to more than twenty-five countries around the world. Since then he has covered stories in over twenty-five more. On his very first trip out of the United States, he ended up in India. Once there, he found himself in the prime minister's residence in New Delhi, interviewing Indira Gandhi.

Steve Wall has covered war in Vietnam, conflicts in Northern Ireland and the Middle East, earthquakes in Peru and Guatemala, hurricanes in Honduras and the United States. He has seen the ravages of famine and the fatal grip of poverty around the world. When students rioted in the Philippines and took to the streets in Australia, he was there. In Mississippi he was threatened and followed by local residents while covering the Civil Rights Movement. Then, while photographing Vietnamese fishermen working on the Gulf coast, he was again threatened to be killed by those opposed to the influx of the new immigrants. Nevertheless, he held his ground to complete his assignments.

Wall's work has appeared in numerous magazines and books, including *National Geographic, Smithsonian, Time, People,* and many others. He has also been a contract photographer with Black Star Picture Agency and covered assignments for United Press International.

For more than a decade Steve Wall sought out and recorded the words and images of some of the most prominent Native American spiritual elders in the United States and Canada. The result of his endeavor was the best-selling book *Wisdomkeepers,* written with Harvey Arden. Wall is also the author of *Wisdom's Daughters* and *Shadowcatchers.* His video productions include *We're Still Here,* on the Six Nations Iroquois Confederacy, *Search for the Grandfathers of Native America,* and *Earth's Song.*

Mr. Wall and his wife of more than thirty years live along the James River in central Virginia. They have two children.